Diamond
Hitch
Days

Diamond Hitch Days

J. N. Hessel

Cover and Illustrations by Gina Phillips

The CAXTON PRINTERS, Ltd.
Caldwell, Idaho
1991

Hessel, J. N., 1910–
    Diamond hitch days / by J. N. Hessel.
       p.   cm.
    ISBN 0-87004-344-7   : $14.95
    1. Hessel, J. N., 1910–   .   2. Forest rangers--
Rocky Mountains Region--Biography.   3. United
States. Forest Service-Officials and employees--
Biography.   I. Title.
SD129.H47A3   1991
634.9'092--dc20
[B]   91-8056
                                                          CIP

Lithographed and bound in the United States of America by
The CAXTON PRINTERS, Ltd.
Caldwell, Idaho
153647

CONTENTS

Diamond
Hitch
Days

Diamond Hitch Days

My era was roughly from the passing of the passenger pigeon to the demise of the magnificent pristine wilderness that was once, as in the days of Lewis and Clark and the first mountain men, known as the Western Frontier.

By the time the passenger pigeon was no more, the fur trappers, gold and silver seekers, buffalo hunters, cattle and sheep drivers, loggers and lumbermen, railroad builders, homesteaders, and mine claimers had had their heyday—and played hell in general and particularly with the Indians, the scenery, the frontier, and especially the pristine wilderness.

Fortuitously the so-called heavy hand of government in the form of the U.S. Forest Service and the national forests clamped down just barely ahead of the last passenger pigeon. In a dandy sweep of unappropriated public lands, mostly over 7,000 feet in elevation, they saved a few million acres of uncommonly remote and inaccessible (even at that late date) mountain peaks and ridges rich in worthless rocks, wild animals, wild flowers, solitude, fresh air, sunshine and little else—but still untrampled by man. What the founders of the Forest Service were after was not worthless wilderness but some last remaining unclaimed stands of magnificent virgin timber and the headwaters of navigable streams, which covered about everything and anything under the sun at higher elevations west of the Great Plains to the Pacific Ocean.

Luckily for me because I came to know them intimately and loved them so much, quite a few of those untrampled-by-man backcountry wilds in the Northern and Central Rockies were just barely, but still within my time. Only a few parts of these vast and rugged domains were accessible and only by rough and variously hazardous foot and horse trails. If venturing off these sketchily blazed routes through the boulders and bush, you had better have a compass and know how to use it. Otherwise, the words of the Indian at the end of one more blind canyon might readily pertain: "Me not lost. Trail lost."

With only foot and horse trails, obviously the only means of transport at that time was by means of a pack on your own back or the back of a horse and sometimes both. The average man gets no particular pleasure carrying a pack on his back. The way I have seen some of them haul back, buck and kick even at the sight of a pack, neither does a horse, mule, or burro. If you put a pack on a burro and give him a chance to think things over, he will sometimes think it is too heavy, buckle at the knees and collapse. When you try to change his mind by lightening the load and helping him back on his feet, he will somehow manage to both kick you and bite you.

What I am saying is that while you will probably not get kicked or bit putting a pack on a man's back, putting one on a horse or mule or burro is another matter. Roping it on so it will stay there over downed logs, around protruding rocks, between close growing trees, etc., and still be there intact at trail's end, is still another. Putting a pack on a horse's back is a strong man's work and no business for a novice. Lifting a hundred pound sack of concrete or box of canned goods to the height of a horse's back is in itself no mean feat. If the horse is skittish and inclined to shy, you had better be prepared for that or any number of interesting events can take place, such as both the cargo and you ending up under the horse's iron-shod feet.

A pack train consisted of a saddle horse and rider with lead rope ahead of seven loaded beasts of burden, generally mules, tied nose to pack saddle ahead— sometimes nose to tail if the horse still had enough tail to make a tie. Packing was kind of a profession and those who followed it were a unique, hard, and often temperamental lot, generally with a sense of humor, but better never crossed. Finding and hiring a good packer was about like finding and hiring a good cook. They were an especially independent breed. Even little things like maybe the way somebody laced his boots could hurt their feelings.

Nowadays, with helicopters and four wheel drives, the place of the oldtime packer is about the same as that of the grizzly bear. Various heroics of some of these wilderness equestrian mountain men brought off in course of freighting to remote trail construction and maintenance camps, fire camps, lonesome lookout and smokechaser locations were legendary wherever two or more people happened to cross trails in that vast silent land. Now they are largely unsung ghosts of paved and unpaved roads and landing strips and heliports where once were only long lonesome trails.

In the professional packer's bag were ties and hitches, variously used for wrapping packages in squares of heavy canvas known as mantis. These ranged from raising or lowering the two sides of a load to bring them at least reasonably in balance, to the prime ultimate diamond hitch which pulled all parts of the load

together, making it as compact as possible and by means
of one more cinch hugging it down so as to be insepar-
able from the horse's back as was humanly possible. Not
uncommonly looking for one more inch of slack, the
packer would seek more leverage by putting one high-
heeled booted foot against the hind leg of the horse and
haul it back for all he was worth which was signified by
a hearty grunt, and caused the horse to not only grunt
but break wind. In case the beast of burden was a mule,
the prudent packer got his leverage in a different
manner or did without.

When properly and finally tied, the long lash rope
where it shows on top of the pack appears as a perfect
diamond. Hence the name for the hitch. Who invented
this dandy hitch and when, nobody knows. It might have
been Lewis and Clark's sergeant in charge of transport
desperately trying to fasten a load of cannonballs to the
back of a recalcitrant Indian pony. Maybe it was an
ingenious mountain man simply in process of doing
what he did most—moving camp. I heard tell about it
first in the course of some of the spellbinding stories told
by my old Uncle Bill. who claimed it was one of the
most useful gifts from the Head Packer in Paradise to
humble man. I was first shown how to throw and tie it
by a Forest Service packer by the name of Ben Rice in
1928—not so very long before it would come to have no
more earthly use at all.

In my time, what was still unsurveyed and virtually
untracked wilderness suffered from the same trauma as
the diamond hitch. I date the beginning of the end of
wilderness as I knew it from a mid-summer morning in
1953 in what was then the Popo Agie Primitive Area of
the Shoshone National Forest—a short day's ride to the
end of the road to Lander, Wyoming, a trade center for
the Wind Indian River Reservation. In other words,
purely God's country in every sense. Years ago in our
overnight camp, I came bolt upright in my sleeping bag
at about 6 am and listened—not to the sweet music of
our horse bells—but to a radio blaring so-called music

punctuated by female screams, male shouts and guffaws. "What in the world," I exploded, "is that?" Hank Payson, the district ranger with whom I was traveling, replied with one word: "Dudes." Grunting and muttering as he pulled on Levis and boots he struggled to his feet and said, "I apologize. I thought this camp was farther down the creek. A dude wrangler has a camp and horse grazing permit up this way and this must be his party of thirty-five rock climbers from Ames, Iowa." "Did you say thirty-five from *Ames, Iowa*? Way back *in here*? Just to *climb* pinnacles?" It was simply incredible! "Aymen," he said. "No more lonesome rocks but good for the dude business." Taking one last look at the magnificent landscape around me, I pulled on my boots thinking silently and sadly: Heaven is no more.

"Everything under the Sun has a given place and a given time. The human can and may have to move around some to find his place and that is possible. His time is something else. He might think he showed up too early or too late or that his span was too short or too long. But move or no move, there's nothing he can do to change his time." If not exact, that's the gist of what Uncle Bill told me, more than once.

After making this uncommonly long, and at age ten somewhat mystical speech, came a customary pause to strike a kitchen match with a dirty thumbnail and a reignite the charge in his big, battered, curve stemmed pipe. While sitting beside him on the unpainted, weather sitting bench outside the door to what he referred to as his "dig," I rightly waited silently and anticipated that, long as it was, the end of the speech was not yet. "These ba'bwire flats ain't yore place, boy, so you got to move a piece. To the farlook country. Up outa the trees to the peak. Where you can feel the good breeze blowin' in yore face an' see a hundred miles in all directions . . . with nary fence anywhere. An' sit there in the saddle an' hear nothin'. But maybe the wheels turnin' in yore head."

The man was my Granduncle Bill—my early idol and oracle. And diamond hitcher from way back when.

Uncle Bill

In that staid little rural community of bib-overalled corn and hog growers, Uncle Bill was neither a native to those parts nor in any sense associated with the plow. With these two negatives against him to begin with plus what were perceived to be quite a few others after he settled in, Uncle Bill gained a reputation for being just plain "no good." It bothered him not one iota. In fact, he considered it an asset which to someone who preferred his own company, it was.

Maybe for my parents and grandparents who were pillars of the flourishing Lutheran church and the community, Uncle Bill was a kind of heathen albatross, but he attended to his own business and never meddled in anyone else's. He pulled his own freight with no help or favors requested or expected from anyone. When it all boiled down, he was reputed to be no good just because he looked people straight in the eye, tipped his hat to no one and believed and lived by his own lights.

In our whole town of almost 500 souls, Uncle Bill to all appearances had only two habitual friends, both "birds of a feather." They were also no good. One, Dave Brazelton, had long ago lost the trail and was just waiting. Dave belonged at the County Poor Farm where he could eat regularly and they could keep him off whiskey. The other friend, Bob Holt, was Indian only by popular suspicion. If he wasn't Indian, it was said he sure acted Indian. Money never meant anything to him either. Every dollar he laid hands on went for gambling, or for guns, or whiskey, or no good women. Bob was much younger, bigger and stronger, and whiter than Dave. He didn't really look Indian. It was just the way he lived and acted. Both Dave and Bob lived in little unkept houses close to the railroad tracks and on the other side.

Sometimes when he felt like it or needed money to pay off a gambling debt or buy another gun, Bob worked for my father, who had more tinsmithing, heating, plumbing and pot soldering work than he could handle even in a ten-hour day except when it came to lifting or repairing windmills. For some reason, he was a "cracker jack" on windmills.

Bob was my friend as well as Uncle Bill's. He was also a cracker jack at turning out a piece of hickory or osage orange into a bow that would outshoot almost any bow any of the other kids around town ever had. The arrows he turned out for me to go with the bow had needle-pointed, knife-sharp metal heads, and shafts with trimmed chicken feathers to make them fly straight. Though loudly condemned by father and mother as no play thing for a youngster (even though said youngster could hardly pull the bow), it made me mighty proud. For rabbit hunting, they (the bow and arrows) were really for real. At fairly short distances, with practice and more muscle, a sitting rabbit was almost certainly a rabbit in hand.

Uncle Bill was really mother's uncle, making him my granduncle. The way they did not associate, you would never know he was grandfather's brother. More or less, he and grandfather looked alike, but beyond that there was very little or nothing.

In appearance, Uncle Bill, standing over six feet and weighing 200 pounds without an ounce of fat showing, was a moose of a man. Actually, with his big shaggy head and a kind of hump in the back at the shoulders, he was more like a grizzly. Temperamentally, the grizzly and Uncle Bill were somewhat similar as well. Keep your distance, or else!

Uncle Bill had hair like Samson before Delilah, bushing down around his ears to his shirt collar, about the color of galena hygrade. What you could see of his face was a big weather-browned forehead, a straight non-prominent nose the same color, and eyes set somewhat wide and deep under eyebrows thick and prickly as porcupine tails. The rest was lost under a jungle of more lead and silver-colored hair. Something like the pictures on the Sunday School lesson cards of the prophet Isaiah or Moses after forty days on the mountain.

What went on under that thatch and behind that hair mask was always a good question. The only inkling came in the eyes. If you asked me the color of Uncle Bill's eyes, I couldn't say—except that they were not dark. More like cat's eyes, blue green grey—maybe. It wasn't the color of his eyes that was remembered. What you remembered was the way they laid back in that bush and bored into you. Mostly they had a look like everything was one hell of a big joke. Just now and then they were different. When they were different, they were smokey ice with thunder in the distance moving closer. This look in Uncle Bill's eyes made whomever they were focused on to get real quiet and start concentrating on an exit. I had it a couple of times, once on yapping when I should have been listening, and again moping when I should have been hustling. I learned to talk less and move fast very early.

The size of Uncle Bill's voice did not match the growl

of the grizzly. When he talked, the words came out surprisingly soft and quiet. The softer and quieter they came out, the more it paid to listen. The way he put words together made the message very understandable. There is a real knack for using just the right word or words at the right time. Uncle Bill had that knack. What he said went direct to the point. At times, it brought down the house, and again, it cut like a knife. When he said something that cut, his voice matched his eyes, smokey ice. This was not often. Mostly Uncle Bill's remarks were kind, helpful and humorous; the biggest jokes were always on himself. With the crowd, though, it was not the general run of honey, but the little bit of acid that is remembered. This is one of the things that kept Uncle Bill untroubled by social commitments or callers. Except for me, this included relatives.

Uncle Bill and I arrived at my point of origin in Illinois, about 150 miles south of Chicago, practically in a dead heat. My date of arrival—September 22, 1910—is documented in the county, church, and family records. The reason it does not show up in hospital records is that there were no such accommodations either at hand or within horse and buggy running distance. At the time and place it was enough that a fully accredited MD was present and officiated.

Uncle Bill's appearance on the family scene, unlike mine, was totally unexpected, totally unwelcome, and never documented. As recalled many years later, he arrived afoot, all of a sudden out of nowhere, with a pack on his back, apparently carrying all of his material possessions. This was not quite correct, as Uncle Bill had a mysterious source of funds never disclosed or discovered. The family, including me, suspected it was a gold mine and wished we knew where. While he was no big or free spender, he always had enough for all he wanted plus plenty for the poker games in the back of Pauley's Pool Hall and the Sunday afternoon crap games in the empty box cars of the Illinois Central siding next to Frost's grain elevator. Plus whiskey. Uncle Bill consumed a fair share of whiskey. He always had a couple of bottles with his groceries in the cupboard on the wall by the stove.

When Uncle Bill showed up right out of the blue, he must have cut quite a figure: Big sweat-marked and weathered broad-brimmed hat, a grimy buckskin jacket with long fringes, and a butcher knife in a sheath on his belt. These were what the family remembered. The natives remembered, too. Not many natives, if any, had ever seen such a get-up. He attracted a lot of attention and created a lot of talk, some of which the family could have done without. Uncle Bill just went on about his business which was buying an acre of real estate and building himself a roof over his head.

In a matter of time, Uncle Bill let out that he had lately wandered down from the Klondike through British Columbia, Idaho, Montana, Wyoming, and points west, eventually to St. Louis, thence northeast to the family establishment. Likewise, in due course, he admitted to gold prospecting in the wildest lands and companies around the world, but mostly up and down the Rockies from Central America to Alaska, mostly with references to Mexico, Nevada, Montana and Idaho—especially Idaho. By the time he turned up on grandfather's doorstep, he had a lot of miles behind him, and years. Maybe in 1910, he was all of sixty, which in those days was quite a few. To me, in later years, he was never that old neither mentally nor physically decrepit in any sense.

How he came, and from where, generally, are known, but why has never been revealed. What shattering prompting was responsible for self-exile from a love life chasing rainbows through mass A-1 wilderness makes a fascinating, never answered question. Why he later committed himself to a land and family not only opposite but downright antagonistic is another.

Most logical, and as local gossip had it, was that Uncle Bill was running from some happening, or more likely, somebody, maybe even the law, and hiding in a place where, by all odds, no one who knew him would ever expect to find him. This romancing was borne out somewhat by the place and manner in which he was finally plowed under, which was near St. Louis on a riverboat with a knife in his back. This happened in the early fall of 1926. I was just turning sixteen. Grandfather left all of a sudden on the evening southbound IC passenger train and was gone almost a week. All I knew was that he went to St. Louis. The rest I did not find out until several months later when I could not figure out why Uncle Bill did not reappear after the usual month or so, from one of his usual September disappearances. The news hit me like it didn't hit anyone else in the family—like a gut shot. To me, Uncle Bill was and always will be, one in a million. He knew and let you know what made the world go round and that he could and would take care of himself.

One of the juicier refinements of local theorizing had a woman in the lead of what or who sent him packing. The hole in this was that where he claimed to have come from, the most notable thing about women was the scarcity, except maybe offwhite women like Mexican or Indian. Looking back, the one thing that seemed to scare Uncle Bill was a woman. He had no good word for any female and seldom had any word at all in that connection. It was sort of like the opposite sex didn't exist, or if it did, best leave it ignored.

I mentioned Indians. Indians, now, were different. To get Uncle Bill going long and strong, just mention Indians. It was the Indian, not the Hebrew who represented God's chosen people. In a place and time when Custer was hero, Uncle Bill violently laid him out as "just another goddamn West Point headhunter, different only because he was more stupid." Also, at the place and time when the Missionary Society was the pillar of the church and community, he bitterly declared both the devout ladies of the Society (including mother and grandmother) and their field agents, as "misguided, meddlin', soul-savin' women." The popularly revered local Lutheran, Catholic, Methodist, Presbyterian, and Baptist emissaries of Lord, God, and Holy Ghost, he most irreverently referred to as "tub thumpers," "bloodsuckers," and "sky pilots." Deep down, Uncle Bill, like the Indian, was actually a very religious individual. He simply objected to having his superstitions organized, supervised, or pawned off on anyone else. "The house of the Lord," he said, "is the whole outdoors; the Earth and the Universe, not some million dollar edifice with a sky pilot behind a pulpit calling signals." At least that was the gist of it.

Father, being one of the biggest contributors and by far the loudest singer in the Lutheran church, and Uncle Bill hauling in the opposite direction, I was left right in the middle—except that I was there for Sunday school and church services three hours every Sunday. For one whole winter, I attended catechism classes every Saturday, when I could have been out hunting rabbits. In church during the sermon, prayers, and singing, I would sit and dream about shooting out all the candles, light bulbs, and various targets in the stained glass windows. What I liked most about church services was the doxology, because it was the last thing on the program. The minute the last amen of the doxology was sounded, I would make a fast break for the alternate exit. The main exit was always blocked by the preacher who took advantage of the doxology to walk out and get set so nobody could get by him without shaking hands. Every now and then you meet somebody who is too nice and cozy to be believable. This preacher was that kind of hombre. I did not like to come anywhere near him, much less shake hands with him. Besides which, shaking hands took time. In breaking out of church after three hours of Sunday school, praying, sermons, and singing, I had no time to shake hands with anyone.

Once it did not work. Once when I was about eleven or twelve on a Christmas Eve following a long drawn out sermon including communion, I raced out the alternate exit and was stretching my legs and sucking in the good frosty air when father caught up with me. He belted me a good one, sort of a right cross to the jaw, and down I went in a big snowdrift. After jerking me up and brushing me off, back he and I went through the alternate exit and out shaking hands with the preacher through the main door. Groggy and bleary eyed as I was, I never saw the preacher, just barely his bony, white hand.

This preacher had a mind narrow enough to split a raindrop. Scripture he could quote by the everlasting hour and did.

Uncle Bill never went near the church, of course. So one day the preacher went to call on Uncle Bill to do a little proselytizing. Uncle Bill opened the door and listened a few minutes while his eyes developed that smokey ice look, no doubt. Then all of a sudden, he grabbed the reverend by the shirt front, whirled him around, grabbed him again by the seat of the pants and collar of his coat and waltzed him tip-toe down the gravel path and out through the gate without a word spoken. When the reverend reported to grandfather shortly after, he was still shaky and claimed Uncle Bill belonged in the County Insane Asylum. Some people like Bob Holt and old Dave thought it was one of the funniest things that ever happened. I thought so, too, but around the family, believe me, I never dared laugh. In the family, it was no laughing matter.

While he did not take much to biblical prophesies, Uncle Bill not only wore the prophet hairdo but indulged in prophesizing more or less himself. For one thing, he took a lot of interest in the weather and was a weather prophet. His trappings included barometer, thermometer, windvane, and rain gauge. He had the names for all the various cloud formations and would quiz me on them so I had them all before I started school. The general difference between Uncle Bill's weather predictions and those of others was that his were less often off the track.

Along with clouds, sun, moon, and stars, Uncle Bill believed occult signs occurred in the sky.

There in the corn country, in those days, when the corn was shelled naturally, you had a great gob of cobs. Cobs made a good fast hot fire in the kitchen range and most everybody had a cob shed in which to store cobs. One of the little chores was keeping the corn cob basket as well as the coal bucket filled morning and night. As soon as I could lift and carry, the corn cob basket was my assignment. I carried cobs morning and night. The cob house was about fifty or sixty feet from the back door and had a low corrugated metal roof on which, in the fall of the year, I dried black walnuts after they were shucked. Under this roof along with the cobs was the outhouse. By that time, we did have indoor plumbing but the plumbing frequently went haywire and a Chic Sale was still something not to be done without. In warm weather, I preferred the outhouse to the indoor plumbing. At night it was possible to sit in the outhouse with the door open so you could look at the moon and the stars and listen to the crickets and dream and think.

One summer night just before bedtime, about nine or ten o'clock, I was sitting there with the door open and the metal bushel basket full of cobs outside the door. The moon was high, about three-quarters, but oddly not especially bright. The stars did not stand out much that night, either. Things were ultra quiet. Not a single cricket. Then—and I would not expect you to believe this—a kind of glow developed off to the left of the moon and much closer. Next—you have seen a red hot brand on a branding iron and know what it look like—a sizzling, and I mean sizzling, brand showed up in the center of the particular light area and stayed there burning into me. The brand was a big curve blade knife with the edge of the curved blade in a business like downward position and lights like jewels on the handle, the handle curved opposite to the blade with two-way finger guards. This is as clear to me today (almost seventy years later) as when I saw it while sitting there in the outhouse. You can think I am looney, but I can still see it. After I had plenty of time to absorb it, the brand turned off as suddenly as it turned on. The glow that framed it took longer to fade away.

A cob-carrying kid eleven years old, I sat there quite awhile, petrified. I sat there until mother called out the back door and told me to get the cobs in and get to bed. I knew enough to know this was nothing to relate to mother, or father, or anyone else—except Uncle Bill. I went to bed and laid there thinking about it a long time before I went to sleep.

When I sneaked off first thing the next morning to consult with Uncle Bill (I had to sneak because by that time Uncle Bill and his establishment were strictly off limits), the picture was as sharp and clear as the night before. Plus a thousand questions. Number one: Had he seen it too? Number two: How did it happen? Number three: What did it mean? I was running out all over.

Uncle Bill did not laugh. For what seemed forever, he sat there on the bench outside the door with his hands on his knees and looked at me, not like everything was a big joke, as usual. He was kind and sort of sympathetic. Finally, he told me to sit down on the bench beside him and he put his big arm around my shoulders. He asked me how the knife looked and I took a stick and drew a picture in the dust in front of the bench. He said it was an old time sword used by the Turks called a scimitar. How come a knife like that, which I had never seen before? He said he couldn't say. Omens were oddball, not often clear cut. Omens were as Greek to me as scimitars. So I learned about omens. Indians, it developed, practically operated on omens. Omens could be either good or bad.

"Mouse," Uncle Bill called me Mouse because I was not built big along his lines. "Mouse," he said, "What you saw, nobody else saw. It was just for you. How come, no one can say. But whoever or whatever it is that runs this whirl-i-gig picked you out to tell you something. You will have to figure out the message as you go along.

Nobody else can. But it does not look good. What it says to me is that there will be more Kaiser Wilhelms and all your life you and the whole world will live with a knife hanging over your scalp!"

I was old enough to know who the Kaiser was. "You mean there will be other wars and I will go to Pensacola, Florida and fly hydroplanes and shoot ducks in the air and on the water with machine guns just for practice like Uncle Paul in the last war?"

His arms tightened around my shoulders. "You will not be shooting ducks," he said. "Just keep all this under your hat. Between you and me."

I have kept it under my hat until now when I am telling you. With what has gone on, and is still going on, Uncle Bill hit the omen dead center and at least one other omen as well.

As it happened, I was the firstborn of five. From the day I showed up, father had me all lined out. I was to be a great MD. That was *his* dream: to be an MD. With troubles in his family and no money, the dream was shot down very early. He made it through the eighth grade in a kind of German school in a little corn town across the Father of Waters in Iowa. Coming from a long line of tinsmiths and metal workers, both in the US and the Old Country (which is what is now West Germany), the best he could do was to keep tradition unbroken. The difference was that he had "drive," and I mean drive with a Capital D. He also had brains . . . plenty of brains to have been the best MD in the USA if he had the backing and where-with-all he built up to offer me. He did not stop with pot mending and gutter making. He moved into heating and plumbing and was a Master Plumber. Then with all the building, he went into contracting. Every spare dime plus all he could borrow went into real estate. A good bit, more than I ever thought was necessary, went for contributions to the church. We squeezed pennies, but *always* had a dollar for church. It all paid off, of course. A lot of substantial church members were putting in running water, and hot air or hot water or steam heating. Father put a new heating plant in the church at cost.

You can see how father and Uncle Bill would not hit it off—Uncle Bill had not been there long enough then so they were not as yet on the outs. In fact, father helped Uncle Bill build his house on his acre across the road from the house where I was born. Uncle Bill's house was not much, just one room kind of cabin, in the corn instead of in the woods. It had no inside plumbing and only the cook stove for heating. Our house was one of the biggest in town, with a bay window and window seat, where mother grew ferns and geraniums, off the dining room. Father had two reasons for selling that house. Number One: he built a house to live in only long enough to find the "right buyer." Number Two: he wanted to get away from Uncle Bill. In this case, the Number Two reason was more likely the Number One reason.

Baptisms in those days were celebrated events. The Sunday I was baptized, as the story goes, the event was celebrated at our house by a gathering, coffee, and cake, in the afternoon. Uncle Bill, not yet having painted the town, was invited and, big surprise, showed up. Hair and whiskers combed, clean shirt, new Levis, new high-heeled boots. Big deal. But not for long.

Uncle Bill looked at me and I guess I looked at him. Anyway, I must have had my eyes open. Then he said something like, "Hmmm. Mountains in his eyes." Father took another look at me like he'd missed something and sort of testy said, "What do you mean—mountains?"

Uncle Bill, still looking at me, said, "Blue eyes—blue as Rocky Mountain skies." Father, still testier, said, "You're not saying this boy's headed for a life out there in that wilderness of rocks and savages where you threw away your life, are you?" Uncle Bill now looked at father and, in his very softest way of saying something, said, "Could be." Then without another word to anyone and no cake or coffee, he walked out. It was the first and last time he was ever in our house.

With the preacher and everybody present, my baptism

was sadly, but well remembered. Based on that, the approximate time of Uncle Bill's arrival was dated.

Most of the sidewalks in town were laid with bricks and no good for roller skating. The streets, including the main street downtown were plain Illinois gumbo—full of wagon ruts when wet and dust four inches deep when dry.

Way out where we lived, about ten blocks from the business district which bordered the IC tracks, we were at the end of a *concrete* sidewalk along a street full of grass rather than dust. The concrete sidewalk and street separated Dick Frank's cow pasture from Odebrect's ten acres of alfalfa. When the grass was somewhat grazed down in the pasture, Franks put their three milk cows on the feed in the street. Most of the time, the only way to tell the difference between pasture and street was the barb wire fence between the street right-of-way and the pasture. Odebrect's alfalfa was not fenced. To keep the cows out of the alfalfa while grazing the street, they were picketed with stakes and ropes. The cows were practically belly deep in grass and red top clover whether in the pasture or in the street. Two of the cows were Guernseys, while the other was a Jersey. The Guernseys were better milkers, but the Jersey was best for cream. If you are acquainted with cows, this is generally the case. I could tell you quite a bit about milk and cream. Morning and night for ten years, I drained bucketfuls of the stuff out of Guernseys and Jerseys and ran it through a hand crank separator.

But the dairy business is off the track. What I am trying to point out is that out there at the end of the concrete sidewalk was the roller skaters' rendezvous; we were practically in the country. The only house near our house was Uncle Bill's, just across the street used for pasture rather than travel. From the time I could walk well enough to be turned loose to ramble around the premises, Uncle Bill's place and Uncle Bill, himself, were like magnets. As soon as I was liberated out the back door, I would do what I was told was taboo and beat it across the street to Uncle Bill's diggings. No amount of scolding or bottom-warming could keep me away.

The word diggings in this case is not just a manner of speech. Uncle Bill actually was a digger. He would never take any kind of a paid job, which nobody could understand because they could not figure out how he made a living. At times, if he took a notion and had a liking for whoever was doing the butchering, he would help with butchering a beef or a hog for a share of the meat. But that was the extent of it. Once or twice, I was allowed to go with him when he was helping butcher a hog. He was the one who always shot the hog to kill it. He never missed. One shot, one dead hog. What I liked best was rendering the lard: cooking grease out of the fat in a big iron kettle hung over an open wood fire. What is left of the fat with the grease out is choice eating. If you have never tasted fresh hog cracklings, you have missed something. Uncle Bill also had a reputation as a sausage maker. He turned it out according to a recipe never divulged.

In addition to sausage making, he had a reputation for a number of things not all on the plus side—like, for instance, poker playing, shooting, and shooting pool. Actually Uncle Bill was a billiard whiz. He did not fool around playing rotation or eight ball or any of the usual simple games, unless some sucker came along who wanted a contest for high states, he didn't. For five dollars a game, he would shoot any kind of pool with anybody, but mainly, it was billiards. At billiards, he could have been a pro. When he was at the billiard table, people would gang around and make side bets on certain shots with those betting against him, generally getting odds. At his age and with no glasses, what he could do with a cue stick and billiard balls was unbelievable. You understand, of course, a good bit of this came to me second-handed. Pool shooting, cards, dice, and dancing were the Devil's pastimes. I didn't dare get caught up anywhere in the vicinity.

The fact is I picked up some lumps for hanging around where he had a first-rate reputation on the plus side. This was his garden. Uncle Bill kept a garden and small orchard of assorted fruit practically on a par with his billiard shooting. That being the heyday of home canning and the Ball and Mason jar, practically everybody kept a garden of one kind or another. Uncle Bill's garden was notoriously the best-organized, most diversified, most productive, best tended, and showiest garden not only in town, but for miles around. You name it and Uncle Bill could and did grow it—bigger and better.

Don't misunderstand. The plaudits did not derive from the *entire* establishment. To the male segment gardening was women's and kid's work. Father wouldn't have been caught with a hoe in his hand for love nor money. For him there was no love and nowhere near enough money in cabbages. Any man who spent practically full time messing with vegetables, fruit, and especially flowers, obviously was missing a few marbles. The main applause came from the stitch and chatter distaff; somewhat on the basis of fisherman and pipe smoker, a gardener of Uncle Bill's calibre could not be all bad, even though the good seldom surfaced enough to be visual.

The garden and orchard was laid out on the sides of a gravel walk from the street to Uncle Bill's front door. Trees, shrubs, flowers and whatever bloomed and grew from the time frost went out of the ground in the spring until the first hard frost in the fall. Beautiful. Back behind the house, this side of an osage orange hedge separating Uncle Bill's acre from Wilbur Burr's forty acre cornfield was an outhouse, smokehouse, and a small shed where the grindstone and garden tools were stored, as well as the drilled well with a hand pump. Everybody had a well, for there was no city water or sewer system in those days.

When the corn grew tallest, fastest during the boiling flatland summer, Uncle Bill spent little time over a still hotter coal range, hot packing and cold packing Ball jars. But except for a few preserves and pickles which were his specialties, most of what he laid by was not canned. It was scattered on screen frames and racks, exposed to sun and air, and sacked. He dried sweet corn, apricots, peaches, plums, apples and pears in large quantities. The only thing I enjoyed more than chewing on his dried fruit was his jerky, thin strips and small chunks of dried beef. Most of this was smoked as well as dried.

The smokehouse was about the size of an outhouse and resembled it in appearance, enough so at night if you didn't know which was which, you could mistake one for the other, but only at a distance. As soon as you came close and got a whiff, there was no mistaking the difference. Nothing I know of smells better than a well-used smokehouse; by the same token, nothing smells much worse than a well-used outhouse. Uncle Bill's outhouse smelled much less prominently than most. It was always scrubbed clean, as clean as the floor in his house, with a can of lime on the shelf next to the Sears Roebuck catalog. Pouring lime down the hole reduces the odor of an outhouse, or at least improves it. A lot of outhouses around town could have done with a lot more lime. (Up-ending outhouses was a popular Halloween prank. The stench sometimes made us wish we had never bothered.)

When the smokehouse was filled with hams, bacon, or jerky, and fired with hickory or apple wood, the down-wind aroma was a scent sensation never to be forgotten. Uncle Bill figured his smoked pork would test up with the best, but tell you that beef jerky was a poor substitute for the real article. The best jerky he claimed could only be made with deer meat, not cornfed cow-meat. A good time later when I made my own jerky, I could agree that deer meat jerky is far more flavorful.

Whereas Uncle Bill had a smokehouse and cured all his meat, we had an ice box to keep fresh meat fresh. The ice compartment took up about half the total capacity of the box. It would accommodate seventy-five pounds of ice. Stu Adams, who delivered ice all over town, came with his ice wagon pulled by an old spavined white horse and filled the ice compartment every other day all during warm weather. The way an ice box was built was most unhandy. Ice went in through a door in the top, with the top being just high enough to make any kind of easy lifting impossible. Hoisting a fifty or seventy-five pound block of ice, with ice tongs weighing ten pounds themselves, and lowering the ice into the box was man's work. Stu, himself, was built like an Olympic weight lifter and needed to be. To get anything in or out of the storage compartment below the ice compartment required either a deep stoop or a knee bend. The average housewife did not need reducing exercises to keep her in condition. Just normal operation of the ice box was plenty. Refrigerators, you might say, like women, have come a long, long way. For better and maybe for worse.

Ice in the wagon was covered with sawdust which had to be washed off before it went into the box. What went into ice tea or lemonade, at our house, was scrubbed as well as twice washed. Mother did not trust it even then; she always figured it was frozen in some pond or river near a sewer outlet and was full of germs. Ice, of course, cost money. The main reason Uncle Bill would have none is that he had been around so much surplus free ice he wasn't interested. A matter of principle. Dried meat, and cured meat, he said, had more staying power than fresh meat, anyway. He was probably correct. A little bit of dried meat will take a man a good long way.

With coaching on where I could set foot and where I could not, what was a weed and what was not, I was not only tolerated but welcomed in Uncle Bill's garden. From the time I can remember, I became more and more helpful; when gardening became less and less interesting, I went. Early in the game I followed him up and down the rows closer than a mule follows a bell mare. He would talk to me more like he was talking to himself. Some things would interest me that I still can remember. He talked about a horse named Ray and a mule called Elmer. "Today," he would say, "Ray and I would go down to the river and bring back a bunch of lunkers." Another time when he might be leaning on his hoe handle and looking at the good grazing in the street, he would say, "Old Elmer'd sure like to get a belly full of that red clover." Later on, I came to know the river was the Salmon. Lunkers could be either salmon steelhead, or rainbow treat, but in size, large only. Working in the garden, sitting on the bench in the shade of the wide eave over the front door of his house, and elsewhere around the premises, Ray, Elmer, Uncle Bill, and I covered rough country, especially in and around some peaks called the Seven Devils [Idaho].

The one thing I did not appreciate were the rattlesnakes which were ever present in bountiful size and number. Ray, Elmer, and Uncle Bill were forever tangled up with rattlesnakes and there were nights when I dreamed and screamed about them. Mother, who never could understand how or where the rattlesnakes came into the picture, would wake me out of a screaming jeemie and say, "Don't think about rattlesnakes. Think about the little blue birds in the springtime." Concentrating on bluebirds can be very tranquilizing, in fact, far more so than counting sheep. Probably one of the least known, but best home remedies for insomnia, it has helped me over many nocturnal mental humps, some worse even than rattlesnakes.

Uncle Bill's garden was educational for me in many ways. Take, for instance, potato bugs. In the days when pest warfare was manual rather than chemical and did not decimate bees, birds, and man himself along with the pests, potato bugs were my first stock in trade. Of course, certain poisons like Paris Green and Black Flag could be had for eliminating bugs even then, but Uncle Bill would have none of these. Even the potato bug, he said, had some reason to be in the total patterns. The only trouble was he multiplied too fast and became too numerous. The idea was to hold him to a tolerable limit, not necessarily to wipe him out completely. Since he had exceeded the tolerable limit and was eating himself out of house and home as well as wrecking Uncle Bill's potato production, the potato bug and I became enemies. Equipped with a quart Mason jar loaded with a cupful of coal oil (kerosene), I went to picking, to cut him down to size for his own good as well as that of the potato. My additional incentive was ten cents an inch for each inch of dead potato bugs in the jar. A fractional inch at the same rate. The potato bug is not especially elusive, but neither is he much for bulk. An inch of potato bugs saturated in kerosene in a quart jar numbered more potato bugs than I could then count.

Despite the fact that both supply and demand may be unlimited, the business of picking potato bugs is no road to riches. It can rapidly deteriorate to a tedium calling to mind numerous alternative pursuits, less profitable but far more enjoyable. Also, at the height of the potato bug season, his environment heats up to the point of discouraging human manual attack. All of the excuses bounced off Uncle Bill like rubber balls off a brick wall. No job, he said, was entirely enjoyable. All jobs had drawbacks and dull moments, at best. It wasn't imperative nor even good sense to pick potato bugs in full heat of the day. The time to pick potato bugs was early morning or evening. On the other hand, if I couldn't take outdoor heat, the cold, wind, rain, drought, and assorted other discomforts, I should get a job like a shoe clerk, under a roof and inside four walls. If I didn't want to pick potato bugs, I could quit, but to quit before a job was finished, or even well started, would make me an "undependable," which was a man built without a backbone, like a wet noodle. The upshot was that I went back to picking potato bugs until the end of potato bug season; I have never cared much for potatoes since.

After the potato bug fiasco, I should have known better. That same summer I fell into the gooseberry trap. Uncle Bill was no gooseberry addict but to round

things out, or for curiosity, or by accident, he supported
half a dozen giant size gooseberry bushes. The size of
the berries was in keeping with the parent plant. And so
with the thorns. One day when the berries were about
ripe, and we were admiring the bumper crop, Uncle Bill
said he would make me a proposition. Unlike himself, he
said, some folks dearly loved gooseberries. If these
gooseberries were picked and peddled from house to
house, they might bring maybe a nickel a quart. Newt
Wimmer who ran the grocery might want to buy some
and sell them across the counter. Maybe as many as a
peck or half a bushel. A peck, according to Uncle Bill,
was eight quarts which at a nickel a quart would be
forty cents. Two pecks, if Newt would take half a bushel
equalled a fortune. Providing I would pick and peddle,
Uncle Bill would sell me the whole crop; and how much
did I think it was worth? I did not think it was worth an
inch of potato bugs, but then again I could see I was
buying a hell of a load of gooseberries, so finally I told
him ten cents. He said, "Sold." And after I paid the
dime out of my potato bug money, I was in the
gooseberry business. I rounded up an empty lard bucket
and a bushel basket and went to work.

While it takes fewer gooseberries than potato bugs to
fill a quart, picking potato bugs is much more pleasurable and satisfying. In the case of gooseberries, there is
not only the same tedium and heat, but thorns to content
with and the only motive is profit. With potato bugs
there were no thorns, and, along with profit, there is the
saving, namely of the potato. Of course it is possible to
put up with thorns and do without any soul satisfaction
if the profit is big enough. At first blush, profit from the
gooseberries looked tremendous. This is where I learned
that all is not gold that glitters: never go into a business
deal without turning it over and examining all the
angles and never buy and pick gooseberries for market
without first making sure of the market. As it turned
out, Uncle Bill was not the only one with a bumper crop
of gooseberries. Everybody else had one, too. After

harvesting half a bushel, I could not sell a quart. Plus being out a dime in the bargain.

When I made the mistake of mentioning the gooseberry disaster to mother, she went steaming across the street and gave Uncle Bill a few paragraphs on a grown man taking advantage of an innocent child. When father heard about it, he said Uncle Bill was the kind who would steal a dead fly from a blind spider. On the other hand, I had nobody to blame but myself; he had told me time and time again to steer clear of Uncle Bill. What he told me, he said, just went in one ear and out the other because nothing was in between, or if so, I never used it. Uncle Bill never offered to return my money. He claimed it was money well spent. For a dime, I learned a lesson that could be worth millions. In September, a few days before his annual disappearance, after all the potato bugs were picked and the unpicked gooseberries had dropped off or dried on the bush, he gave me what looked like a dime, but turned out to be a ten dollar gold piece, for what he called, "beginning to get smart."

After I had done something up to Uncle Bill's expectations for a change, he would say, "That's good. You stick around and we'll make a man of you yet." Variations on this had to do with teaching me "what makes the world go round," "how to hold up your end," and "to use your own think tank." These were necessary so I would "never have to go looking for a handout" or "depend on hand-me-down answers." While he would give a down-and-outer like Old Dave practically the shirt off his back, he held a deep conviction that the average reasonably healthy man had no right or excuse for getting himself into any such sorry condition. The sick, maimed, and blind left him painfully uncomfortable. He would walk a mile around to avoid a wheelchair case.

One day, at about the age six or seven, while running to fetch a hoe from the tool shed, I somehow tripped and piled smack into a stack of clay flowerpots. Pots and parts of pots flew in all directions. One part laid open my right knee, where the scar is the reminder "to keep your eyes open and watch for a clear track" to this day. It was a dandy cut and a bloody mess. I did not, like the Indian, just sit and grunt. I grabbed the wound, jumped up on the good leg, and howled like a castrated hound. This brought Uncle Bill on a high lope; with a firm grip on my neck, pressure on the right pressure point to stop the blood, he gave me a few choice words pertaining to what worse thing would happen if I did not shut my yap. Once things quieted down, which was quick, he picked me up, packed me into the house and laid me on the bed with orders to lie still. After washing the blood off with cold water, he doused the cut with some brownish stuff out of a pint bottle that was liquid fire. If he had not been practically sitting on me, I would have hit the ceiling. Also, I could taste blood from biting my tongue keeping my yap shut. Following this, he pushed the edges of the cut tight together and told me to take hold and keep them that way. While I did this, he converted part of an old bed sheet into a compress and bandages and applied them to the cut. When father hauled me off to the doctor for professional treatment later in the afternoon, the doc said Old Bill had done an A-1 job. The only thing he could have done different would have been to put in a few stitches for which, by then there was no need.

The next day, when I showed up at Uncle Bill's feeling like a cripple returning to the scene of battle, he gave me the big joke look and a pat on the back. "Mouse," he said, "When I poured that whiskey in that cut I thought you might take off and never be back. You stick around and we'll make a man of you yet."

Any catalog of Uncle Bill's sins would have shown gambling high on the list. When it came to cards or dice especially, word had it that he was not one for any amateur to tangle with. This was consistent. Not only with cards and dice, but across the board, he was no man for anyone, either amateur or professional, to tangle with. He had convictions and would back them to the limit. The way he bluffed was sneaky. Just when you were sure he would never bluff, he would run one and more times than not make it work. His luck, furthermore, was at times phenomenal. Bob Holt swore that Uncle Bill could draw two cards to an inside straight and hit it when everybody else drew blanks.

Uncle Bill's hands did not exactly match the rest of his anatomy. The fingers were long and fine like a piano player. He would pick up a deck of cards and practically make it talk. He took care of his hands. Whenever he worked, he wore leather gloves.

Anything worth doing in Uncle Bill's code, was worth doing right—top notch. Even when the stakes were beans or matches, he did not play cards simply for amusement. He was a competitor with one objective: to come in first. This is not saying he was a poor loser, nor a whoopee, rub-it-in winner. Win, lose or draw, he outwardly maintained a matter-of-fact stance, which to some could be very irritating and downright disconcerting. One thing did get to him—an uncertain, indecisive player who slowed up the contest. He, himself, made instant decisions. Anytime a player with obvious paralysis of the decider entered the game, Uncle Bill would soon pick up his chips and let himself out.

Any and all games of chance, there and then, of course, were illegal. What went on was mostly a small change harmless pastime-type poker beneficently tolerated in back rooms of pool halls by the local law or occasional extemporaneous crap games like those on a warm winter Sunday afternoon in an empty box car on the IC siding, not easily detected or worth raiding. Just now and then, the stakes became slightly racy with as much as a hundred dollars in the pot.

Unbeknownst to anyone other than Uncle Bill and Bob Holt, I started gathering card and dice savvy about as soon as I learned to read and count. Uncle Bill and Bob, especially on poor weather days, played cribbage by the hour for a dime a game. Cribbage for a kindergarten beginner is a fairly complicated contest, but cribbage was easy for me. A big incentive was Uncle Bill's crib board. The board and pegs were made from prehistoric mastodon tusk ivory from Alaska. The ivory was black on top shading down through brown to white. I liked to think about what the critter must have looked like when he was alive and still wearing his tusk. Uncle Bill showed me a drawing of a healthy mastodon in one of his books. It was very impressive. In the live state, of course, a mastodon's tusk was all white like the elephant. When buried for a few hundred or thousand years, the ivory takes on the color of whatever it is buried in like black dirt, gravel, or whatever.

Like everybody else, Uncle Bill had some definite ideas on what should and should not be included in the educational curriculum. In his book, the whole business of gambling in all its common forms, including cheating and how to cheat, should be exposed to the student before the eighth grade. Like with drink and dope, he said, ignorance and intolerance led more people astray than knowledge. A course in stud or draw or craps, with the teacher acting as dealer, at about the fifth or sixth grade, would be very popular, especially when the teacher was caught with too many aces or loaded dice. I was very fortunate. I got the course and the teacher was an expert.

The spectrum of wagering is practically infinite. Uncle Paul, who graduated in agriculture and was supposedly an expert in everything that had to do with agriculture, including grains, once moved into the grain market. What he knew about grain apparently he did not know about the market. He lost his shirt. Playing the grain market, however, is fully respectable and no sin. It is not in the same category with cards, dice, and horse racing in any sense.

One of the less likely shades of the wagering spectrum in which Uncle Bill, Paul Groves, and I became unprofitably involved had to do with pigeons. Paul owned and operated the barber shop in town. He was a good barber but more he was a pigeon fancier. For the price of a shave or haircut, if you cared to listen, you could get enough information on the merits of various species of pigeons, food requirements, breeding habits, flight speed, and homing instincts to fill an encyclopedia. If you didn't care to listen, you got it anyway.

The pigeon is a fascinating bird, and up to a point, an engaging topic of conversation. For one thing, the common everyday slate blue pigeon that overpopulates cities, haylofts, and belfries is mainly good for nothing other than target practice in the country and amusement of bench warmers in city parks. Although edible, he has a skimpy carcass. To a pigeon fancier or squab producer, he is the very least of more than a hundred varieties. What we are talking about here are pouters, fan tails, homers, racers, and porkers. Some of these are beauties and grow almost as big as a white leghorn chicken or, at least, a large bantam. My all-around favorites of Paul's collection were the white king and red carneau.

The variety that almost broke my neck was either homer or a racer. Neither of these is particularly outstanding in appearance and I have never been sure which is which or whether they are one and the same. My understanding of pigeon racing and wagering is equally scant. All I know is that Paul somehow fast-talked Uncle Bill into going in with him on the purchase of a high or fast flying purebred pigeon to be entered in competition and get them both into big money. When this highbred stud arrived, it shortly developed he had very lowbrow tastes. By some disastrous mischance, never fully explained, this bird flew the comfortable Groves coop and came to roost with the hoi polloi in the belfry of our Lutheran church. The roost was a kind of attic area above the bell under the belfry roof. The reason I came to be clued in on all this and to be brought into the act, was the size of the trap door that gave access through the belfrey ceiling to the belfrey attic. It was home to many local, run-of-the-mill pigeons. This trap door, for a pigeon, was quite roomy and for the average man, very tight. Why it was put there in the first place is a good question. Why it was left open makes another. Still another, most critical at the moment, could a small boy equipped with light and gunny sack, on a dark June night, get through it? At the offering fee, a pair of white kings to start my own business, I figured it was quite possible. Access to the bell tower was through a more commodious trap door in the high ceiling of the church vestibule inside the handshaking main door. The heavy one-inch bell rope dangled through a hole in the ceiling close to this trap door down to within about four feet of the vestibule floor. A built-in ladder climbed the wall close to the rope from floor to trap door. Another ladder could be seen ascending from the floor of the open bell tower to the lesser entrance to the pigeon roost. All very handy.

While the church doors were locked, one of the basement windows was not. Once through the window, a door could be unlocked from inside. One of the three of us might have asked permission of the preacher to enter and retrieve, but all things and the company considered, cooperation of the preacher was doubtful. At best, he would probably insist on a church board meeting for a vote, but which time, regardless of the vote outcome, the prize pigeon could be gone. Since the preacher's parsonage was separated from the church by about 100 yards of pasture for his driving horse, the chances of detection from this quarter were remote. From all other quarters detection was equally unlikely; all other houses nearby were at least a block away. Anyway you figured, a midnight raid in the dark of the moon looked like a cinch. On the other hand, you will recall that old saw about the best laid schemes of mice and men going haywire and it is no joke.

Once school was out and summer set in, I set up my wigwam in the orchard back of the house we were living in at that time. This wigwam was made with a big wornout living room rug with a few holes in it, good for ventilation, but not very waterproof. On good hot nights, I was allowed to take a few old quilts and bed down in it. Good hot nights in Illinois are more numerous than not throughout the summer. Compared to my normal upstairs bedroom, even with all the windows open, my tepee, pitched under the kiss of a green gage plum and a Jonathon apple was cool as a desert cave. Cool, too, for ducking out with no embarrassing questions asked when need arises for recovering a costly errant bird.

When I arrived at the rendezvous near the spirea shrub, under the stained glass window depicting the good shepherd leading a flock of woolies on the west side of the church, I was so cool I had goose pimples. It was dark as the inside of a black cow and quiet as a moment of prayer. The two pigeon owners, armed with the necessary light and gunny sack, were present and ready.

With the light muffled to a candle glow, I slid through the basement window into the room where the Ladies Aid held their potluck suppers. Having spent yea time there, I knew the layout of the basement and whole church like the back of my hand. I could have made my way around with no trouble even without the light. The only part not familiar was the bell tower and I was about to learn that. The basement stairs came up to a small room accessible from the outside by way of the back door. The church had three doors: the main handshaking door, the alternate exit also at the front, and this back door. I unlocked the door and Uncle Bill and Paul came in. It was the first time either of them had been in the church—maybe the first time they had been in any church. Two other doors, in addition to the outside door, led out of the back room. One went to the pulpit area where the preacher performed and the other went to the main part of the church filled with rows of long white-oak pews. As well as being long, these pews were hard and slick-polished; they were very uncomfortable to sit on and next to impossible to sleep on.

The three of us went out into the pew area with me in the lead with the muffled light, next Paul, and then Uncle Bill bringing up the rear. At that time of night in that light, a pew looked more uncomfortable than usual and actually sort of spooky. I began to wish I were back in bed in my tepee. We went through the two swinging doors from the pew area to the vestibule where the bell rope dangled from the ceiling and the ladder went up the wall. The plan had me going up the ladder first, with Paul, who was not as old or as big as Uncle Bill, following me up with the light and the sack. Uncle Bill was to stay below and sound any necessary alert.

When I came to the trap door in the vestibule ceiling at the top of the ladder, it was a heavy door and took some doing for me to get open. About the time Paul decided I had better come down and let him go first and open the door, I finally pushed the cover clear and crawled through, coming face to face with the bell. The size of the bell hanging there in its stanchion was surprising. Considering the weight, I wondered how anybody ever hoisted it up there. How church steeples and bell towers are constructed and equipped always has been a marvel and a mystery to me. A steeple, jack, or human fly as they are called, either has not heard of the law of gravity or is overready to meet his Maker. Like the highwire act, it is a last gasp occupation. At least, that is what I was thinking while Paul crawled through the hole behind me. We stood there for a minute and he said, "I never thought that bell was that big. Must make a heck of a racket standing here beside it. Think you can get through that hole up there?" The door in the belfry ceiling looked bigger from the bell level than from the ground. I said, "Sure," and went up the ladder with him behind me. The door was big enough and then some. Paul, himself, could have gone through it. Up near the top, he passed me the light. I eased up and poked my head and shoulders through, slow and easy. Right then things started to move—away from the hole in all directions. I turned on the light. In an area about fifteen feet square and three feet high, pigeons in all stages from egg to adult were everywhere. The floor was paved with a two-inch crust of pigeon droppings ranging through all stages from freshly deposited to powder dry. A few light sleepers took to the air, stirred up the dust, hit the roof and fell back. Generally though the light seemed to be a blinding tranquilizer. Most of the community sat tight. Below me on the ladder, Paul sotoed, "Can you see our bird?" I said, "I think so. Way over in the corner. Wait till the dust settles." The dust was in my nose. I tried but could not stop a sneeze, which woke up more sleepers who flew up and around and against the roof stirring up more fertilizer and creating a racket I was sure could be heard not only all over our town, but six miles away in Sidney. Backing down for fresh air, I tied my handkerchief over my nose and told Paul to come on up and block the hole while I tried to corral the purebred. I could see that the ceiling was very flimsy and that I would have to maneuver on the two by four rafters or fall through and land on the bell, making a racket that would sound in Mattoon, twenty miles away, as well as Sidney. I will not bore you with any more details except to say that ever since those next ten minutes, whenever I have heard the expression, "That's for the birds," I think of where it should have derived.

Having finally caught and sacked the bird, Paul and I did not dilly-dally making the descent with me in the lead and Paul behind carrying the bird in the bag. The bird did not like the bag. He flopped around trying to fly. When you are in a hurry descending a ladder, holding the top of a gunny sack with a flopping bird inside with one hand, and trying to close an overhead trapdoor with the other, anything can happen. In this case, it happened. Just as I bottomed out and turned the light on so Paul could see better to shut the door, the door shut on Paul's fingers. The bird picked this exact time to make a big flop in the sack and it is not surprising that Paul lost all hold on the ladder. The only thing that saved him was the bell rope. Twisting around, he grabbed the bell rope and managed to hang on. I have always been somewhat sensitive in a negative way to lightning and thunder, but no lightning or thunder ever left me paralyzed as the bong of that bell overhead at midnight.

Uncle Bill grabbed the end of the bell rope and Paul, still hanging on to the sack with the bird still flopping around, came sliding down. Very slowly and carefully, Uncle Bill eased up on the rope. Then, I can tell you, we got out the back door and made a run up the street about half a block to some big lilac bushes overgrowing the sidewalk in front of Guy Williams' place. About the time we hit there, a light went on in Guy's house and looking back, we could see a light in the preacher's house, also. Next a light came on at Hudson's place across from Guy and we hurried along up the street toward Paul's dovecote, a block up and half a block down an alley. By this time, it was safe to talk and Paul swore and said, "That goldarn door. I got three mashed fingers." Uncle Bill puffed and shook and I thought he was winded from the run. Then he doubled up holding his belly and I knew he wasn't winded. He was laughing more than I had ever seen him laugh. I said, "I better beat it, back to bed." Uncle Bill choked out, "Okay, Mouse. You did good. Real good." As I took off, Paul said, "Yeah, I should have let him shut the darn door."

Sneaking back to the tepee, round about I noticed the Rices next door to our house had a light on and I wasn't surprised to see one upstairs in our house, too. Mother was the lightest sleeper ever. At breakfast, the next morning, she said, "Joseph, did you hear that church bell in the middle of the night?" "Church bell?" I said. "Well, Dad didn't hear it either. The strangest thing. Just one loud ring." A lot of other people also thought that it was strange, especially the preacher.

Most of my trouble came in trying to explain why Paul Groves would give me a pair of expensive pigeons—even though I was careful not to take possession till a couple of weeks had elapsed since the strange midnight bong of the church bell. Father went so far as to ask Paul about it. Paul told me he told father he just wanted to get others around town interested in growing pigeons and let it go at that. Father was no more interested in pigeons than in gardening. Pigeon business, he said, was purely monkey business. Nobody but a barber would get mixed up with it. That was the end of it—except that neither Uncle Bill or Paul would ever talk about what went on with their pigeon once we got him back where he belonged. I was left to wonder and am still wondering.

Uncle Bill's interest in racing was not confined solely to pigeons. If wagering was involved, it covered anything that flew, swam, ran, crawled, rolled, or skated on ice. For one thing, it extended to humans and specifically me.

Sizewise, I started out with little or nothing to brag about and was more or less a slow grower all the way. While the fact that I was a flyweight was obviously somewhat disappointing to Uncle Bill, he said the outlook was not entirely hopeless; in a showdown, a man's size could be very deceiving.

One day in late June, we were sitting on the bench in the shade of the wide eave, taking a five after some hoeing and weed pulling in the garden. Uncle Bill's big gloved hand reached over and covered my skinny little knee. "Pretty soon we have that Fourth of July town picnic coming up," he said.

"Yep. Last year I beat everybody in the foot race and won the three dollar prize."

"Think you can do it again? Some of those kids are a lot bigger than you are, and older. This year, you'll be in the seven to ten year old race and you're only seven and it's a longer run."

"No matter. I can run faster than any of 'em."

"Maybe we ought to practice a little and see if you can run as fast that far."

"Sure," I said. "Where do we practice?"

"Over there on the roller skating walk," he said. That's how I won two prizes that year: one from the picnic and one from him. How much he won I never knew, but being the smallest and one of the youngest in the race, as well as close kin, the odds were right, you can be sure. After running twice a day, twice as far as the required distance for a week before the big event itself, he had me tuned up like a jack rabbit and it was strictly no contest. My total take amounted to a whopping fortune, but the two dollars I got from him, in addition to the three dollars from the picnic was a secret just between him and me. It was the start of a running career that lasted through college—from which I never made one thin dime, only pretty but worthless ribbons and medals plus a few headlines. That was the last year the running contests at the Fourth of July picnic at the last remaining small grove of original hardwood trees constituting the town park, were held. Rumor had it that this too was on account of Uncle Bill when, with like a lot of other things for which he was blamed, he was mostly innocent.

I say Uncle Bill had me tuned up like a jack rabbit. Of course, there were no jack rabbits in Illinois—then or ever. The rabbit in Illinois is the cottontail. The jack is bigger and faster on his feet than the cottontail, but not as good to eat.

At that time in that part of Illinois, cottontail rabbit hunting was a popular sport. As a matter of fact, the cottontail was about the only game left to hunt. There were few bobwhite quail, but not many. One day in the spring, late in the afternoon, we heard a kind of drumming noise coming from the cornfield back of Uncle Bill's cabin. Uncle Bill listened a little and said, "I'll be darned—a sure enough prairie chicken. Let's go see if we can spot him." So we eased out through the

osage orange hedge a little ways and saw this bird that
was blowing up a yellow balloon under his bill every
now and then and flapping his wings while he did a
little up and down dance, which was where the sound
was coming from—the wing flapping, I mean. We
watched for a few minutes and Uncle Bill sadly shook
his head. "Poor old boy," he said. "I bet there ain't a hen
for miles around." As Uncle Bill explained it, this was a
rooster prairie chicken trying to drum himself up a hen
and build a nest. He said the country was once prairie
chicken heaven with thousands of them around, but
market hunters had whittled down the flock to only a
very few here and there. As a matter of fact, that was
the one and only prairie chicken, with all the miles I
covered rabbit hunting, I ever saw in that part of
Illinois. I never forgot it, and like Uncle Bill, the sight
of it made me very sad.

According to Uncle Bill, the market hunters once
hauled prairie chickens, rabbits, and other things like
ducks and geese off to market by the wagon load! Now
the prairie chickens were so few nobody hardly ever saw
one. Rabbits were no longer numerous enough to make
market hunting worth the chips. He said the day would
come when they would be just like the prairie chicken.
It wouldn't pay to take a gun and go looking for one
even for the pot. He sure enough had it figured out. A
man goes out with a gun today in Illinois and about all
he gets is exercise without even fresh air or clear
sunshine.

You take the like of migratory game such as ducks
and that was the time in Illinois they were getting so
scarce the only way to get real good shooting was to set
out shelled corn along a pond or waterway—bait the
poor birds and shoot them on the feed ground. Some
landowners who had a piece of water on the place would
set up traps like this and charge hunters who could pay
to come and shoot. I know because I went once with my
Uncle Paul, who worked in Chicago, and it made me
sick. Now and then I would run onto a duck or two

along a puddle and get off a shot but never downed a duck. That kind of shooting was okay. It was giving the duck a sporting chance, but I couldn't stomach the baiting. It was anything but sport. Might as well shoot chickens in the barnyard.

In those days there were still quite a few rabbits in the cornfield and they were fat and toothsome, to say the least. They didn't have mechanical pickers that vacuum every kernel of corn. With hand shucking into a wagon pulled by a team of horses or mules, a lot of nubbins were left in the field for cottontails to chew on.

I can't remember what age but as soon as I was able to walk a mile or more, Uncle Bill took two pieces of one inch by four inches and two pieces of one inch by six inch boards about two and a half inches long and built a box trap which we baited with half an ear of corn left in the field. We set it along the hedge between his house and Wilbur Burr's cornfield. The door on this trap was hinged to a piece of wire across the top of the four inch by six inch entrance by means of a couple of small staples. When the trap was set, the door would be propped up inside the trap with a thin piece of corn stalk. The rabbit entered to eat the corn at the far closed end of the box, knocked down the prop on the way in, down came the door and he was meat for the table.

To get yourself in the rabbit trapping business, in addition to the trap, you needed a light club. The handle of an old broom was ideal. With the rabbit in the trap, the trap was handily upended, door end up. You reached in, grabbed him by the hind legs, hauled him out of the trap head down, and put a quick end to his mistake with a clean hard whack of the club behind his ears.

Until getting into the trapping business, I thought the only sound a rabbit could produce came from thumping with his hind feet. If you have never heard the scream of a rabbit when pulled out of a trap, dangled head down and about to meet his maker due to a behind-the-ears whack with a broomstick, you probably think the same thing. The first time I heard the scream, I dropped the rabbit and it got away. It is a blood curdler original. The only thing anywhere like it that I have come onto is an eagle scream at some lonesome place when you had no idea there was an eagle anywhere around. Of course, with trapping rabbits you more or less get used to it. Not every rabbit would let go with the scream.

The only thing that gave me about as much of a start as hearing my first rabbit scream had to do with a skunk. It was also my first skunk. I caught this skunk by his right front leg in a spring-jaw trap at a mink set. His getting himself into the trap was a mistake right at the outset. Standing well back out of normal skunk spray range, I leveled on his head with my single shot .22 rifle. When I let fire, down went the polecat, apparently to his total reward.

Never having removed a skunk from a trap, much less transporting one from the wild and removing his hide, the thought occurred to me to unfasten the long chain from the stake and head for some skunk-skinning expert like Uncle Bill or Bob Holt without laying my own hand on said skunk at all. Since there was about four inches of snow on the ground dragging the skunk in the trap at the end of the chain would damage the pelt no way.

So I took out at a normal pace through the dead, downed corn stalks pulling my questionable prize behind. I had not gone far when it suddenly occurred to me that the weight of the drag had strangely become much lighter. I looked at what gave over my shoulder, and there was that skunk up on three good legs very much alive and keeping up with his foot in the trap with no dead weight at all. Apparently instead of hitting him between the eyes as targeted, my .22 slug went off center and creased his skull just enough to temporarily knock him down. Suddenly the relatively long chain on the trap was way too short for safe company with my catch. The instant I recovered from my paralytic surprise I dropped the chain, shifted my feet into high gear, got a big tough corn stalk caught between my legs and fell flat on my face still well within spray range of a big healthy polecat. This is when I found out I could cover ground on hands and knees about as fast as upright on two feet. Luckily, in the meantime, my quarry was apparently still in a daze and did not move. Wiping the snow off my gun and making sure there was none fouling the barrel, I got off a shot from a prone position and *this* time my skunk was down to stay.

When finally I arrived at Uncle Bill's dragging the skunk, he took it out of the trap and showed me how to take the hide off without getting the scent all over the hide, or the skinner, either. He said it was a big prime hide without much white and should fetch a good price. Then, since he never missed anything, no matter how little, he wanted to know how I got the knees of my pants so dirty and he noticed some dirt on my gun. Even though I had decided not to, I had to tell him what all happened. Like the night when Paul Groves got his fingers caught in the trap door of the church belfry and slid down the bell rope, he huffed and puffed like he was out of breath and not much sound, which is the way he laughed when he laughed real hard. He put his arm around me and huffed and puffed some more and finally said now he had heard everything—and then some.

The way to shoot a rabbit was not with a shotgun but with a .22 rifle to catch him sitting and pot him through the head before he broke from cover. This saved a lot of mess and meat, but called for quiet stalking, which in a field of down dry cornstalks crackling underfoot is not easy. The ideal time for rabbit hunting was after a fresh snowfall when they are easily tracked to their chosen hideout and generally sit tight till the hunter can spot them within easy shooting distance and take good aim.

With what the family consumed, a few neighbors with whom I had standing orders for rabbits at regular intervals and the one butcher shop (otherwise known as the "meat market") in town, my outlet for cleaned rabbits at twenty-five cents each was constant and in my estimation quite lucrative. Competition was practically nil as not many troubled themselves to build the traps, carry them two at a time several miles to set out in the cornfields, run the line every cold winter morning and pick up and clean the catch before school. At one time, I had as many as a dozen traps, which was a few too many for easy daily checks and caused me to cut back to eight. As soon as the corn was shucked in October or November, I lugged the traps to the fields and before the ground thawed to mud come spring, I lugged them home again. My total take decimated the local supply of rabbits little if any and was always within the legal limit—which at the time amounted to almost no limit at all.

When it came to toothsome game, Uncle Bill claimed that a well-fried, corn-fed cottontail beat all. Maybe the only thing better, he said, was a well-fried fox squirrel or red squirrel living mainly on black walnuts or hickory nuts.

By walking the rails and crossties of the IC railroad west from town about two miles, you would come to the only year round trickle of water anywhere near. This three-foot wide, foot deep drainage ditch, appropriately named the Black Slough, ran about as much black soil in solution as water. In summer, it was dammed up at a spot slightly wider and deeper than usual, for what was known as swimming or more accurately, mud crawling, by the lesser males of the community, who disported there in the nude. Since the dam was constructed only of old doors, planks, and sod, it leaked badly and backed water up in a puddle three to four feet deep.

The Black Slough supported only a few minnows that could be caught with a cheesecloth net and carried home to die in a fruit jar of water. There, too, were a few frogs that never grew legs big enough to be edible, and every now and then a crawdad or two. A few lost mallards were attracted to its surface as a temporary place for rest and reorientation. The compelling item of interest to me was the rather plentiful resident population of bank-dwelling muskrats and the fact that the course of the trickle seemed to constitute a kind of highway for mink on the move. Along about 1925, when I was fifteen, a Grade A large muskrat hide shipped to Sears Roebuck was worth two dollars and fifty cents. Never having heard or dreamed of what is now known as Junior's weekly allowance, this was a small fortune. Once on a cute type of set (trap), recommended to me by old Dave Brazelton, I caught a No. 1 large brown male mink that brought twelve dollars, which was like striking the mother lode. Uncle Bill claimed it was not the unique set that fooled the mink, but just that he stumbled onto the trap when he had his mind on something else—probably a female. Mind-lock on a female, he said, would get you stumbling into all kinds of traps and I should never forget it. Let the mink be a lesson.

This advice may or may not have had something to do with another item for which I developed an early and long-lasting fascination: namely, all manner of firearms. Hanging on a big spike driven in the wall above and a little to the right of Uncle Bill's bed, was a wide black gunbelt gleaming with cartridges. Attached to the belt was a black leather holster out of which protruded the ivory grips of a large calibre (I learned later it was a Colt single action .44 calibre) pistol. The elevation of the spike, length of the belt, and direction of the handle of the gun, were such as to facilitate quick and easy reach of this cannon by anyone sitting or reclining on the bed. From the lower end of the holster dangled a couple of leather thongs whose purpose I also learned later was for tying around the wearer's leg somewhere above the knee, thereby holding the holster tight against that part of the anatomy.

As well as being within reach of anyone lying on the bed, this weapon was in reach of a small boy standing alongside of the bed. The first time I reached to touch same, I well remember. Out of nowhere a big paw hit my outstretched hand knocking me to my knees, leaving me feeling like my arm was certainly separated from the rest of me at the right shoulder. When I looked up, more or less in a daze, Uncle Bill's face was not six inches from mine and that smokey look was ablaze. Pointing a finger at the gun, he said, in a tone of voice like a hiss of a snake, "Never, never touch." After a little pause in a soft relaxed touch, "Until I tell you, you can." While he stood over me silently, I picked myself up and took a seat on the bed holding onto my lightning struck arm and looking at the wall hanging sort of petrified, like the gun itself rather than Uncle Bill had hit me. After about a minute of quiet concentration, I looked at Uncle Bill and slowly and very positively got out, "Never—until you tell me." "Good," he said. He went over to the stove and poured himself a cup of coffee and brought me a handful of dried apricots which took me awhile to eat. I learned my lesson.

A few years later, when I was maybe eight or nine, I busted in on him one day when he had the gun out of the holster, running an oily rag or the end of a wire through the barrel. Shells out of the gun were scattered next to him on the kitchen table. I shut the door carefully behind me and stayed put just inside. Neither one of us said a word. Uncle Bill finally put the empty shell chamber back in the gun, gave it a couple of test whirls while I watched and out of nowhere said, "C'mere Mouse—let's see if you're strong enough to lift this thing." I couldn't believe my ears.

Advancing to the table cluttered with shells, oil can, and cleaning rags, I said eagerly and confidently, "I'm plenty strong." Carefully pointing the muzzle away from both of us, he held the smokepole so I could take hold of the handle and the instant I had a hold, he let go his hold and my gun-holding hand dropped from horizontal to almost vertical. The weight was unbelievable. By using both hands I was barely able to bring the thing at arm length up to eye level and point it at the window.

"Don't touch the trigger," he said. "The gun might be loaded."

"It's not loaded," I said with the barrel wavering around in circles still more or less pointing at the window.

"Did you check to see if it's loaded?"

Giving up the pointing exercise, I carefully handed the hardware back to him and pointing to the shells on the table said, "All the shells are right there on the table."

Holding the gun by the handle and giving it a quick shake he flipped out the cylinder and what appeared left me dumbfounded and scared skinny. There was a shell in every chamber. Reaching out and touching the exposed casing of a shell not believing what I was seeing. I got out, "It can't be. I was standing there watching you every minute."

"Uh huh," he said. "But somehow the gun *is* loaded. Does that teach you anything?"

"Yes sir," I said emphatically. "When you pick up any kind of gun, stop and look to see if it is loaded—never trust *anybody!*"

"Correct," he said, "on both counts." Taking the gun and slipping it into the holster attached to the gunbelt hanging on the wall by the bed, he added, "One more thing. *This* gun is *always* loaded. And *never* forget it."

Except for just one time, many, many years later, when I would have sworn on a stack of bibles the gun wasn't loaded and shot a hole in the lower level concrete floor with a 410 shotgun, I never did forget it. Luckily, the hole was very minor and located in a dark corner of a room where it was never noticed. One night on a bird hunt with an old shooting pardner in whom, as a safe gun handler, I had ultimate confidence, he shot a hole through the ceiling and roof of our one-story motel room with a 12 gauge automatic. I was watching his every move and standing suspiciously clear of all the action. Unfortunately, the action occurred in the midst of a veritable cloudburst and repairs of shot and water damage to the ceiling and roof turned out to be quite expensive.

A few years still later, Uncle Bill buckled on his cannon without wheels and took me out in the country to a big hayfield with a big stack of baled hay that we could shoot into without fear of bouncing bullets into a farmhouse. Even by resting the gun on a corner post brace, I could not hit a gallon can at ten paces. Old as he was and without his spectacles, Uncle Bill hit four out of five small-sized condensed milk cans in five shots so close together they sounded almost like one. He shook his head saying he should have hit all five. This gun, he said, was not a gun for boys and that I shouldn't feel bad about not being able to hit the gallon can. My time would come. For about two days after this target shoot, my hearing was not the best and mother worried that I might be going deaf, never suspecting that I might have reason. The near detonations of a .44 call for leather ear drums.

Other than as an item of merchandise with rather favorable mark-up and rapid turnover, in a hardware store, father hated guns with a passion and hardly knew shotguns from rifles. We never sold handguns of any type as a matter of principle, regardless of customer demand or profit. He refused to stock handgun ammunition. Grandfather occasionally took a day off to hitch his horse, Prince, to the buggy, take his long bamboo pole and drive six or seven miles to the Embarras (locally referred to as the Ambraw) River after catfish and sunfish. Father had no time for fishing or hunting. The name of his game was "getting ahead" and he played it to the limit—in a hurry every minute. Hunting and fishing, he said, never got anyone anywhere—but I noticed he always ate his share of the rabbits I supplied for the table.

One time when I was excitedly after his permission to go on a camping and fishing trip way over on the Sangamon River, twenty or thirty miles away, he said that was a lot of foolishness. The best campground in the

world was a good warm bathroom with hot and cold
running water and a comfortable flush commode. After
their altercation, Uncle Bill never said much about
father but when I told him that, he sadly shook his head
and said father was "a man in a hurry trying to pull
himself up by the bootstraps"—someday he would "pull
the straps clean out of the boots and that will be that."

Father went like mad early morning to nine at night,
six days a week, but he never turned a tap on Sunday.
That was the Lord's day—forenoons at church, after-
noons reading the *Chicago Sunday Herald Examiner*,
and a nap. Very frequently the nap was very helpful as
there was another church service Sunday night. By the
time I was seventeen, I had enough hours in at church
service to keep me in good standing with the Lord, God,
and Holy Ghost for the rest of my life. It has always
been a mystery to me why a man can't get the message
in a few short lessons, but I guess it is like Uncle Bill
once said, "the tub thumpers know you have to give
people lots of religion because they leak. Look at the size
of the Bible. It takes a lifetime to do more than thumb
through it, and there is grist for the human mill on
every page. I just don't want anybody to tell me how to
grind it."

So much for all that church business. I was talking
about guns and how father had no use for guns whatever. The bows and arrows Bob Holt turned out for me
as a beginner kept me occupied and pacified for a
couple of years or more when finally at about age eight I
managed to wheedle a Benjamin handpump BB gun out
of the stock at the hardware. This acquisition was a
thrill never forgotten. Along with it came a long pointed
finger lecture from father about what would happen if I
aimed it at anything other than an empty can or
English sparrows, shot through any windows, or created
mayhem with said weapon in any other fashion. What he
didn't know was that under instruction and careful
surveillance of his hired hand Holt, I had been shooting
cans and sparrows with a much more lethal airgun in

the Holt arsenal for six months or more already; his lecture, more or less, went in one of my ears and out the other.

English sparrows populated the town in swarms, especially around barns and granaries. On the other hand, they presented a relatively small and elusive target. Considering the short distance over which it was possible to achieve a fairly flat trajectory with a lead BB propelled by the total air possible to pump-up in the Benjamin, my chances of materially reducing the numbers of this feathered pest were not much. This fact soon came home to me and resulted in (1) my looking for larger, more likely, and experimental targets and (2) wheedling for a more powerful and accurate firearm, for instance a single shot .22 calibre Stevens also in stock at the hardware dispensary.

Number 1 of these not only delayed the realization of Number 2 by at least two years, but caused me to accumulate a scar on top of my left wrist that I still wear, and to suffer the most severe application of a razor strap to my tender butt I ever received—and I received not a few. Also, when I went running to Uncle Bill with the awful truth, he not only invited me off his premises but told me never to come back till I could convince him that I had "all my marbles back." During the dressing down he gave me, his eyes were as steely and his voice as soft as the time we came face to face after he knocked my hand away from his gun. This time I did not dare to face him. I just turned and ran through the hedge and out as far as I could run into the tall corn. The whole world had fallen around my ears and I sat and cried my heart out.

To begin with, in a part of the yard next to the grapes we had a big red plum tree and close by, a smaller sweet pear. In the uppermost branches of the plum tree a couple of mourning doves picked out a site and built a sizeable nest. With time on my hands, the Devil got into me and set me to thinking it would be interesting to shoot this nest out of the tree. With a mere BB gun of course this was impossible. But with a BB gun plus a center fire .45 calibre bullet I had stumbled onto in the weeds behind Bob Holt's shack and had been carrying around in my pocket for ballast, I might just be able to get the dark deed committed.

Carefully selecting the crotch of a couple of limbs on the sweet pear tree about head high and seemingly made to order for launching the business end of the bullet at the nest. I sighted in the target till convinced the projectile was dead on, then gave a couple of pumps on the BB gun, aimed the gun at close range at the cap in the center of the casing—and pulled the trigger. There came a deafening blast that caused the sitting mourning dove to lift off in a flurry, but no visible damage to the nest. All the damage I suddenly realized had come home to roost on me. Utterly amazed and dumbfounded and strangely not hurting at all, I see blood running out of a ragged round wound in my left wrist and spilling in a frightening red stream down my left hand. The explosion not only flushed the bird out of the nest, but mother out of the kitchen. Noting all the gore, she grabbed my good hand and started running with me across Cain's backyard for the doctor's house, conveniently located only about half a block away.

I was never sure whether it was the cartridge casing or lead nose of the shell that reversed and hit me, but whatever it was the damage was very superficial, despite the horrendous bleeding. It went through the thin skin and flesh on top of the wrist and laid there on the bone. The good doctor picked it off, bandaged the break in my hide and sent me on my way.

It was not for this misdemeanor that I got strapped by father and lambasted by Uncle Bill. At worst, I was simply separated from the BB gun for a month or more and lectured on evil temptations and dangerous unpredictable logistics of a bullet detonated without guidance from the crotch of two limbs in a small sweet pear tree. The doctor said it was lucky I got whatever in the wrist instead of the eye. The preacher claimed it was a miracle and manifestation of how the Lord had his arms around little boys who go to Sunday School and church every Sunday. Uncle Bill disgustingly said I just got what I had coming to me for shooting at a bird on the nest in the first place.

The sin that won me the blistered butt from father and temporary banishment by Uncle Bill was not perpetrated until probably a year later—long enough after the abortive missile launch so that it had almost faded from memory and, of course, the BB gun had been redeemed. This time, as I came around a corner of the house one day and say my younger sister, Kay, sitting on a metal bucket playing in the sandpile with her back to me, the Devil really got with me. He whispered in my ear, "Sneak up a little closer behind those bushes and bang a BB on that bucket. It will give her a start and she won't know where it came from. Very funny." When I pulled the trigger, I gave her a start all right. Knowing the gun always shot a little low, I aimed a little high to compensate and it was a little too high. The BB missed the bucket and hit her in the fleshy part of the posterior. She let out a howl, jumped about two feet high, and took off for the house for all she could go. Except for one little item. I might have said she must have been stung by a bee or bug of some kind, but the BB had just enough poop to penetrate what little she had on at the point of impact as well as the hide and just enough flesh to stick where it hit. All mother had to do was pinch the sides of the wound and out popped the incriminating evidence. In the short time it took her to perform this very minor operation, apply a little disinfectant, and come looking for the gunman with a yardstick in hand, he was long gone.

When hunger finally forced me to come out of hiding among the bales of hay in the mow of the barn, along towards sundown, I was prepared to take my medicine but not quite the size of the dosage administered. Try as I might to make the truth stick, I could never quite convince anybody that the shot was surely innocently aimed at the bucket; the fact that it targeted in otherwise was purely accidental. The fact that anybody, especially Uncle Bill, would surmise I might stoop so low as to purposely intentionally aim to shoot my sister or anybody else was a hard, unjustified blow. There went the BB gun—I never knew where but am pretty sure it went in pieces to the dump. In final analysis, I considered it good riddance. Like Uncle Bill disapprovingly said when I first went running over to show him my prized possession, "That thing is neither fish nor fowl. You mess around with it long enough and when it comes to real shooting you won't be able to hit a bull in the rear with a scoop shovel."

Many years later after Uncle Bill had gone under and I had gone to the Northern Rockies in Montana, our friend Bob Holt suffered a similar trauma. I never did get the particulars entirely straight, but somehow Rob was down in the near vicinity of the widow Odebrecht's cow barn trying to get some kinks out of somebody's large calibre handgun. The gun went off unexpectedly and, just as you might guess, down went Edith's prized Jersey milk cow, deader than a nit. Pronto Bob went home, packed his arsenal and what other few belongings he had worth taking along in his old Model T truck and left town. Nobody ever found out where he went nor ever heard from him again. With all her land and money, it didn't hurt Edith Odebrecht one little bit to buy a new milk cow, but she was madder than a hatter and tried to get the sheriff to go after Bob and make him pay for the dead cow. Luckily, the sheriff was too busy with other matters and never did much about it. At least he never caught up with Bob. You can be pretty sure poor old Bob had barely enough ready cash to buy gas for his take-off much less to pay for a milk cow.

I can be very sympathetic with Bob because the gun I acquired about a year after the bucket-in-the-sandbox fiasco and the end of the BB gun, must have had the same defect as the gun he was tinkering with when he accidentally killed the cow. This gun was a Winchester

.22 repeater rifle with a rust pitted octagon barrel and stock that looked like it had been used for clubbing snakes in a rockpile. After some hard bargaining, I bought it plus a box of shells from a juvenile acquaintance for one dollar and seventy-five cents, with no questions asked as to where and how he, himself, had come in hand of the thing. I smuggled this prize purchase into a hiding place in the haymow of the barn and smuggled it out for company on lone, long rambles over the countryside at every chance.

The trouble with this gun was in the firing mechanism. Even with the safety on, you could never be sure when it might go off. The only safe way to shoot this antique was to wait until the target was clearly sighted before putting a shell in the chamber. This took some ins and outs with shells as there were times when the target would disappear before you could get the gun loaded. Sometimes in the excitement of the hunt, I tended to forget the outs.

One evening as I was winding home from hunting crows out at the slaughterhouse, operated as need by my rabbit buying friend, the village butcher, and located about two miles from town. I forgot an out, and, only by the grace of God and good gun handling, missed shooting one of my toes off. I carried the gun in the crook of an arm with the hammer in the safety position and the business end pointed at the ground, at what turned out to be not quite a far enough distance ahead of me. The thing went bang unexpectedly and for no reason, other than that was what it was in the habit of doing. There was a .22 bullet hole in the toe of my boot not a sixteenth of an inch from what was inside. I would bet this is exactly what happened to Bob—except that he did not happen to miss hitting the cow.

Of course, a .22 bullet does not make much of a noticeable hole in leather and by covering it with enough grease, it can hardly be seen even at fairly close range. As far as the hole in the toe went, I got by just fine till one day sitting on the bench under Uncle Bill's front door overhang with my legs stretched out and both feet in plain view with some of the grease worn off the toes of the boots. And right out of the blue, after the two of us had been sitting there quite awhile eating dried pears and saying nothing at all, he says, "How the heck, with what, when, and where did you shoot that hole in the toe of your shoe?" I pulled in my feet in a hurry, looked at my boots like I had never seen them before and say, "Shoot? What hole? Where?" And he says, "You know darn well what hole. Where're you hiding the gun?"

The upshot was that I was forced to tell him the whole truth—start to finish—the truth. Also, I had to go haul out the gun from hiding in the barn and sneak it over to him on the basis that he would "fix what ails it quick and easy." When I delivered my precious field piece, he took it in hand, checked to see if it was loaded, leaving the breech open, looked at me and asked, "How would you like to trade it for a brand new one?" It was an incredulous proposition and having learned to be a little cautious of his dealings, I said, "You mean you'd trade me a new one for that old one—straight across?"

"That's the deal. I get this gun. I get you a new gun. You keep it here and whenever you want to use it, you come here and check it out."

I said eagerly, "You bet. It's a deal."

"Okay. This is now my gun? I can do anything I want to do with it?"

I said, "Yes *sir!*"

Right away he walked over to the fence, got a good hold on the barrel of the gun, took a long swing at a post and broke the gun to smithereens. Of course, I couldn't believe my eyes—smashing a good gun like that. Picking up the pieces, he brought them back and handed them to me. "Go throw that junk in my scrap pile and don't ever let me catch you with a man-killer like that again."

That's how I finally got the beautiful little Stevens single shot off the rack in the hardware where it hadn't been sold in over a year. Uncle Bill got one of his poker playing buddies to go buy it from father and gave it to me to keep at his house. Not having to sneak it in and out of the barn was a big help. Of course, the day finally came when the gun and I were "found out," but by that time I was old enough and had redeemed myself enough to be allowed to keep the gun in a specified corner of the basement at home. Be it known to all my younger brothers and sisters, however, that nobody was ever to touch the filthy thing but me. I was never to load same for firing until far enough from the bedground, where, if I shot anybody in the family it could only be me. And certainly sooner or later it would be me. Of such are the perils of parenthood.

I say I redeemed myself. Redemption came in a strange and wonderful way. Along with a passion for all outdoors, a sinful aversion to attending Sunday School and church services, and a love for guns, I was oddly endowed with a quick and facile brain. How quick and facile I was to demonstrate come the eighth grade.

In those days back in 1924, it was customary in the county to hold a kind of an educational grade school roundup in the form of a bodacious all day written examination in which all eighth graders in the county participated, as a requirement for graduation to high school. Said exam covered everything from orthography through physiology, arithmetic, grammar, geography, history, to penmanship and drawing.

About 150 enrollees, male and female, from schools all over the county were entered the time I took the thing and it was considered quite a feather in the headdress of the teacher who brought home a winner. In every school there were two or three up and comers and as a part of the get-ready, there was a lot of special prepping of these possibles two or three weeks or a month ahead of the writeoff.

In my case, I had a tough old girl teacher by the name of Jakeway. She not only ran a tight ship with an eighteen-inch, white oak ruler, but really was a teacher, a real credit to the profession. Not even the dumbest dumbbell left her class without learning plenty.

Her prep class amounted to an hour before school for a full month previous. She asked the questions and the few of us she was drilling wrote the answers on the blackboard as fast as we could write. Of course, she didn't get any extra money for this overtime and effort and we got no extra credit. Anybody in the class could come to the prep sessions, but nobody was forced to do it and it wasn't held against you if you didn't. Only about four of us showed up and for those of us who did, she made it fun and games even though we worked like beavers. She had a way of making you want to work for her—just for the heck of it, if nothing else.

Come the day of the exam, the whole class was taken up to the big city and a few of us at least were ready. The only exam I ever took that was tougher was the all-day written junior forester exam many years later after graduating from the wrong college. I should have graduated from a School of Forestry rather than Liberal Arts & Science.

At any odds, one day not long after the day of the exam, I was out at my sand-filled jump pit practicing pole vaulting with a flimsy bamboo pole that used to come with rugs, when mother hollered at me from the back door that someone wanted to talk to me on the telephone—and she was really excited. When I got a footstool under me so I could get up to the horn on the hand-grind wall phone and had the receive to my ear, imagine my surprise when there on the other end of the line was Miss Jakeway—and I wondered what the hell have I done wrong now. Then she said, "Congratulations, Joe. You have won the Kaufman medal." Not yet being sure whether this was good or bad but sort of thinking I might be in the clear, I asked her, "What is the Kaufman medal for?" and she said, "For ranking No. 1

in the county on the examination. Your grade was 96.5." After thinking this over for a minute I said, "I didn't win the medal. You did. All I did was write the exam." And handing the receiver to mother I said, "You talk to her. I want to go back to vaulting."

The medal she was talking about was a bum medal because I didn't get to keep it. All it amounted to was that I got my name engraved on it and it was passed on to whoever was No. 1 the next year. But there was a big to-do about the No. 1 business. I had to get my picture taken all dressed up in a new knicker suit and new shoes and a tie and everything for the paper and father's Master Plumber magazine. Father thought it was all great stuff and put his arm around me but it didn't change his thinking about going to church every Sunday, nor guns, nor hunting and fishing, one little bit. All it did was get him to thinking more strongly about some other things—like I was starting out exactly on the right track for making a great MD. He said he knew I had it in me all the time. All I needed was to get that "hunting and fishing foolishness out of your head and settle down to something worthwhile." That kind of Uncle Bill, Bob Holt nonsense "never got anybody anywhere."

When it came to Uncle Bill, I never would quite figure out whether he thought coming out a winner in mental gymnastics was good or bad. When he put *his* arm around me, it was more like he did it sympathetically than enthusiastically and I was a little surprised. If he thought it was good, he sure enough didn't think it was *all* good. Among other things he said now I had poked my head up where people could shoot at me and in a way I had really put my foot in the fire. Without keeping my guard up, I could get caught in other people's ambitions to the place where I might get to thinking they were actually my own. In a way, he said, sort of like he wished he himself had been among the lucky few; it was better to be born with no brains at all. In the end, though, he rewarded me with a silver dollar just as I had counted on him to do.

As usual, what he had to say about getting caught up in other people's ambitions was right as rain. For a kid with a brain like mine, the feeble three-year village high school was no way good enough for me. Instead of finishing out only the fourth and final year at high school in the big city ten miles away, I must attend there from the beginning. At the start, father personally delivered me to the principal of the uptown educational institution with positive instructions to said mogul to shape my curriculum so as to fill me to running over with everything needed preparatory to medical school and becoming the "best MD in the USA."

Over those four years, I got the works and managed to work in a lot more—captain of the track team, president of the senior class, and National Honor Society at the first clatter. None of which to the surprise and utter disgust of father caused a rupture of my love affair with field and stream, guns, hunting, and trapping one iota. On the contrary, after four years of the big city, I was sick to death of the whole shooteree and more siwashy than ever.

Even at that late date in the civilized state of Illinois, a little Indian teaching could save your life. If I had not been favored with a smattering of how-to-stay-alive-anywhere-in-any-kind-of-weather type of education learned from Uncle Bill, I would not be here today and neither would Jim McKeon. Jim was a road maintenance employee of the state or county, maybe about fifty years old when I was about sixteen.

Anybody who has lived there and has had a chance to visit a few other areas like say Montana or Alaska in winter knows that a full-blown blizzard in Illinois compares quite favorably with blizzards most anywhere. The temperature might not drop quite as low and a few other factors may be somewhat less spectacular, but when the chips are down, a midwest blizzard at its frigid howling best does not take a backseat to any winter torment wherever.

As I recall, it was the winter of 1927 in late January

or early February when this blizzard hit our part of Illinois, and liked where it lit well enough to hang around the better part of a full week. The temperature went to twenty below and the wind blew like Katy-bar-the-door whipping a fine snow mixed with black dust into drifts long and deep. Most of the roads were drifted shut and except for milking and feeding chores all the natives with any sense stayed strictly indoors close to the stove warming their toes.

Armed with scoop shovel and chains, I made out over the ten miles to school in the family Model T sedan Monday through Thursday, okay. But come Friday, the way the wind was shaking the glass in the storm windows and more snow in the air, trying to go it along was pure crazy. I knew this guy McKeon with the road department made the run everyday and thinking he might really be off his nut and go, I called him and found out he was as batty as I thought. You bet he would like to have me go along. There were a couple of drifts where I could help shovel snow.

So we togged out somewhat like Eskimos about to make a dogsled safari—but as we found out later, not near enough like said Eskimos and here we go in McKeon's Model T trouble-shooting truck. We kept going with only one drift to shovel our way through about three miles this side of the big city. The trouble with this drift, which was in a fairly deep cut, was that it kept backfilling about as fast as we shoveled and seemed to grow bigger minute by minute. The Ford Model T truck had a heater off the manifold but with the wind like it was and the temperature like it was, what little heat came off the manifold froze before it ever reached the heater outlet. By the time we pulled up in front of the school, my toes and fingers especially were like icicles and I was shivering like a case of St. Vitus' dance.

McKeon said we had better start back a little early on account of the early dark and "that damn drift in the cut" that "might be trouble." His idea of early was 3:30.

Much to my surprise when I entered the school building, it was deserted. The word failed to reach outlying villages, but all classes and activities that day were canceled due to the storm. At least they still had a fire in the furnace and the place was warm. The day wasn't wasted as I had plenty of reading to catch up on.

Come 3:30 and there was my taxi and driver right on time. The wind had let up slightly and the temperature had come up to five above zero during the day. The stuff coming down from the heavy overcast had changed from large snowflakes to a kind of frozen mist—not sleet, still snow but a very fine variety that stings bare hide when you face into it. Of course, in town where the wind could not get a clean sweep there was one kind of weather and out in the open flat was another, as we shortly discovered.

A Model T truck is no Salt Flats racer under the most ideal weather conditions. In about a foot of snow with chains on the rear wheels it just barely outruns a turtle. At that time of year, with the prevailing black cloud cover, the time required to get to "that darn drift that might give us trouble" used up most of the remaining so-called daylight. When we got to the drift, it was no longer a drift but a white wall about eight feet high and twenty feet wide.

Samson, himself, with a full head of hair, and a scoop shovel in both hands could not have shoveled a truck trail through it. Sometimes these Illinois drifts got hard enough to drive right over the top without scooping. A little testing showed that this drift was not yet in that category. The other alternative sometimes feasible was to go around. Due to the close proximity of a barb wire fence to the top of the cut on both sides this measured was ruled out, too. So there we were Friday night, seven miles from home and flat out stuck. Either we hiked that remaining distance or we turned around and went back to a hotel in town. Since the cafeteria at school was closed, I had had no lunch. My belly button was beating on my backbone, but neither of us had money enough to buy a room and a couple of meals.

Obviously, despite the blizzard, all the signs, except the frigid howling weather pointed home. So we made the blue ribbon bonehead decision to head for home, but Jim did not think he had enough denatured alcohol in his go-mobile to keep the engine block from breaking. We had a chance to cool off while he crawled under the vehicle and opened the petcocks on the radiator and the engine block.

My blood was already congealing, so while this operation went on, I ran short distances up and down the road waving my arms and slapping my hands against my armpits. Then finally, after what seemed like eternity and a day to open a couple of petcocks, we took off— crosswise of the blowing snow with heads sticking hunched down in our coat collars and backs half turned against the arctic onslaught, feet headed in one direction while facing another. This can get you into all manner of trouble: like stumbling into a road culvert and falling flat on your face in a snowdrift.

The road, itself, was one of those early Illinois half-tracks, hard surfaced and in this case, concrete one lane nine feet wide only. When the other lane thawed out in the spring or during wet weather, this unpaved track became a quagmire or Illinois gumbo. Accomplished drivers traveling the wrong way on the pavement, on encountering an oncoming vehicle, would speed up to meet the man with the right of way. At the last possible moment before a collision, they would cut out into the mud and pray for enough momentum to get back on the hardtop. If momentum failed, you were just plain hub-deep stuck and went looking for a man with a team of horses to pull you out. Depending on how well you might know the man, this emergency service could be quite expensive—especially if the happening occurred during the milking hour or at night.

In winter with a high wind, the concreted part of the highway was swept fairly clear except for a few drifts. Breaking trail was not much of a problem on this particular hike. For the first four or five miles we humped along at a fairly good pace. Jim was equipped with heavy four buckle overshoes as compared to my sixteen inch lace hunting boots which made walking much easier. Albeit, as heavily greased as they were, they afforded far less protection from the cold. The thing I worried about most was frozen feet. Maybe mostly on account of his overshoes, Jim started falling behind and the farther we went, the behinder he got and I would have to wait longer and longer for him to catch up.

You understand, of course, that we were passing farm houses every half mile on mile along the route—most of them set back from the road a good distance but all within striking distance had we a mind to turn in. The only thing we had in mind was to get on home and this numb rumdumb single-mindedness etched in ice crystals on the think-tank screen all but did us in.

About a mile and a half from the north edge of home base, I looked back from my leading position and my *compahdre* was nowhere in sight. This was the first time I had lost him entirely. I let go a holler but the wind, it all went east and not north in his direction so there was nothing for it but backtrack. And about two hundred yards back, there he was sitting on a road culvert with his head in his hands.

"Hey Jim," I hollered from a distance, "Come on. We're almost home." He didn't even lift his head. I went on back and shook him by the shoulder and he finally came to. "I had to sit down here and rest a little." His voice was so tired and weak I could hardly make out what he said. "These darn overshoes are heavy as lead. I think my feet are frozen."

"They're not as frozen as mine with no overshoes. Come on. Get up. We're almost there. Move—you've got to keep on the move."

After thinking a minute, or just taking another little rest without thinking, he got on his feet and we were back on the move. This time I stayed with him to make sure I had him along. About now I was hungry as I was cold. The two pains I'd say were equal. My mind fastened more on just making it to Jim Sower's Drug Store and shelling out a dime for a large size Baby Ruth candy bar than on getting home to a warm fire. What old Jim was thinking about, I'll never know. He might have been walking in his sleep but walk he did—for most of a mile to another road culvert. Then down he went again—head in hands. And I was really scared ... scared because I was remembering one miserable winter afternoon when I was over at Uncle Bill's place and he and Bob Holt were stoking the stove, drinking coffee and whiskey, and swapping lies about the coldest weather in recorded history and their near misses in freezing to death.

I remembered Uncle Bill saying that of all the ways a man could go, freezing to death was the easiest out of any. In fact, it is really quite pleasant. You just go to sleep without a care in the world and no pain and presto, you were gone. The one thing you must do to keep from freezing is to never give in to the desire to sleep. If you do, it is curtains every time.

Obviously, Jim was to that condition of pleasant dreams and shortly becoming a block of ice. Something desperate had to be done. I shook him and hollered at him and shook him again but all he would do was grunt and try to wave me off. I hated to do it but finally I hauled off and kicked him in the leg just above the top of his overshoes. This brought his head up and I let him have a good healthy slap in the face. Good medicine. I had him up on his feet and mad. "You little so-and-so. I'll get you for that." He came staggering after me, with me keeping just out of reach hollering that he couldn't touch me with a ten foot pole and threatening, if he stopped, to hit him again. His mad lasted almost to where we had it made but it got less and less and he kept staggering along slower and slower, bending so far forward as to almost fall on his face. Just as I could see a godsent light in a window of the fartherest north house in town, he did just that—fell flat in the snow. By the time I got back to him he was luckily up on his hands and knees shaking his head and mumbling something that made no sense. "Jim," I hollered, "I can see a light—just one more time." And hoisting him under the arms for all I was worth, he came upright again but was weaving around like a drunk and obviously had no more idea of where he was or what was going on than the man in the moon. Getting his arm around my shoulder and packing as much of him as I was able, we inched along to that light. Somehow I got him up the front steps to the door and gave a couple of kicks on the door by way of knocking. The door shortly came open to a nice lighted warm room with a couple of people and I just let Jim fall right on in on the floor. Then without a word of explanation, I got out of there heading for that candy bar. I heard somebody on the porch hollering at me but I had made my delivery and now I was going to eat. It was about a quarter-mile to Sower's Drug and another quarter from there home and all that got me there was that candy bar. When I got to the drug store, my fingers were so numb I could barely fish the dime out of my pocket or hang onto it after I did. Since I was strangely in no mood for conversation with Sower or anybody else, I fumbled the dime on the counter, picked up the bar, and departed. I tore the paper off the candy with my teeth as I went back out in the blizzard. Old man Sower told others and told me personally later that I looked like walking death and if he had known what I had been through, he would have never let me out of the store.

By the time I made it home which was somewhere around 7:30 or 8:00 p.m., I had consumed the candy and was no longer hungry: only teeth-chattering cold. Somehow I got the door open and inside without falling in like Jim and wound up standing on the big hot air register in the floor almost directly above the furnace with people helping me off with my clothes. I knew I should not be standing on that register. If my feet were frozen, as well may be, that was the worst possible place to be. Uncle Bill said one of the first things to do was to rub them with snow. Since my hands were numb, I could not unlace my boots and Mother got the boots and socks off and brought in a dishpan full of snow. The feet were pretty damn white and stiff, but since I could still move my toes I did not think they were frozen. After a little of the snow treatment to feet and hands, we progressed to soaking them in lukewarm water and warmed towels. Eventually I got as much feeling and flexibility back in the extremities of all four of my major appendages as ever.

The next day there was a short piece in the city paper about the road foreman and the high school student who walked seven miles home through the blizzard suffering nothing worse than minor frostbite in hands and feet. Apparently the people into whose hands Jim had been unceremoniously delivered had phoned in the story. What they got and what the paper printed was only a little part of it. After getting back on his feet, which was several days later, Jim stopped by the hardware store and privately told father the whole of it. He told father to have me stop at his house. As far as he was concerned, I had saved his life, and he had a little gift for me in appreciation. When I went over to see him the next weekend, I was a little hesitant thinking maybe the gift might be a punch in the nose. The fact is he had found out from Jimmy Sowers that I had stopped there for a Baby Ruth bar and right on the spot had bought a whole box of these bars and had them there to give to me. I told him the last thing in the world I wanted to do was to kick him and hit him, but it was the only thing I could think of to keep him from going to sleep. He said if I hadn't hit him, he would be asleep for keeps and he was just grateful as anything. He didn't know it and nobody else did but I was darn sure if it hadn't been for my listening to Uncle Bill, in all probability we both would have been asleep for keeps.

If Uncle Bill had not gone into the eternal sunset and I had a chance to discuss the close call with him attributing the happy ending to simply a little know-how picked up from him, I am pretty sure of just what he would have said. With a peculiar knowing half-humorous smile in his eyes, he would have said, "Hunk uh. It was just that you and old McKeon still had some time showing on your clocks." Uncle Bill held that close calls were a dime a dozen and along with bellyaches were a normal expectable adjunct to life.

The summer after Uncle Bill's final September-October pilgrimage, a local entrepreneur engaged in a straw-baling operation, having in hand what looked to be a sound contract for tons and tons of baled straw for use in the making of paper. Lowest man on the production line was the "wire puncher" who punched wire through holes in the wooden blocks that separated the bales and when twisted, held said bales together. For a nine hour day, six days a week, this tedious chaff and dust-blown chore commanded compensation of three dollars plus a farm dinner a day—in those days an amount eagerly sought after by any teenager wanting work. Luckily, I landed the job. After six weeks and miles of wire had been punched the job ended. All hands were paid their due. Then the papermaker renigged on the contract; the affable, honest middle-aged enterpriser went financially bellyup, put a Colt .45 to his head, and pulled the trigger. Uncle Bill would have shrugged ("He got the signal. His time was up."), and sent the widow an anonymous hundred dollar bill which would have been a godsend.

Whatever happened to that beautiful ivory-handled gun in the black tie-down holster on the black gunbelt that hung on Uncle Bill's bed, I never found out.

Aunt Helen and Her Brother Brad

More than once Uncle Bill said to me, "Mouse, you are in the wrong place. With your bent for the outdoors, like me, you are hemmed in here. You belong in the mountains, the Rocky Mountains! Like the Salmon River country in Idaho." He never gave a hint as to why he himself had left the mountains and his obviously beloved Salmon River country, especially.

The one time I saw him really lose his cool was when I reported to him about father taking me to the principal of the big city high school and telling him he was to give me everything I needed preparatory to the study of medicine in college. Uncle Bill surprisingly, furiously, exploded, "You're no more a sawbones than I am!" Then, just as suddenly and seemingly contrite, he put an arm around my shoulder and hugged me roughly against his hip. "My trail," he said quietly, "and your trail did not cross just accidentally."

The summer following my "wire-punching" summer (1927), my Uncle Paul happened to be managing several meat markets for a chain in the state of Minnesota. More or less facetiously he proposed that insofar as it had been decided for me that I was to cut meat sooner or later, I might well begin by breaking down carcasses of pork, beef, and mutton—thereby acquiring a raw feel for and rudimentary understanding of the construction of the human animal. Father thought this was not only a fundamentally sound educational opportunity but physically advantageous. For twelve dollars a week plus room and board, I would put in a six day week, seven to seven, Monday through Friday and seven to eleven on Saturday. I would learn how to cut steaks the same thickness top and bottom, and trim the last ounce of meat off bones and convert these scraps into hamburger and sausage by the No. 3 galvanized washtub fulls. In a letter only to me, Uncle Paul added the most attractive inducement of all: Sundays and holidays would be devoted, not to church going, but to fishing in some of Minnesota's most likely lakes. The final week before the start of school, we would run up north to the Boundary Waters Canoe country and finish the summer off with a guided canoe trip and fishing in a fisherman's paradise.

Compared to anything I had ever known before, the features of Minnesota appeared paradisiacal in themselves: the clear blue lake populated with game fish rather than lethargic catfish; the evergreen forests filled with deer, moose, wolves, and bears rather than rabbits. More than anything else, the forests fascinated me. Only one item was lacking. There were no mountains. I had never seen a mountain any more than evergreen forests and sparkling blue lakes. The way Uncle Bill described them, there were no mountains.

It was on the Fourth of July when we were on the way back to St. Paul after having spent Sunday and the morning of the Fourth fishing for walleye pike in a lake called Mille Lacs that I merely happened to mention that it was too bad Minnesota had no mountains—and opened the gates. My Aunt Helen, whom I thought was the most beautiful woman and the best cook in the world, looked around from the front seat where she was sitting next to Uncle Paul. "If you want mountains, you should go where my brother is, to Missoula, Montana. That's in the middle of some of the wildest mountains in the world." After a minute, she said, "You know, that's an idea. If you want mountains, how would you like to work in a National Forest? They have some summer jobs. I'll bet Brad could tell you how to get one."

There in the back seat of the car, I was now wide awake and more than a little excited. "You mean your brother is a ranger?"

"Not a ranger. He's with the Northern Rocky Mountain Forest Experiment Station—doing wood products research. That's part of the Forest Service, too. But he could tell you what summer jobs are available and where to apply. I could write to him and see what he has to say."

Now I was really excited. "Getting to the mountains is what I most want to do. Working in the mountains—Oh boy!"

"Don't get your hopes too high," Uncle Paul put in. "Brad had a degree in Forestry from the University of Michigan. You won't even be eighteen next summer and I bet you have to be eighteen at least to get a job with the government. Most of those summer jobs probably go to college students studying forestry. Joe's not going to study forestry. His dad has him all lined out to study medicine."

"Oh, poo," Aunt Helen told him disgustedly. "I'm going to write Brad and find out. It doesn't take a Ph.D. to use an axe or make a trail. Joe doesn't want to be a meat cutter all his life—cooped up inside four walls of a doctor's office or hospital." Aunt Helen came from a little town on the upper peninsula of Michigan where her people had operated a successful trading post for years. She had gone to Wellesley back east but she was no dummy about axes and trails. I wanted to give her a big hug and kiss.

"Please do write and find out what he has to say," I said urgently.

The response to Aunt Helen's letter to her brother Brad came faster than even I had hoped and despite Uncle Paul's repeated warning not to get my hopes too high, left me floating on Cloud Nine. Because there were so many better paying jobs available the Forest Service had trouble recruiting summer help that summer and might encounter the same problem next year. Somewhere in the Northern Rocky Mountain Region including Montana, northern Idaho and eastern Washington, where he worked, it might just be that the Service could put me on. The pay would be minimal but in case I might be interested in studying forestry in college, the experience would be a big help. He said if I was still interested to write to him about this in January. If I were still interested...! The possibility of getting to the mountains with a job when I got there was precious beyond compare. Pay was of no consequence. If only I had a chance!

I could not thank Aunt Helen enough and went back to my boning bones and hamburger and sausage-making dreaming dreams of next summer living and laboring in a fantastic mountain wilderness with deer, elk and bears behind every bush!

Come New Year's day of 1928, which I thought would never come, I composed and typed (several times) a letter perfect letter to Mr. Melvin Bradner at his home address in Missoula, Montana—and on January 2, along with prayers for prompt delivery, dropped it in the mail. While desperately trying to put my best foot forward, I tried to keep it as much to the point and concise as possible, as I had been taught to write a business letter in typing class the past year. In total, this life or death epistle—extolling my virtues and abilities from running the hundred yard dash in ten seconds to cutting and selling T-bone steaks—amounted to one typewritten page. In conclusion, I admitted to being no Paul Bunyan, but one tough kid believing he could hold up his end on any kind of job the Forest Service might have to dish out . . . And please tell me where and to whom to apply. As to the reply, I had trepidations aplenty, but all in all I considered it a darn good day's work.

When, after what seemed like a year, but actually was only about two weeks, thrill of thrills, came Brad's response. On reading the first paragraph, I was a mile high and walking on air. My letter was sufficient in itself for an application for summer work. The ranger on the Rock Creek District of the Missoula National Forest by the name of Lou Nichols had happened by his office one day and when Brad showed him my letter, he had taken my name and address saying he was having trouble recruiting summer help and would write to me about the last of March and that "he can probably put you on! Let me know if you get the job."

Between the joyous receipt of this letter and getting a final yes or no from Ranger Lou Nichols, whom I envisioned as some kind of mountain-man god, each passing week seemed never to come or go. March is a thirty-one day month . . . Four full weeks and more. Week one went by and no letter. Week two and three, still no word came. Week four and I was almost reduced to tears. With still two days to spare, the red letter day was March 29. An envelope came, complete with its official Forest Service insignia consisting of a shield centering an evergreen tree that could be anything from a fir to a pine.

I had thought my letter to Brad was a model of concise composition, but this one from Ranger Lou was the epitome. It consisted on one paragraph as follows:

> I have your application for summer work. If satisfactory, sign the enclosed Agreement for Employment. Return one copy to me by return mail and report for duty the morning of June 15. I will be at the Bonita, Montana train stop to pick you up.

After perusing this vital communication several times to be sure I hadn't missed anything, I turned to the attached "Agreement for Employment" and examined this rather lengthy and finely printed document in detail—including the form number and place of printing. Of immediate interest was the fact that the Forest Service, U.S. Department of Agriculture would pay me for my labors the enormous amount of sixty-five dollars per month plus "subsistence" yet! This was the first time I knew that the Forest Service was in the Department of Agriculture but thought it was probably a good thing—which it was. On looking it up in the dictionary, I found that subsistence meant "the barest means in terms of food, clothing, and shelter needed to sustain life." Without clothing it turned out to be barest means—providing you were up to cooking the food yourself and had no aversion to housing in a warehouse or tent.

For all this I agreed "to perform to the best of my ability any duty to which I may be assigned"—which included everything from digging post holes in loose gravel to turning out a batch of edible biscuits. "That I will work on any fire, in any capacity directed at my regular rate of pay"—apparently day and night till I drop in my tracks (which often proved to be the case). "That eight hours on the job shall constitute a day on trail, improvement or other regular work. In cases of emergency, I agree to work any required number of hours per day on fire suppression when requested to do so and may be held subject to fire duty on Sundays and holidays." I agreed to eight hour days, six days a week and Sundays and holidays depending on the weather.

"That I will not smoke during the period of fire danger, designated by notice of the District Forester as from May 1 to September 30, except at campgrounds and improved places of habitation." (I once knew an eminent forester mindful of these smoking restrictions but aching for a smoke after three hours in the saddle, suddenly pull up and dismount at an obviously safe spot beside a creek. "By gosh," he said, "right here is where we establish a campground. I'm going to have a smoke.")

Having read that neither Indians nor white inhabitants of the wide open spaces were given to wasting words and not to be outdone by the scarcity of same in this exchange, I replied forthwith:

> Thank you for your March 24 offering of summer work. As requested a signed copy of the Agreement for Employment form is enclosed. I look forward to working for you and the Forest Service and to your picking me up on the morning of June 15 at the Bonita train stop.

Also, as requested, I posted this response to Lou's exciting missive within hours on the same day it was received—by return mail!

Very strangely, I thought, as I was preparing my reply and Agreement for Employment for Ranger Lou, I was reminded of Uncle Bill's saying, "your trail and my trail did not cross just accidentally." Aunt Helen's trail and my trail did not cross just accidentally either. I did not say anything about this when I wrote to her but thought all the time I was writing that the spirits of the mountains were reaching out to me and no way were to be denied. Uncle Bill, I knew, would have very certainly agreed.

On the same day I received the firm offer of a job at Bonita, of course, I elatedly notified Brad and asked him to let me have his every suggestion for getting myself properly outfitted for the assignment.

In the meantime, before ever having directions from Brad there was one item of equipment I knew I could not possibly do without. Even though an extravagant outlay in view of my meager means, I must acquire this essential in celebration of getting a job in the mountains if for no other reason. Secretly, I had been putting aside a dollar here and a dollar there for this purchase for more than a year. Most of the necessary amount I had saved from my meat-cutting income the past summer. Now, taking this money from where I had it squirreled away in a coffee can under a loose floorboard in the barn, I counted it once more and next day took it to the city where I went to school. The minute the school day was finished, I hurried to the big hardware store where I had seen this article displayed and had gone back and drooled over it several times. Under the glass in the counter of the gun department, it was still there.

To the man behind the counter, I pointed to the object of my affection and said, "I want that Colt Woodsman .22 automatic pistol." The cost was about thirty dollars. It was the loveliest, most exciting purchase I had ever made. Smuggling the first part of my get-ready kit into the house, I slept with it under my pillow where I could caress the deadly blued barrel and walnut grips. If father had known, he would have been furious. With all my correspondence relative to a job in the mountains 2,000 miles from home, he was furious enough already. Although he had never been west of Kalona, Iowa, where he was born, he referred to Montana as, "that land of rocks and savages."

Brad's reply to my letter asking for pointers on getting outfitted for the job contained much of vital interest and importance.

> Lou Nichols is an oldtimer who came to the Forest Service when it was first established. Previously he had worked for the Texas Rangers. He is known to be a little hard on beginners but will get you off on the right foot.
>
> Other than towels and toothbrush, I doubt if you can buy the essentials of what you will need in the way of clothes in Illinois. After you leave Missoula, you will probably not get back to town for three months, so you should take everything you will need for that length of time. Plan on a

day or two to buy what you don't have in Missoula.

Bonita, Montana is little more than a name on the map. It has a post office and a general store of sorts that stocks a few groceries and other staples, but is no place to shop. The Bonita Ranger Station, head-quarters of the Rock Creek District, is about five miles up the road toward Mis-soula. Buy your railroad ticket straight through to Missoula and take the local that stops at Bonita, twenty-five miles or so back to that point. The fare is not much.

Unfortunately, we will be out of town when you arrive, so we will be unable to meet you at the depot. But someone will be at the house, so plan on sleeping there and leave your suitcase with whatever clothes you will not be needing for field wear.

Basically, you should have a good pair of hobnailed or corked hiking boots, a couple pairs of Levis or tin pants, a couple of cotton work shirts and one good heavy wool shirt. A wool or tin cruising jacket is also a must. You will need several pairs of wool socks, a pair of leather gloves, a hat (preferable with a fairly wide stiff brim), and a pack sack for carrying all you cannot wear. A strong sharp pocket knife is essential.

If you have any money left, get yourself a fly rod, reel and line plus a few Paul Bunyan bags and grey-hackle-yellow wet flies. Rock Creek is a great trout stream and you should learn how to catch them.

Again, except for whatever you may already have, wait to buy what you need when you get to Missoula. See Jim Brooks, Supervisor of the Missoula Forest at the

Post Office Building and ask him about getting a shot for ticks.

This most illuminating and helpful communication cleared up several previously hazy items regarding purchase of the train ticket. As to outfitting, at least I had the boots—even though yet to be "hobnailed or corked" whatever that might be—still the correct boots. These boots, for which I had worked, scrimped, and saved were expensive sixteen inch lace Russels with a low heel and full moccasin toe, and of which I was very proud. As I shortly discovered, for the right kind of boots, they were all wrong. The high lace top interfered with free play of the calf of the leg, the low heel gave little or no instep grip on logs or rocks, and the beautiful moccasin toe quickly wore off causing leaks.

In my Illinois ignorance, little did I know that regardless of whatever else he might wear, a glance at woodsman's or mountain man's boots at that time told almost all. The correct boot had a low six or eight inch lace upper, smooth toe, hard tough heel counter, and heavy leather sole with heel high enough to hook over a log or rock and hold.

The boot that told most was one immediately recognizable; it was handmade to order from a submitted foot outline by the small but famous White Boot Company of Spokane, Washington. There were a few cheaper imitations of this boot available, but not in the same class by any means. For foot comfort, foot protection and long wear, it was the top of the line beyond a doubt.

An offshoot of the heavy White "logger" was the lighter narrower-toed even higher heeled White "packer" made especially for the horseman, who, with his string of horses or mules, moved all manner of cargoes from the road head to all parts of the mountain wilderness available only by trail. Cargoeing and packing was an art and a profession unto itself (now unhappily practically extinct). Both the "logger" and "packer" boot were as waterproof as a leather working boot could be built. With liberal fairly frequent applications of Hubbard Boot Grease, they could be kept that way.

Always included with new White loggers and packers came a pair of false tongues to keep sticks, dirt and debris from accumulating under the laces. When properly fringed, these added a decorative touch of foo-foorah over the instep and toe. The degree to which the false tongue might be fringed and to which the fringe might be worn and curled, told something about the wearer as well. The laces were made of leather thongs.

When the boots had given the wearer their all, they could be returned to the maker for rebuilding as good almost as new at a fraction of the original cost which, to be sure, was not minimal (about thirty dollars), but to the woodsman who properly valued his feet as one of his main assets, it was no more than a sound investment at any cost.

I eventually found out all this about proper woods boots. Likewise, in due course, I learned that by what he carried with him in his packsack, the experience of a mountain man, logger, packer, or forester might also be relatively accurately assessed. The most experienced carried the least possible in the way of extra wardrobe and effects. The trick was to have along on the body and back every essential needed for an extended stay and any eventuality likely to be encountered in the back country, yet to have as few of nonessentials and to be light as possible.

Until arriving in Missoula and making observations of what the well-dressed woodsman seemed to be wearing, I thought erroneously that I had the correct boots. That summer, in view of my limited budget—but never after—I had to and did manage with those boots. The hat (though of downtown Illinois variety with a wide but too limber brim and ridiculously wide cloth band) also got me through. Socks and shirts, I had already in good supply. Towel, wash rag, and underwear were no problem. Other supplies included pocket knife, tooth-brush (but no toothpaste—salt and soda would see me all the way), fine-tooth pocket comb, safety razor (could and would use soap for lather), and a small steel mirror.

Though long before the days of Levis in Illinois, I never-the-less knew what they were. Uncle Bill was probably the one and only who wore Levis rather than bib overalls in Illinois. A wool "cruising" jacket and especially a "tin" cruising jacket and "tin" pants were real puzzlers. These, like the leather gloves and trout fishing outfit, could wait. The "tick shot" was another unknown—fortunately—because had Mother been aware of what was in store by way of infectious "ticks," she would have had a tizzy.

The wild flushes of joy and excitement occasioned by my sporadic receipt of mail from Montana, the winter and spring of 1928, were not shared around the Illinois hearth and home. Father angrily blasted each incoming letter. My unseen dreamland, he raved, was "nothing but a land of rocks and savages." "How," he wanted to know, "do you propose to pay your way out there? Who pays for all those (German word presumably meaning oddball) clothes you must have?"

His Plan A had me profitably and securely pinned down that summer painting radiators for hot water heating, and otherwise assisting with his plumbing and heating business.

As to financing the far journey to Verendrye's "Land of Shining Mountains" and the track of Lewis and Clark, I figured I had enough, if not plenty, of my own resources. Net dollars hoarded over the years in my savings account totaled almost $135.

I had determined the one way and roundtrip and

cheapest railroad fares to get there, long since. Without sleeper, the two-night and most of three day's train cost amounted to only about half the total of my savings. If necessary, with board and bed furnished when I arrived, I was prepared to get there flat broke. I later discovered flat broke was the financial condition of most of those signing on for summer work with the Forest Service.

Springtime in the Rockies has rightly been acclaimed in verse and song as a time of renewal. With several hundred thousand acres of wild land to look after, for the ranger it was a time of "hurry, hurry, every chance you get." Following the snow melt, there were miles of trails to be cleared of winter windfall; saddle and pack horses and mules to be brought in from the winter range and fitted with new shoes; summer pastures and hayfields to be irrigated; plus a thousand and one other big and little chores to take care of.

To accomplish all that needed doing on the district during the open summer months, the ranger was given a meager, closely guarded allotment of funds for hiring a packer, headquarters guard, a small trail/road maintenance and construction crew, two or three lookouts and smokechasers. He thought it was great because at the outset, he had no summer help at all. With all that help on the protection end, he, himself, could be free to get out and check on a couple of timber operators to make sure they weren't filching more timber than they paid for and that they were cutting stumps to the prescribed low height. He could ride half a dozen or more grazing allotments to make sure the permittee wasn't running more cows or sheep than he paid for. He might even get some of the dreaded reports and other paperwork pecked out on the typewriter. It was the paperwork that really killed him.

So for a packer, Ranger Lou Nichols hired Bucky Harris, a heck of a hand with horses and mules, who had a mini-ranch up the road. Harris had a little trouble with the bottle on occasion, but he was a winner when it came to mules. Lou hired Earl Barry for his head-

quarters guard, bullsmoke, and general assistance because Barry had a couple years experience on the
district and as a graduating senior at the University of
Montana School of Forestry, he could run a transit and
scale logs. Em Hauswirth, who owned and ran the
Bonita General Store and Post Office with his wife (Miss
Maud), could build anything from a birdhouse to a log
cabin out of little or nothing, went on the summer
payroll as road, trail, and construction foreman. Benny
Curtis, the trapper up Rock Creek, would return for
another season as smokechaser out of Grizzly Creek
Station. A hiker who could go day and night and knew
the country like the back of his hand, he could also not
only effectively handle a shovel and Pulaski tool on his
own, but line out and supervise a crew of emergency
firefighters recruited off Butte's Skid Row—no mean
feat.

The two lookouts on Quigg Peak and Sliderock Mountain, a couple of forestry students from Oregon and
Georgia, would be back. To fill out Hauswirth's road
and trail crew, there was the Mad Russian who shacked
up all alone each winter on his few acres below Kitchen
Gulch, Julius Cairn, a tough old French-Canadian loner
who trapped a little and worked his small gold hole in
the side of the mountain up Welcome Creek, and, of
course, Alphonse Gratton, a bull of the woods type, also
a French-Canadian and friend of Cairn, who did everything from tail maintenance and construction to operat-
ing the horse-drawn road grader. Finally, there was
that greenhorn kid fresh out of high school back in
Illinois by name of Hessel to help Barry and be general
flunky around the station. Not much force probably, but
since Brad would recommend him, better than someone
who would be underfoot and just fill a hole in space.

If by some miracle a little more money for hiring
seasonal help might materialize, plenty of itinerant
loggers, miners, and other pick and shovel help would
be along looking for work. All in all, Ranger Lou
Nichols, with what money was available, was in fairly

good shape. Not able to reach out and accomplish much in the way of improvements, he had at least enough for a skeleton fire protection force and maintenance.

The most direct and fastest way from Urbana, Illinois to Missoula, Montana was via Illinois Central rail to Chicago, a transfer in Chicago from the IC Terminal to Union Station, from whence straight through via Burlington Route and Northern Pacific of Milwaukee Road to the mini-metropolis of Western Montana at the mouth of Hellgate Canyon.

The ultimate in luxury rapid transit to the Northwest out of Chicago were the plush, all Pullman trains with observation car, silver service diner, and one or two mail cars, pulled by behemoth coal-fired steam locomotives. Drive wheels on these colossal movers were bigger in diameter than I stood tall, and came equipped with a steam whistle audible for miles.

The one featured by the Northern Pacific was proudly known as the North Coast Limited and that of the competing, nearly parallel, Milwaukee Road, as the Olympian. Approaching the backbone of the high Rockies from the East, the Milwaukee Road switched from steam to electricity for the climb over the Divide, and in summer the Olympian pulled an extra fresh air observation car uniquely open on all sides.

For less favored penny pinchers like me, somewhat slower and less luxurious trains made up with only a couple of Pullmans, numerous day coaches, several express cars, no observation car, and sometimes a diner ran over the same rails. Comparing not having enough money for likes of a fly-rod and flies at trail's end to spending two nights sleeping in a hard cushioned day coach, I would take the day coach and tough it out.

High school graduation ceremonies took place on the night of June 10. By leaving the following morning, I was allowing one full day for outfitting in Missoula prior to reporting for work at Bonita on the morning of the fifteenth.

Surprisingly on that morning of June 11, stating that

he happened to have business in that part of town anyway, Father allowed he would furnish me transportation to the depot. I had the warming thought that this gesture might indicate a thaw in his icy attitude toward the expedition. But, no way. The several miles from home to station were covered with never a word exchanged between the two of us. Only, as he paused at the passenger's parking long enough for me to haul my one suitcase out of the back of his truck, did he say, "When you get enough of those rocks and savages, come on back to civilization." And I said, "Okay, I'll write you a letter." With that and a wave of the hand, he was gone. Even though missing a parting good luck handshake and especially a parting good luck dime, I had no trouble momentarily standing there suitcase in hand watching him go, fighting back any tears. When the chips were down, I ruefully guessed maybe I was as stubborn as he was, and went on into the depot waiting room. My train to Chicago was about due.

Through Chicago, across Wisconsin, part of Minnesota, the expanses of North Dakota and eastern Montana, the train seemed to travel at a snail's pace and stop at every crossing. A few of the stops were long enough to allow passengers and crew time for a short meal at depot beaneries which, in those days, were often the best place to eat in town. Saving my money, I ate soup, plenty of free soda crackers, and milk. Mostly, it was navy bean soup, and potato. Only once, I banqueted on a large, hot beef sandwich that, even though swimming in a greasy gravy, tasted like it had come straight from a gourmet kitchen. Lucky for my pocketbook, my stomach was anything but delicate and I was not addicted to eating simply because the clock said it was time to eat.

If the train had seemed to crawl and linger across the flats, the minute I could make out in the hazy distance what I thought might be, and eventually actually turned out to be, real honest-to-goodness mountains, it seemed to simply spin the wheels and get absolutely nowhere in its approach to what I was looking at. Yet the fence posts and telephone poles along the right of way were zipping past my window at a rapid rate.

This phenomenon of seemingly getting nowhere while actually traveling like a bat out of hell, though I was totally unaware of the fact, was my first introduction to what I later learned was the "far look"—a love and craving for which I was to carry with me the rest of my life. Those first dim outlines of ragged snow-capped rises in the landscapes on the horizon as I would later find out, were at least, amazingly, over one hundred miles in the offing.

When finally the foothills were attained and the train reached into the Rockies themselves—even with all Uncle Bill had told me and the reading I had done—the tremendous dimensions of the unfolding scene exceeded every expectation. I could not drink in details of the steep, evergreen-forested slopes, great rock slides, boulders, and clear rushing streams fast enough. To me, it was a whole new world, indescribably beautiful, with a new, exciting view around every turn.

Crawling up the east slope of the Continental Divide, some of the turns were tight enough to see not one, but now two great locomotives laboring up the steep rails ahead and a part of the coaches behind. Patches of snow appeared under the trees attesting to the rapid rise in elevation and the near approach of the Divide. Then abruptly, we were over the Pass and easing down the even steeper and more crooked west slope track into the fabled hell-roaring mining town of Butte. That first awesome sight of the workings of the "richest hill on earth" was a never-to-be-forgotten experience. Surely, I thought, Montana must be rightly named the "Treasure State."

From Butte, the train leveled out down a watergrade following the fall of the Clark's Fork of the Columbia— past the belching smokestack of the Anaconda smelter, past Golf Creek where the Frenchman, Benetsee, made the first discovery of gold in 1852, and not so far down the river from Gold Creek, we flashed past a sign saying, "Bonita," my place of rendezvous with Ranger Nichols only a couple days hence. Though trying desperately to glimpse as many of the fascinating physical attractions of the passing scene as possible, the train arrived in Missoula with me feeling I had missed far too much.

Stepping down from the day coach to the platform of the Northern Pacific depot, I looked down a surprisingly wide thoroughfare that was the main street of the city of Missoula. From what I could see, it was not much of a city, as I knew cities, but more of a large, low horizon, comfortably-sized sight. I was strangely flushed by a feeling that rather than being a newcomer, I had just returned home.

Following a brief orientation discussion with the friendly ticket agent, the Bradner domicile, where I had been invited to pitch my camp, was easily, if somewhat distantly, targeted.

Sitting on the flat at the foot of Mt. Sentinel, rising abruptly to the East, the community of possibly, optimistically, 10,000 souls was split by the broad, east to west flowing Clark Fork of the Columbia—with the business section on the north bank and the residential section, including the small University of Montana campus, on the south. Higgins Avenue, the town's wide main steam dead-ended at the NP depot on the north and ran straight south through the center of the business section, arched over the river and the Milwaukee Road tracks via the long Higgins Avenue Bridge, and continued on out for about ten or twelve city blocks through residences to vacant sagebrush flats—where it changed abruptly from hardtop street to rough gravel road.

The address I hoped to reach was on a cross street to the east of Higgins "out toward the University." A mile and a half or more distant, a taxi was the fast, easy way indicated to get there, but the early afternoon was bright and warm, and the smell of the air strangely sweet, crisp, and invigorating. After the long, confining train trip, what I wanted most was to stretch my legs.

With far more time than money, I ignored the advised taxi, picked up the suitcase, and headed south from the depot down Higgins through the business section afoot— eyeing a free striding fellow pedestrian traveling in the same direction ahead of me, with avid interest.

Carrying what I suddenly recognized as a "packsack" on his back over a red and black plaid wool jacket (must certainly be a cruising coat), and wearing a well-weathered soiled and beat-up grey curl brim hat, the man interested me. His entrancingly different garb was highlighted by his faded khaki canvas pants crudely chopped off at the eight-inch top of heavy, high-heeled, laced boots.

As later I learned, these heavy canvas, highly water resistant britches were the "tin" pants confusingly referred to in Brad's outfitting letter. With double protection over the knees, it was said that a pair of these pants was never properly "broke in" until they were covered with enough tree pitch, grease, and grime to become sufficiently stiff to "stand alone." The coat of a similar water resistant canvas material, frequently suited-up with the pants, was known as a "tin" coat. Probably the best of both were styled and manufactured by Filson—a company catering to loggers, cruisers, woodsmen, and foresters throughout the big timber country of the Northwest, and rightly famous for the fine quality of its products over many years. The Filson "tin" cruiser vest with its many handy pockets, like the coat, was woods wear nonpareil.

Also, as I later learned, the descriptive word for abbreviating the original length of pants legs in the fashion of the pedestrian preceding me down the main street of Missoula that spring day of 1928, was "stagged" and the purpose: to avoid hooking overlong pants legs on snags while hiking through brush or walking the length of downed logs, either fresh felled or long dead and windthrown.

On the south corner of the second cross street from the depot, I suddenly came face to face with a window full of everything the well-dressed woodsman, sportsman, logger, miner, or cowpoke of the Northern Rockies might wear for either work or play—everything on my shopping list and more. Never had I seen such an enticingly different and desirable wardrobe array. Taking careful note of prices, I excitedly thought my needs might well total less than my available dollars.

Progressing with mind-boggling outfitting possibilities, a few doors farther down the street came a "hock shop" window full of watches, rings, cameras, binoculars, musical instruments, and especially a display of used guns of all types and calibres. Prominently, among these weapons was one almost a dead ringer for Uncle Bill's bedside companion—even to the ivory grips and black holster with dangling leg tie-downs. I would dream about owning this formidable Colt hand cannon all summer. As luck would have it, the gun which I needed like a hole in the head, would still be there in the fall and I would have it—all for only ten silver dollars. There and then, under the pawnbroker's distinctive three silver spheres suspended over his doorway I knew, beyond a question of doubt, that Missoula must be the most wondrous hub of the most wondrous remaining wilderness outdoors in the universe. At that time I was not wrong. Miraculously, I was there and part of it.

Wandering reluctantly on from the enthralling gun display, I went several doors past the window of one of the successive shops and, suddenly remembering, came up short and retraced my steps. In the window, more or less ignored, while bemused with other thoughts, there had appeared an assortment of resoled shoes and low-cut boots. The fact that the soles and high heels of one pair of said boots were oddly studded with short sharp spikes had finally registered; I must go back to this shoe repair shop and have another look at what strangely pertained with these boots. If perchance what I had overrun might be hobnails or what Brad had called "corks," I would enter, open my suitcase, haul out my precious high-topped boots and give this shoe repairman some business. On second look at the boots in the window, I deducted that what I was looking at, definitely were not hobnails, but must indeed be corks.

Inside, the little bald-headed proprietor was busily occupied at his sewing machine at the rear of his shop and in no hurry to wait on another customer. Finally, he put aside the boot being worked on, came to the counter, and silently waited for this intruder to state his problem. Not a little flustered I pointed to the boots in the window and got out, "Are those what you call corks in the soles of those boots in the window?" Taking a step back and spitting a stream of tobacco juice into a sandbox next to the sewing machine, he nodded affirmatively and wasting no time on idle talk and as though any darn fool would have known they were corks, simply said, "Corks." Accepting the fact, I lifted my suitcase up on the counter, opened it without any more words and extracted my boots.

"I need to get these boots either hobnailed or corked— if you can do that by about noon tomorrow." Picking up one of the boots and examining it as though the likes of it he had never seen before, he tossed it back on the counter and said, "No good for corks—hobnails, maybe."

"How come no corks?"

"Soles too thin. Corks won't hold."

"Okay. Put in hobnails. Noon tomorrow?"

"Umm."

Handing me my part of a claim ticket, he set the boots aside, spit again in the sandbox and returned to where he had left off at his sewing machine.

Picking up the suitcase, considerably lightened without the boots, I browsed on down the remarkably wide and unhurried street, remembering that I had forgotten to ask how much this hobnailing job might lighten my already flyweight pocketbook. Finally, I walked toward the long bridge on the down river side, past the Florence Hotel, a major landmark four or five stories high, among the one and two story business establishments up and down the street, past a motion picture theatre, and there was the river—in flood stage, fast and roily, but strangely unlike all the Illinois rivers I had ever seen and not actually muddy. If a man knew how to handle a canoe, I thought it might be dangerous but good for a canoe. Water borne, uprooted trees and debris moved with the current seemingly fast as the mill tails of hell. It was wild. Where all that volume of water originated and where it was being emptied had to be equally wild.

Leaning over the bridge rail and watching and hearing the historic water go by, I let go a suppressed whoop of answering joy and excitement to the sight and sound of the magnificent welcoming torrent. I would get to know this river, the lands of its headwaters and feeder creeks and tributaries if it took the rest of my lifetime. This was the challenge and the promise, And the barest of beginnings. This I knew as I felt the wild racing river also knew.

Suddenly the long train ride and a gnawing in my belly for want of nourishment caught up with me. I was tired and ravenously hungry. Slowly, I trudged on across the long bridge, also spanning the Milwaukee Road tracks just as they reached the imposing station on the river level some distance below.

Magically at the south end of the bridge, across the north-south arterial from me appeared a small bakery from which I shortly emerged with a sack holding six large sugared doughnuts and a quart bottle of milk. A block farther up the street on an inconspicuous series of steps leading to the side entrance of a vacationing high school building, I settled for a one-man picnic.

Packing the sack containing an empty milk bottle and two uneaten doughnuts under one arm and carrying my suitcase with the other, I arrived at the Bradner address promptly at 5 p.m. which I considered an appropriate time. A first ring on the bell brought no response. With the second, the door was thrown open by a young, plumpish, nor especially attractive female with a towel wrapped around her head.

"Oh," she said, out of breath and in great haste, "You must be Joe. You're to have the bedroom next to the bath. I'm going to summer school and live upstairs. Here's a key to the house. I'm late for a date, so come in and make yourself at home. Go straight down the hall to the bath and bedroom."

And before I could get a word out, she turned and ran up some stairs. Nor ever reappeared.

The assigned bedroom was more sumptuous than any bedroom I had ever put foot in. One look at the frilly satin bedspread on the dandy wide bed made me know if I ever took the bed apart, I could never put it back together like the original make. With the way I had been taught, one never slept in a bed without leaving it made up as good as before. Then I saw these two beautiful soft heavy blankets on the foot of the bed and the problem was solved. The blankets were all I would need. Following three rough days and two nights in a day coach, I could have slept comfortably on a marble slab. The thick rug made the floor look like a feather bed.

Those blankets had a familiar look and suddenly I remembered—Hudson Bay blankets—identical to the one I used last summer in St. Paul. The number of little black stripes stood for the number of pounds each blanket weighted. These had four stripes. The blankets were first used in the early days for trading by fur trappers, working at the Hudson Bay Company up in the Hudson Bay area of Canada. Anyway, they were elegant blankets.

Unaware that it would be my last for the next three months, I first of all subjected myself to a deep hot bath. Little did I know that where I was headed, hot water was not easily come by and used mostly for essentials like washing dishes and laundering clothes—only rarely, if ever, for bathing the body. After pouring the water, I was in and out as quickly as possible. The sensation of being clean of train grime was one thing, but the absolution required to obtain same was no pleasurable indulgence for me. The temperature of water next to my hide has forever been a shock—too hot or too cold, never just right. The only possible time a good hot soaking can really be appreciated is after about two or three weeks on a sweaty, filthy forest fire line.

Ducking out of the bath into the bedroom, I dug out freshly laundered pajamas and while slipping into them got to thinking that here, too, might be surplus baggage for the mountain man packing his all on his back. How wrong and how right leaving them behind turned out to be, I was quick to discover: wrong, because they are a wonderful divider between the human hide and the rough WWI surplus wool blankets furnished without sheets in those days for Forest Service bedding; right, because pajamas were definitely not what the well-dressed mountain man wore between the blankets.

In following years when, for comfort's sake, I spit in the eye of decorum and carried pajamas along and wore them, I suffered many a mean jibe and questioning look from diehard companions. Several times I was crudely called upon to account for this unorthodox night attire. "Hessel," I was asked (more than once), "why do you pack along that useless fancy dude get-up just to sleep in? Ain't long underwear good enough or are you just out to scare the bears?" To which my answer, first, was explanatory, "I don't wear long underwear and these darn blankets feel like they were made of porcupine quills." Later on, I simply answered, "Go jump," which seemed to suffice.

At any odds, that summer I did not pack along pajamas. That day, with the luxuriously soft Hudson Bay type blankets, I did not need pajamas. I spread one of the two blankets on the floor, wadded up my dirty clothes for a pillow, pulled the second blanket over me, and by 6 p.m. in broad daylight was dead to the world. So ended that 13 June 1928 with a long unlikely transposition from cornfield flats to snowcapped mountains—and a part of my life already seemingly detached, strangely foreign, and far removed.

Opening my eyes to my first mountain morning was like being reborn in a glorious new world. Never had the sun been so brilliant so early, nor the air so crisp and cool in June. It was actually chilly—so chilly I hesitated to leave the warm blankets. But with the hands of the small clock on the dresser at 6:30 a.m., I had things to do; to a teen-age greenhorn, they were very important things to do.

Goaded by the uncommon chill in the air, I shaved and dressed quickly in my Sunday best complete with suit-coat and tie. Blankets carefully refolded and placed back on the foot of the bed, I stole into the immaculate kitchen, left the empty milk bottle rinsed clean in the sink, and by 7:10 was off and hiking. First, I had to discover the flat-out walking time from my town camp to the distant NP depot, where tomorrow I had an early train to catch for the twenty-six mile reverse run upriver back to Bonita. Second priority was to satisfy the gnawing in my belly for something other than doughnuts for nourishment.

With my long track and field experience, I developed a constant interest in how much time was required betwixt a starting line and the finish tape. Heel and toe walking was one event I had never had much experience with nor any special interest in. That was soon to come. While horses might be available for travel from here to there by rangers, packers and a few others in the Northern Rocky Mountain Region of the Forest Service, at that time peons like me traveled the mountain trails on shanks mares. What few roads had been built were very sketchy both as to length and standard. Laboring and sweating up steep trails and easing down descending grades over long distances was a way of life. Hikes of ten or twenty miles per day were common and up to thirty miles not especially unusual.

A slow-walking man or burro travels uphill and down at the rate of about two miles an hour. A good strong ambitious hiker travels twice that distance in the same time and if he is really in a hurry to get somewhere, can push over moderate distance up to five miles per hour. These times compare favorably with that of the average mountain horse, for a mountain trail horse is valued far more for his walking, rather than running ability. Rarely there will be a walking horse capable of six or seven miles an hour over good mountain trails and fairly long distances. I have been aboard just a few. Generally the average is much less—especially if horse and rider are "pulling," i.e., leading a string of three or more pack horses or pack mules, which more often than not in the Forest Service was the case.

Probably a record, if actually true, was set many years ago by Bob Marshall, the first head of the Division of Recreation in the Forest Service, and the man for whom the Bob Marshall Wilderness Area on the Flathead Forest in Montana is named. Marshall, it was said, hiked seventy miles over mountain trails in twenty-four hours—which is a truly great feat. I met this remarkable man once socially at a Forest Service party in Missoula and again about ten years later in Washington. Physically, he looked capable of turning the trick. But shortly after my second meeting while still in the prime of life and apparently good health, he came suddenly to the end of the trail due to heart failure in a Pullman sleeper berth on a night run between Washington, D.C. and New York City.

On that bright June morning back in Missoula in 1928, at a sustained rather rapid pace, I made it to the NP depot ticket window where Higgins Avenue dead-ended in exactly thirty-four minutes. This required that I must leave my place of stay probably no later than 6:15 a.m. next morning in order to eat a bite and get aboard the Bonita train, departing at 7:25 and "generally on time." As usual, since I am famous for always arriving for train, plane, and other departures with plenty of time to spare, I decided, to be safe, I would leave promptly at 6 a.m.

Ticket to Bonita in hand and pocket sagging with seven heavy silver dollars (change from one of my few remaining ten dollar bills), I back-tracked down Higgins several blocks to a likely looking chop house of which, in passing, I had made a mental note. What I had noted was that this place appeared to be patronized by eaters who looked like they could afford a fare on about a par with what I might afford, eaters informally attired in woods and work-related wear.

On entering and taking a seat on a stool at the long well-populated counter, I immediately wished I hadn't. In my coat and tie I felt ridiculously conspicuous. I was eyed by several adjacent companion breakfasters.

"Coffee, boy?" Standing with a heavy white mug and coffee pot on hand, ready to accommodate, the ancient aproned male behind the counter looked at me, I thought, like I might very likely be one who never touched the stuff. And he was dead right. I had never learned how to stomach the hot black brew.

Not a little embarrassed to admit it within earshot of fellow guzzlers, I faintly said, "No, thanks. Just bring me some ham and eggs—and do you have some milk?"

"Sure, boy. You got ulcers like me, huh?"

"Yeah, ulcers." Ulcers, I gathered, had some favorable relation to milk drinkers, and if so, I must also have them.

Later, during the Dirty Thirties, I ran into a few notable bargain meals, but never before nor since have I been faced with a bigger platter of ham, eggs, hash browns, toast and jelly, nor a bigger glass of good cold milk, for a mere four-bit piece.

"You get around that, kid, and you won't have no more ulcers for awhile."

And "around it" I "got" to the last little crumb. After three days of sketchy food intake, it was a feast to end all. I was hungry.

The old timer, as well as waiter, was cashier and I

suspected, if need be, probably cook and dishwasher. Not only that but I later learned he owned the joint, and was rightly famous for his meals and prices among knowledgeable wood hicks for miles around. Breakfast was fabulous but his steak dinners (suppers) were simply beyond compare. When I shelled out one of my slick-feeling silver dollars and received my four bits change he advised seriously, with a wink, "Don't take no chances with them ulcers, kid."

All he wanted and got for a tip was a big well-fed grin. "Great breakfast," I told him. "Be sure, I'll be back." I kept that promise more than once.

As I passed by the woodswear store where I had decided to start my exciting outfitting, the urge to enter and begin buying was almost too much to put off. On the other hand, I did not want to be burdened with bundles while taking care of the No. 3 objective on my program: To go see Jim Brooks, the forest supervisor, in his office at the Post Office Building and find out about the tick shot.

Though I had no way of knowing at the time, a forest supervisor in the Forest Service organization was a big potato—top hand in the "field" administrative set-up.

When Theodore "Bull Moose" Roosevelt became President, he moved the small so-called Forest Reserves out of the Department of the Interior into the Department of Agriculture and vastly increased the acreage by carving out great selected tracts of choice timberland and the erosion susceptible headwaters of navigable streams from the Public Domain. The name, "Forest Reserves," was change to National Forests. To protect and manage the new enlarged public timber and watershed lands in their new home in Agriculture, he created the USDA Forest Service. As the first Chief Forester over the new wild public holding, he appointed his forestry-minded and educated friend, the energetic and peppery Gifford Pinchot, later Governor of the State of Pennsylvania. After viewing European forests and studying forestry under the scientific European foresters, he had the original National Forest and Forest Service vision. Congress bought and approved the new concept and set up, over howls of the timber barons who were then cutting out and getting out of the East, Lake States, and South, and heading for the great stands of cheap public timber in the Rockies, California, and Pacific Northwest. The general public, in their mad rush to make a fast buck from other than timber, for the most part could have cared less.

In 1905, when all this was coming to pass, trees, soil, water, range, fish, and wildlife in the general public view were still in practically limitless supply, and sometimes in the view of homesteaders, trees were a plague on the land. The word, "conservation," as applied to national resources on wild mountain lands especially, had barely been coined. Outdoor recreation, like climbing mountains for exercise or just to see if you could get to the top and back again without breaking your neck or freezing to death, was the pursuit of fools. Skiers who took to the cold and snow, merely for the fun of it, were "flatboard idiots." Anyone who had time (other than possibly on national holidays) to hunt and fish, except for meat and hides, was a ne'er-do-well or a rich demented dude. Forest, range, and prairie fires caused by careless loggers, range riders, those wanting to get rid of snakes and ticks, and dry lightning, raced and raged over millions of acres, killing everything, including people, in their path and nobody, practically, cares. Smokey the Bear and the smoke-jumpers were far in the future.

On the other hand, in creating the National Forest system and the Forest Service, T. Roosevelt and Pinchot did not, at least did not intend to, create a preservationist monster. National Forests, as opposed to National Parks, were set aside in the public interest for productive use of all inherent renewable resources: using soil to grow continuous crops of trees and growing continuous crops of grass and shrubs for grazing by domestic livestock and game.

It was a good plan and looked fairly simple to execute. In addition to the basic uses such as growing timber, grass and shrubs, and keeping the headwaters of navigable streams from washing down on the flats, multitudinous legitimate uses of the wild National Forests lands showed up that were never dreamed of. Likewise conflicts arose between uses that could not possibly be reconciled to the satisfaction of all parties involved.

What T. Roosevelt and G. Pinchot wrought has turned out to be nothing so simple as a preservationist monster. It has become a fire breathing dragon. Since the masses of outdoor recreationists, bird lovers, armchair ecologists, and long haired environmentalists have swarmed into the act, production of trees and grass have been moved to the back burner. Pinchot's original work force did not have to face up to overwhelming numbers of wilderness lovers. They had the wilderness, more or less, all to themselves, so much so that sometimes they would catch themselves answering their own questions.

If not being overrun by wilderness lovers, however, they had plenty of other things to worry about, like looking down the business end of a trespassing rancher's six gun. Though never a gun toting outfit, there were some tight occasions both on the range and in the woods when the early day Forest Service ranger wished to high heaven that he had one, and later thanked the good Lord he didn't. Even a livestock operator or logger caught stealing grass or timber seldom had guts enough to shoot an unarmed representative of the U.S. Government in cold blood—not even a forest ranger.

After gathering a small staff in Washington, D.C. dubbed the Chief's Office, Pinchot set up headquarters in places like Missoula, Montana; Denver, Colorado; Albuquerque, New Mexico; Ogden, Utah; San Francisco,

California; and Portland, Oregon. District offices were headed by a potentate called the District Forester. In the line of command the District (now Regional) Forester answered only to the Chief Forester. On down the totem-pole, the District Forester designated a Forest Supervisor to head up each of ten or more National Forests, comprising a District, with each supervisor having to answer only to the District Forester. In the so-called "Stink Hole" at the bottom of the administrative pole came the Forest Ranger with four, five, or sometimes a couple more rangers under each supervisor.

The Chief had a staff of Assistant Chiefs; the District Forester had a few assistant District Foresters; the Supervisor usually had an Assistant Supervisor plus a few clerical aides. Other than his limited seasonal summer help, the Ranger was strictly on his own. No need for a steno to fill out a few reports or a bookkeeper to keep track of a few bucks spent on seasonal help down on the farm. A ranger, at $900 per annum, furnishing his own horse and riding gear, and no expense account, got a lot of satisfaction just being lord of a quarter million (or more) acre spread.

In 1905, when Pinchot was setting up his outfit, college trained foresters were in very short supply. In the United States, at that time, forestry as a profession was practically unheard of, let alone taught in institutions of higher education. Of the few turned out at Ivy League schools, Pinchot managed to corral most for his top echelon. But to fill all the slots in the field, even few as they were, he was forced to compromise for men who had simply been exposed to a semblance of forestry and watershed and range management, like loggers, cowboys, homesteaders, prospectors, and frontiersmen of all types. The number and generally high caliber of men who answered his call for practical down-the-line assistance, especially in view of the low pay, long hours, and expectable hazards, was amazing.

To pass the early day ranger examination, a man had to be literate to the extent that he could write a diary,

and read, understand, and explain to users the rules and
regulations under which the national forests were operated. He had to demonstrate knowledge of how to cruise,
mark, and scale timber and logs. Finally among other
requirements, he had to display proficiency with an axe,
crosscut saw, rifle, and rope. Lack of ability to put a
pack on a horse and make it stay proved the downfall of
many an applicant.

Those who passed this exacting practical test were
known in the Forest Service as the "Old Timers" or
"Early Day Originals." Those who lasted proved to be
one of the most close-knit, not to say "clannish," loyal,
self-sacrificing, proud, tough, and honest group of
civilian employees in the history of American government. Many were promoted to Forest Supervisor and a
few to even higher positions. This group dug the holes
and planted the posts—frequently in the solid rock of
public opposition—for today's tremendous National
Forest System.

J.B. Halm was one of the heroes of the catastrophic
fires of 1910 in Idaho and western Montana. I was one
day privileged to shoot geese from his blind at Nine
Pines Reservoir in the shadow of the Mission Mountains
with him. He was one of very few of the notably
close-mouthed "Old Timers" to articulate the nature of
the breed. In his all too brief reminiscences, he says: "In
those early days of the Service, I was impressed by the
unselfish loyalty of everyone, the enthusiasm with which
they worked and sweated, carrying their food and beds
on their backs, traveling the dim forest trails mostly
without horses . . . rain or shine, day after day sleeping
under the stars, or in winter in soggy leaky cabins with
roofs sagging under ten feet of snow. Sometimes we ate
from the same pan and slept under the same blanket;
and snowshoed with hundred pound packs for days, wet
to the bone . . . when the snow was firm and the going
was good, we laughed at our hardships, poked fun at
each other's weaknesses and mistakes, and filled the
woods with song. We shared dangers, toiling beneath

those great white or black billows of smoke . . . adding our mite of strength to control the fire demon and stop the destruction . . ."

When it came to down-the-line recruiting, obviously Pinchot did well; since all promotions came from within, the Halms were the stuff from which supervisors, regional foresters, and the Chief, himself, came to be made. Forestry school graduates were attracted to the Service like a magnet and for years on end, the Forest Service drew the cream of the crop. In all its history, the Service has never had a Chief who has not been a professional forester or had long previous experience in the Service itself. This is a proud and critical distinction.

To my everlasting benefit, Ranger Lou Nichols was one of those diamond hitch, "Early Day Originals." Forest Supervisor Jim Brooks, on whom I was destined to call regarding a tick shot that day in June back in 1928 was not. He was one of the new breed of cats. Scarcely six years out of college, he had passed the new, most technical, all-day written, Junior Forester examination with a high mark, and gained rapid promotion from District Ranger to Forest Supervisor. At the time he was the youngest head of a National Forest in the country—an outstanding accomplishment. The Missoula Forest was not one of the heaviest work load Forests, but heading it for a starter was certainly a challenging assignment.

The attractive young lady first encountered on entering the door marked, "Missoula National Forest—Supervisor" in the large greystone Post Office Building, welcomed me with a bright, "Good morning." And, on announcing my name and business, she gave me a warm across the desk handshake. "You're the boy Mr. Bradner mentioned. Mr. Brooks is free. You can go right on in. I think he was expecting you sometime today."

On proceeding somewhat hesitantly through the indicated door, I stood in a plain carpetless, brown-linoleum floored cubicle sparsely furnished with a large white oak desk, swivel armchair, two straight-backed visitor chairs in front of the desk and a couple of glass-door bookcases filled with assorted official-looking tomes. The yellowish walls, aside from a big window behind the occupant, were covered with large hanging maps. His eminence, the supervisor, was sitting in the swivel chair deeply absorbed in a scattered mass of maps, papers, and books. Bright tie loosened, collar unbuttoned, and fresh white shirt sleeves rolled up, he seemed to see me, without taking his eyes off the protractor with which he was at work. "Be with you in just a minute."

Sitting on the edge of one of the two hard, uncomfortable visitor chairs, I waited while he quickly consulted a slide rule and made notations on a ruled white pad. Looking up suddenly with a broad, friendly smile, he stood and held out a hand across the clutter. "Howdy," he greeted. "I'm Jim Brooks. Sorry to keep you waiting. You must be the young man from back east headed for the Rock Creek District and looking for a tick shot."

Rising quickly to take his outstretched hand, I confirmed his supposition and stammered out a confused thanks for giving me a chance to work on the Missoula National Forest.

"'Fraid you're out of luck on the tick shot right now. The Lab's run out of serum and that's the only place you can get it. The docs up at Hamilton are doing a great job, but they're short-handed just like the rest of us. Plus they need to expand their facilities. Do you know anything about spotted fever?"

"All I know is that Mr. Bradner said I should get the shot. I take it the ticks somehow must cause the fever."

Brooks, behind his large horn-rimmed glasses studied me silently for a minute. He was a big raw-boned, rather flush-faced man, easy to talk to and, young as he was, more or less on my age level. I thought at his age he must be great.

"I don't want to scare you unnecessarily, but it's pretty serious business. You get the fever and it's a hell of a death. You just burn to a cinder. Next to the Bitterroot country just over the hill, the Rock Creek District is one of the worst. We had three fatal cases up there last year—a sheepherder and a couple of stump ranchers. None of them had taken the shot, but even a shot is no guarantee against contracting the fever. A shot may make it easier . . . may save your life. Right now, they're just more or less experimenting with the serum and actually don't know. Most all of us take the serum if it's available. Makes your arm swell up and get darn sore for a few days."

"What do these ticks look like? Where do they come from?" I queried.

"It's the common wood-tick: round, flat, brown, hard-shelled, about the size of the head on a small tack. You pick 'em up going through the brush, sitting on a stump or down timber. They seem to be attracted more to light than dark colored clothes. Most of them don't carry the fever. Those that do seem to get it from contact with the Rocky Mountain wild goat or some other animal. Sometimes, you can feel 'em crawling on you. Sometimes not. They fasten on and burrow in sucking blood. Once they take hold, you can't pull 'em out without leaving the head and even if they aren't infected with the disease, that can cause a simple infection. A touch of iodine or turpentine will sometimes make them let go and back out. If you get 'em off in less than twelve hours, there isn't much danger. Come in after a day in the field, strip down and look yourself over every night. Most cases seem to be with individuals who aren't especially clean—wear long underwear day and night without changing for long periods. And the ticks seem to follow the snow-line, liking humid or wet conditions. As the country and brush dry out, they seem to disappear. The worst season is in the spring of the year. There's no doubt you should have a shot if we could get you one, but I think if you just watch out for them and look yourself over every night for the next month or so, you'll be okay. It's one of the hazards we've been living with and no preventative shots for years."

"Sure," I said. "I'll take my chances."

The supervisor smiled a little and changed the subject. "You're getting a pretty early start on being a forester."

"Yes, sir. Thanks to Brad and Ranger Nichols—and you. I'm sure looking forward to the work."

"Nick's an old timer who came to the Forest Service from the Texas Rangers, some years ago. He's a widower with his family grown and gone. Had a horse rear and fall backwards on him about a year ago and spent sometime in the hospital. Rock Creek's a great trout stream. Take a rod and a few flies along. You may have a little free time to fish."

"I'll need someone to show me how it's done. I never fished for trout."

"You'll find someone. All those natives up there are fishermen." He stood up and again held out his hand. "Glad to talk to you and sorry about the tick shot. Good luck."

As I left the Post Office Building, feeling a little apprehensive regarding no tick shot, the large-faced wall clock read only 9:35 a.m.: more than enough time for clothes shopping. Uppermost in my mind was Brad's and Brooks' exciting comments on the Rock Creek trout fishing. As if in answer to my thoughts, as I progressed from window to window along a side of Higgins I had not previously investigated, I came to a sporting goods establishment. In the entrance was a showcase featuring three magnificent fresh fish the likes of which I had never seen before, and seldom ever would. Laid out on a cake of ice, they were beauties to behold—silvery grey with a pink stripe along the side—these were my introduction to trophy size trout. The card atop the glass over the center lunker read, "5 pounds 4 ounces. Caught on Paul Bunyan Bug. Rock Creek 6/12/" In other words, just day before yesterday.

After ogling the catch in every detail for some minutes, I entered the store resolved on purchasing a Bunyan Bug if it meant parting with my last precious dime. I had no more idea of what a Bunyan Bug might be or the tackle and method necessary for presenting it to a trout than the man in the moon. Brilliantly demonstrating my total ignorance, I said to the affable, slightly portly man behind the counter, "I need a Bunyan Bug."

"Salmon fly? Grasshopper? What make of bug did you have in mind?"

Momentarily dumbfounded on learning that the bug was not simply a bug, but a wide variety of bugs, I confessed, "I don't know one from another—which do you recommend?"

"Depends," says the man, "on the time of year and where you're going to fish. Right now, I'd say this one here—the salmon fly."

What was the salmon fly type of Bunyan Bug, looked to me like nothing resembling any kind of bug in my acquaintance—a small cylindrical piece of orange and black painted cork with some stiff short grayish hair stuck through it at right angles, tied to a long shanked barbed hook of a size not for Illinois sunfish. "You mean that's the thing those trout out there in the box were caught on?" I asked incredulously.

"That's the thing. Doesn't look like anything a trout would ever hit but it does the trick." The salesman paused. "Of course there's a knack in knowing how to fish it. Those fish were caught by an expert, Norman Means. He called himself Paul Bunyan and makes the lure. That's how come the name, 'Bunyan Bug.' When he fishes it, he gets in the creek with high waders and sometimes goes in over the waders. The bug is cork and floats with the current—cast it up and across stream and work it downstream with the current into the holes."

With no other customers in the store, the knowledgeable salesman apparently had nothing else to do but talk to his only client—even though the client was obviously a teenager not likely to be indulging in any big purchases of the tempting merchandise. Sensing an opportunity for improving his lack of know-how in a most fascinating pastime, the teenager invited the salesman to continue elaborating on the taking of trout by honestly stating his total ignorance of the art.

"Maybe," I said hesitantly, "if you have a few minutes, you can help me a lot more than just with the bug. This is my first time West. I came yesterday from Illinois to take a job on the Rock Creek District of the Missoula National Forest and I'm green as a gourd. I've fished for mostly sunfish in Illinois and once for walleyes in Minnesota, but never for trout. In addition to the bug and flies, what all do I need? And how much does an outfit cost? I haven't much money. And still have some field clothes to buy."

Putting both hands on the counter on which he had laid out his bugs, the kindly bug purveyor looked at me with new interest. Here might be a customer of some consequence—if not at the moment—in time to come. Relaxed and smiling, he held out his hand, "I'm Bill Gates."

"Glad to meet you young fellows going to work for the Forest Service. That's one good government agency with good people. A lot of them trade in here. Going up to Rock Creek you've *got* to have a trout outfit. Never started putting one together from the fly end, but let's see what we can come up with. Not much money—hum." Reaching into a drawer behind him, he brought out a small coil of transparent thread-size material looking like it would in no way bear the weight and battle of the trout out front.

"This is a gut leader. It's tapered from big at one end to fine at the other. Tie the bug to the fine end, like so." Passing the fine end through the eye of the hook, he deftly fastened the leader to the lure with a knot like I had never seen before, clipping off a short piece of surplus leader with a fingernail clipper. "Handiest gadget there is for a trout fisherman—fingernail clippers," he said. "You need a nail clipper. Now this leader is heavier than some and longer, about seven feet, than some. I personally like a long leader, a tapered leader.

There's flat-same size on both ends leaders, like flat and tapered line, a lot cheaper, and not as good, either to cast or as invisible to the trout. You ought to learn to tie that knot."

Taking another bug and another piece of leader, he handed them to me. "Put the end of the leader through the eye of the hook about an inch or two. Now come back, wind the end around the main leader three or four times, back and through the loop above the eye of the hook. Hold the end and pull the leader tight. A surefire knot. Practice that a few times while I take care of this customer." He left me tying, clipping, and retying the knot to wait on another customer who had walked in and was examining price tags on a rack of fly rods. Shortly having taken care of the customer, he was back with several small boxes of various type flies.

"After you get the bug tied to the leader, we tie the leader to a line. This here is a cheap flat untreated line, hard to cast. And this is a more expensive treated single taper line. They're several types of tapered lines: double taper, shooting, etcetera. Right now all you need to know about is this single taper. The small tapered end of the line is tied to the thick part of the leader like so." And slowly he tied the leader to the line using a different knot and showing me in detail how to make the knot as he went along.

"Now," he said. "Before we go any farther, we've got to back up. There's several kinds of trout fishing, all different, all requiring a different type of outfit. Dry fly, wet fly, spinners, and God forbid, but there's trout fishing with bait, worms, hellgrammites, grasshoppers, even dough balls. Don't knock it, some of the biggest trout brought in here are caught on bait using a simple snelled hook, flat leader and line, no reel and any old kind of pole, even to a cut willow. Unless I really needed meat, I wouldn't stoop to any kind of bait—it's not sport fishing—purely meat. Now personally I'm a downstream, wet fly fisherman . . ."

Between customers, my lesson went on through level

winding and automatic reels (automatic recommended); split bamboo rods—two jointed, seven foot, seven-and-a-half foot, eight foot (seven-and-a-half foot, four jointed recommended as best all around and easiest to carry); flies—wet, dry, hair, feathered, streamers; hip boots, waders, creels. For over an hour, he went on, giving enough on trout fishing and trout fishing outfits to fill a book with me hanging onto every word and absorbing every detail. While worrying more and more and becoming more uncomfortable, wondering what all this tutoring and final outfitting in sum total was about to cost, I started to visualize at minimum an outlay far exceeding my total remaining capital. Woodswear outfitting was still first priority and still unaccomplished.

At the moment we had progressed to the relative desirability of nets for landing the lunker, merits of various types of nets, and method of using a net, when I happened to note next to the stock of nets, a stock of the Number 1 item on my shopping list—pack sacks.

"Now there," I said, "is something I need most—a pack sack. Pick me out a good medium size inexpensive pack sack. After I buy that and a few things to put in it, maybe I'll have a little left for fishing equipment."

"Ah, ha," said my fishing professor, pawing through the pile of assorted sacks, "right here. $3.65. But never let it be said buying necessities stood in the way of you putting together a fishing outfit when you're going up to Rock Creek." Holding the brown canvas pack sack in one hand and putting his other arm around my shoulder, he regarded me with mock questioning seriousness.

"It might have to be said," I laughed. "A fisherman can hardly fish without pants."

"Tell you what. You go get what you need to put in this sack. And even if you're dead broke when you finish with that, you come back."

"I can never thank you enough for taking so much time to fill me in on trout fishing. I'll be back."

Shelling out four silver dollars and taking the sack

AUNT HELEN AND HER BROTHER BRAD   111

unwrapped underarm, I exited and hurried up the street to the woods wear establishment the helpful sporting goods proprietor had recommended as probably my best place to shop. The time was now past 10:30 and shortly after noon I must pick up my hob-nailed boots.

In the clothing store, I encountered the same unhurried easygoing welcome as at Roy's Grill and Gates Sporting Goods. After ringing up a sale to the one other customer in the place, the proprietor, a dapper gent with a small close-cropped mustache, came wandering forward to where I was admiring a large stock of cruising coats as though he might have cared less to make a sale.

"Howdy," he greeted with a smile. "You need a few of those cruisers those morning?"

"Just one," I smiled back, "and I doubt if I can afford that."

"Never mind the cost. Which one do you like?"

"You better believe me. The cost has got to come ahead of what I might like. I like that solid maroon-colored coat." Taking the indicated jacket off the rack, he held it up as though seeing it for the first time.

"I'm not sure you want this coat. It doesn't have the double back—no pocket in the back."

At this point like with Gates and trout fishing, I confessed to complete ignorance about cruising coats, told the man my destination, and asked the expert to pick out what he thought would be best all around at a price I might be able to pay.

"Goshamighty," he said, "you get up there on Rock Creek you'll be working with Em Hauswirth. The fish are really hitting up there right now. You like to fish?"

"Nothing I like more. I just came from Gates Sporting Goods. He recommended your store."

"Good for old Gates. But no wonder you're short of money. He probably sold you the whole store."

"Only thing I bought was this pack sack but he sure did give me the dope on trout fishing, about which I was as ignorant as about these coats. Like I told him, I can't fish in the nude. What little money I have, you'll get most of it."

"Well, when you get up there, you get next to Hauswirth. He's road and trail foreman on that district and a fishing fool." Holding out a bright red and black plain jacket: "Try this coat. It's got four pockets in front, one in back, and one inside. You can't get too many pockets."

The coat fit just right and eyeing it in the glass, I thought it was the finest I had ever seen. "Oh, boy!"

"Perfect," he said.

"Yeah perfect, but I don't know if I can afford that quality coat or not."

"I said never mind the price. That's the coat. Now what else do you need?"

"A couple pairs of Levis and some leather work gloves."

"What size Levis?"

"I haven't the vaguest idea."

Whipping out a tape, he checked my waist and inseam dimensions at a glance, and picked a pair of Levis from a pile. "Try these on. Right over there in that closet."

When I changed into them, the waist had about an inch of slack and the legs were at least two inches too long. Stepping out of the closet, I said, "Away too big."

"Uh. The second time they're washed, they'll fit just right. Always buy Levis two sizes over your actual size. They really shrink."

"I'll look damn funny with the legs rolled up like that."

"You will 'til you fall in the creek or put 'em through a wash. Don't worry about how they look now. Coat and two pairs of Levis. Gloves now should come as near fitting your hand as possible."

Never having owned a pair of leather work gloves, I would never have known. "Try this small size glove. They differ some by make, and they may stretch a little with use." The glove he handed me seemed a good fit. "Index finger a little long. Try these." The second pair fit even better and felt good and snug on my hand like no glove had ever felt before.

"Okay," I said. "Now let's see if I can pay my way out of here with a few dollars left for hobnails and a couple of meals."

Returning to his cash register counter and doing some quick arithmetic on a scratch pad, he looked up and announced, "$27.50."

"Um, um," I moaned, "Let's look at some cheaper coats."

"You like that coat I picked for you?"

Running my hand enviously over the fine wool texture of the bright plaid coat lying on the counter, I said, "Yessir. I sure do like that coat. The only question: Can I afford it?"

"After a hard winter, nobody has money this time of year. But you have something as good as money and that's a job. Tell you what. Pay me half now and the rest when you come in the fall. And take that coat. I can sell you something for less but that's what you need."

"You mean you'd trust me 'till September?" The proposition was incredulous. "You don't even know me. I might never show up."

"You'll show up okay. The minute you hit town. I make a few mistakes on people, but not many."

I took off my tie. Then my suit coat. And stuffed both into my newly acquired pack sack. "Where I came from people don't generally trust people like out here. Put the pants and gloves in this pack sack. I'll take and wear the coat and pay the whole bill now. The way I was taught, if you can't pay for something on the spot, you go without 'till you can." Taking out my flat pocketbook, I extracted my last two twenty dollar bills and handed him the money. "Ever so many thanks for offering to trust me, but I think I can get by."

Obviously pleased and amused, he put the money in the cash register and helped me get the pack sack over the coat. "A little warm today for a cruiser."

"Maybe. But not too warm."

"You remember now. Get with Em Hauswirth. Get him to take you fishing and tell the no good old man I'll be up and tangle lines with him sometime this summer."

"I'll sure tell him." I ran my hand lovingly over the cruiser once more and gave him a satisfied grin. "Sure is a dandy coat."

Giving the jacket a tug downward in the back to take out a wrinkle under the pack, he said, "You'll wear that coat a good long time. Anybody wants to know where you got it, you tell 'em right here." As I went proudly out the door, he waved and I waved. "Come back and tell me about the fishing when you get in next fall," he said. I nodded and went out thinking the business of outfitting for any expedition of any kind had to be one of the best parts of the outing. I still think that way. However, the thrill of acquiring my first cruising coat with my last few dollars was never quite repeated. It has always been a mystery to me how such small items can stand out as the most memorable in a man's life.

Another thing, I could not help thinking I had to be heading by some lucky turn of fate, for one of the greatest trout fishing streams in the West. First Brad, then Brooks, then Gates, and finally my trusting clothes outfitter, Yandt, had warned me to be prepared for the fishing in Rock Creek. And there in Gates' sidewalk showcase, I had seen the fabulous indisputable evidence.

In all truth, Rock Creek is, or once was, a famous trout fishery. Also in all truth, in the two, too-short and busy summer seasons I put in on the Rock Creek District, the opportunities I had to test its many tempting riffles and holes were extremely few and far between. At the time, I could scarcely throw a fly or a Bunyan Bug ten feet from the end of a rod without getting tangled in the brush or snagged on a rock.

Back on the sidewalks bordering the still surprisingly and excessively wide Higgins Avenue, in my bright red and black plaid wool coat on a warm day in June, and with the unaccustomed pack on my back, I was aware that my get-up anywhere downtown in Illinois would certainly have attracted the stares of all and sundry. If highly conspicuous and incongruous there, on-coming pedestrians here in western Montana, I noted somewhat disappointedly, never gave my brand new costume even a second glance.

Over a period of time, I discovered the cut of a man's wardrobe in this, the Treasure State, was a poor means of measurement either of his status in the community or at the bank. The pedestrian sporting an elegant new cruising jacket might be a nobody, without a spare dime, while the man in the well-worn boots and faded work shirt sitting next to you while breakfasting in Jake's Place might be a well-heeled timber operator or rancher.

Uncle Bill, according to the family, and to their everlasting chagrin, "dressed like a bum." When once I innocently asked him why he never "dressed up," his violent answer surprised me. "To heck with that foo-farah and buttons and bows," he spat out. "So long as a man's dressed for the weather and protected from bugs and thorns, it don't make any difference what his cover is made of or whether it's cut one way or t'other."

I thought Uncle Bill would have approved of my purchases especially the Levis and leather gloves. The coat, too, except for the bright red color. As to that he would have said, "Goshamighty boy, in that outfit a blind man can see you comin' or goin' a mile away, even in heavy cover." In his day, concealment rather than advertisement of one's presence was uppermost. In my time with the arrival of the trigger-happy big game hunter who cannot differentiate between a standing or moving deer, horse, or human even in an open meadow, it is just the reverse.

The time now being about the noon hour I decided, in retracing my steps to Gates, to stop by Silent Sam's Shoe Shop and learn the bad news on how much my hobnailed job would set me back. If the boots were ready, I would add them to my pack and save some steps. As it happened, my scarce-worded cobbler was driving the last few nails as I walked through his door. Placing my claim check on the counter without any greeting so as not to disturb the peace, I stood there and waited until he finished the job.

After a few minutes, he distastefully eyed the product of his labors, came and set the boots on the counter and looked me in the eye.

"You planning to walk any timber in them things, don't do it." With this long speech, he turned again and spat a stream of tobacco juice in his sandbox.

"I'm going up to Rock Creek out of Bonita. You think I'll be walking any timber up there?"

"Um," he grunted, noncommittally. "Fishin'?"

Vaguely sensing something highly contradictory to exterior appearances in this question, I answered cautiously, "Work for the Forest Service."

"Umm. Mighty good fishin'." Still unwilling to accept the unbelievable, I got out, "You, a fisherman?"

A half humorous light lit up his sharp old eyes as though not wanting to expose the semblance of a smile on his tobacco stained lips, he turned away for another discharge into the sandbox. With an expression on his face still somewhat like the satisfied cat, who has swallowed the mouse, he faced back again with the question still unanswered and said, "Hobnailed. One dollar."

I gave him the money, put the boots in my pack, and hurried to Gates. In my red coat and pack sack, I idled around examining price tags on fly rods and other items in his inventory till the proprietor, my fishing authority, was free of customers.

"Do you happen to know that shoemaker up the street, on the other side just below Yandt's?" I ask confidentially.

"You mean old Bixby up at the Lonesome Pine Shoe Shop?" Gates laughed. "What'd he tell you?"

"It's what he didn't tell me. Is he by any possible chance a fisherman?"

"He *wouldn't* tell you," said Gates, "and you'd never

guess it by dealing with him, that old boy's a fishing fiend. He's got a beat-up Model T truck and takes off for somewhere every fishable Sunday. If the mood hits him he'll close up shop and head out for two or three days during the week. He's probably caught more and better fish than anybody in these parts, not excepting Norman Means. Gives all he takes to local charities that run a kitchen in conjunction. Just one little hitch in the way he fishes—he uses bait. Maybe that's one reason he never talks about it."

If Gates hadn't told me I would have never believed it.

"Now," Gates continued, "Let's ask you a question."

"What's that?"

"How come you didn't buy a *red* coat? Was Yandt all out of red?"

It was my turn to laugh. When I asked him seriously what he thought of the coat, Gates said Yandt had done me well. With his approval, I was more than pleased. In the end, I went out of the place with a cheap steel rod that telescoped from seven feet to three and which Gates said was such a poor excuse for a fly rod that he was embarrassed to show it to me. For a reel, I selected a Martin automatic, with which he said any purist trout fisherman would never be caught dead, but with which I landed many a trout over a number of years. The reel was loaded with the cheapest treated single taper line he carried in stock. I bought two catgut tapered leaders six feet long rather than the recommended seven feet because a foot in length amounted to about ten cents difference in price, and I purchased only one expensive Bunyan Bug of the salmon fly variety which my adviser warned rightly that I would quickly lose and not be able to replace, and three gray hackle yellow wet flies that he said was not half enough. That was it. Without the landing net, I was left with no paper money and a scant two dollars and sixty cents in my pocket.

With Gates' wishes for good luck on the job and admonitions to report in on the fishing whenever I might get back to town ringing in my ears, I took one

last parting look at the stimulating Bunyan Bug catch
on the ice in his entry showcase and headed south across
the Higgins Avenue Bridge.

Now that I was outfitted as advised by Brad—at least
to the limit of my means—before the train ride on the
morrow, I still had pressing things to do. First priority
was getting back to the Bradner residence, drawing a
tub of hat water not for another bath, but for soaking
one of my two new pairs of Levis. Yandt had told me
that to really shrink Levis, to soak them in good hot
water.

As to the bath, with the help of my new red wool coat,
the pack on my back, and the midday sun, I was so
bathed in sweat that, barely halfway across the bridge, I
was forced to shed the coat and add it to my back pack.
Where my one and only suit was wadded up in the
bottom of the pack, I meticulously folded the precious
cruiser across the top.

The lunch hour having come and gone without my
indulgence I again stopped at the neighborhood grocery
at the end of the bridge and bought cheese, crackers and
a pint bottle of milk. As I exited with these items in
hand, it came to me, almost revelation-wise, that I had a
packsack on my back made expressly for packing all
and sundry. All it once it dawned on my why the logger
ahead of me coming from the depot packed his indis-
pensibles on his back rather than in a suitcase. In
addition to putting the load where it belonged, it left the
hands free for taking a chew of snoose, rolling a
cigarette from a Bull Durham sack, warding off brush
and bugs, and any number of other essential uses for
unencumbered arms and hands. The homely brown
canvas bag with the shoulder straps and apparently
unlimited capacity suddenly appeared to me as the
greatest invention since man. It was a small mystery to
me with all the dead rabbits I had to pack dangling
from a belt why I had never even heard or thought
about it. Also, I became aware of this highly useful,
convenient, and comfortable accessory and how back-

ward the so-called civilized populace of Illinois could be.

The "rediscovery" of the woodman's old canvas pack-sack and its present widespread use is humorously amazing to say the least. What wonders have been wrought in its improvement from the single crude sack to current multiple-compartment models made from brightly colored weatherproof nylon would set many a deceased back packer spinning in his grave. This includes improvements in packframes—from rough heavy wood and canvas to ingeniously cushioned plastics and aluminum. Yet the prime ultimate wonder is not so much in the stunning construction of the present day backpack, itself, as the contents, including everything from powdered soup to the papoose. As was, backpacking was a man's province, but no more. Ms. now packs her own warbag on her own back and man is glad of it. No one, regardless of sex, should miss this unique opportunity to sprain the spine and indent the kidneys. Having had my day with the standard forty pound smokechaser's packsack on my aching back uphill and down over long distances, I will do my packing on the back of a horse.

When Yandt told me, matter of factly, that soaking Levis in hot water would materially reduce them in both length and girth, he was in no way exaggerating the shrink. As I immersed, puddled, and sloshed my new britches in the hot tub, what was happening looked to me like the reduction might be too much. Also, an item Yandt had failed to inform me about was the effect of hot water on Levi dye. The blue ring around the spotless white tub was as frightening as the shrink. As the water turned more and more indigo, I hastily pulled the plug, extracted and wrung as much water as possible out of the pants and, with some Dutch cleanser, discovered in the cabinet under the sink, set about removing the telltale dye. By the time this strenuous chore was completed, more or less satisfactorily, the postshrunk Levis were almost dry enough to test the fit without hanging them on the backyard clothesline. Slipping out of oxfords and suit pants, I straightened the wring-wrinkle out of the more than a little damp Levis and pulled them over my shorts. Amazingly, the rolled up overlength was now a just right instep length, the legs formed over my knees from the knee up as snugly, almost, as my leather gloves fit over my fingers and the waist barely missed on the too-big side being my exact girth.

Unfortunately and surprisingly, along with all the rest of the astonishing shrink had gone, the buttonholes. Only at the point of no return could I force the metal buttons through the original openings. Indeed with the old all button Levis, no matter how stretched and torn, there was forever this difficulty of fastening and unfastening the frustrating metal button fly. A man with bladder or diarrhea trouble did best to just leave the fly unfastened. Failure to do so could result in disaster with a capital D.

Man's decision-making ability has never been so severely tested as when deciding what to take along and what to leave behind, at the last minute, before launching off for several months to somewhere remote from and inaccessible to, the big and little necessities and conveniences of what he knows as home. Invariably somewhere along the line whatever he decides will be wrong—which after a few similar forays, he will recognize at the outset. Just as leaving my pajamas behind was a mistake, taking along my polished street oxfords was also a mistake. Those shiny brogans were extra baggage. I had ample time and opportunity to consume the complete unabridged works of Shakespeare, but failed to throw in so much as the current issue of the *Saturday Evening Post*. I starved all summer for reading material. Be it said, however, I *did* get there with film for my camera and shells for my gun.

By the time I had again cleaned vestiges of dye from the bathtub, dried my faded and shrunken Levis in the sun, and made all my right and wrong decisions in transfers from suitcase to packsack, the sun was drifting down over the yardarm, even despite the surprisingly long evening. Deciding against making one more long haul downtown to Jake's place for supper, I cleaned up the remnants of my cheese, crackers, and milk, spread my two blanket bed on the floor, and vaguely wondering where the student housekeeper in the attic had disappeared, I was again soon fast asleep. It was a day to be long remembered.

What "corked" boots can do to the soft pine floor of a bunkhouse or cook shack of a logging camp might well be imagined. Even a small dose of cork-booted traffic reduced door sills and floor to fine splinters in short order. Over the entry to one logger beanery that I remember, there hung a sign, "No Corks or No Eats." It meant either go to the bunkhouse and change shoes or cache your calks and eat in your sock feet. In this era of the nature boys and girls, I am always reminded of that sign by signs in beanery windows reading, "No Shoes— No Shirt—No Service." Such was the decorum of the logging camps of that time, that the loggers would have either stomped the undressed nature lovers like cockroaches or run them out of the woods. Both breeds apparently are equally strong-minded but physically, logger vs. nature boy, there is no contest. I shudder to think.

The next morning, I also shuddered to think what those newly hobnailed soles of my boots might do to highly polished hardwood floors. Rather than testing, I sock-footed to the basement to park my suitcase in an off track spot and donned my warned-of low heeled and high topped boots on the bottom step of the front porch, at the end of the concrete sidewalk. If one has never walked in hobnailed, or especially calked, boots on concrete, the feeling is somewhat like when first getting on roller skates—except for being a little more sure your footing is not going out from under in both directions. The tendency is to try to walk softly, which is utterly impossible. Often, you put the foot down flat with as little give in the ankles and knees as an arthritic and this results in a most unnatural and peculiar gait. Hobs or calks, especially new and sharp corks, are meant strictly for in the mountains and woods, not on city sidewalks. After clomping along the long stretch between my erstwhile bedground and Jake's Place, I was thinking I might be crippled for life.

Slipping the pack off my back, I set it against the wall behind an empty stool at the far end of the counter, hung my cruiser on a handy coat hook above same, and bellied up to be served with my Illinois hat pushed comfortably on the back of my head. Though it was strictly forbidden in my upbringing to ever wear a hat in the house, and more especially at the table at anytime ever, I had quickly noted on the morning before, that in Jake's Place, it was apparently the fashion, if not the rule, to do so. Uncle Bill had once told me that "hat or no hat, what comes off the griddle tastes just the same," and I saw no reason for stepping out of line by eating bareheaded.

Old Jake did not bother to offer me coffee. He simply arrived with a big glass of milk. "Ulcers any better this morning?" he greeted. I shook my head and said sadly, "Uh, no better." Equally seriously and sadly Jake said, "Too bad, what'll you have?" "The same as yesterday. Ham and eggs." Here ham and eggs also meant large quantities of hash brown potatoes, toast, jelly and milk or coffee whether you wanted them with the ham and eggs or not. Had I known of the no milk, all ham diet ahead of me or imagined that this might be my last store-cooked meal for the next three months, I would have turned green at the very mention of ham and ordered a T-bone steak with a side of lemon meringue pie and angel food cake, plus not a glass but a quart of good fresh cold milk.

When, decked out in my new red cruiser with brown packsack on my back, I went to pay my way out, Jake said, "Goin' somewhere?"

"Yeah. Got a train to catch to Bonita."

Dubiously shaking his head, Jake said, "You watch

them ulcers. Stick to milk and whiskey. Don't drink no water or coffee. They'll rust your pipes." And handing me the change from my last silver dollar, he put in, "Good luck. You come back and see me."

"Be back in September," I replied. "Take care of the cow."

The morning train out of Missoula to the black and white sign along the right of way that said "Bonita" was known as the "milk train." If it took on or put off any of the white stuff on the way as far as Bonita I couldn't see it from the dirty window of the dusty coach. The only milk I saw for the next three months was condensed type, out of an Eagle-brand half pint tin can, long since out of the cow.

But milk or no milk, the morning Missoula-to-Butte-and-back local was vital to the sparse population for miles away on both sides of the Clark Fork. It was the sole carrier of eagerly awaited mail, Sears Roebuck and "Monkey" Wards merchandise, freight, and incoming or outgoing natives and newcomers, up and down the line. The train's arrival at all the crossroad stops was a daily event attended by the postmaster or mistress, most of the local merchants, the Forest Service ranger or his representative, other dignitaries, and most anybody with time on his hands and nothing else to do.

Following a clashing, jerking, hesitating start, and working up enough steam for a couple of loud whistles, the train leisurely cleared the outskirts of Missoula, speeded up to about thirty miles per hour, cut the steam, and coasted into Milltown, barely ten miles distant where it came to a sudden, jerking, grinding stop and sat panting as though even this little run was just too much. Milltown, at the confluence of the Blackfoot River with the Clark Fork, naturally was just that—the site of a large sawmill. Part of the interesting operation could be seen from the train window—to wit, a huge gathering of big logs floating in a large pond with several men equipped with long pike poles dangerously jumping from log to log herding said logs one by one to a point where they were picked up by a continuous chain and carried up a chute into the mill. The screaming sound of saws could be heard even inside the coach at the train stop.

At an important stop like Milltown, the pause of over twenty minutes by my guess, was long enough to occasion the man in the seat next to me to comment that the "darn train crew must have gone fishing." I agreed. Just as it appeared that we might sit there until the crew had caught a limit and I might not arrive at Bonita till noon, if ever, the loud call of "Bawwd" came from our conductor. Five minutes later we loudly, with much jerking, huffing, and puffing, again laboriously got underway. This time under full steam and at up to thirty-five miles per hour, we made ten or twelve miles all the way to the stop at Clinton where there was not only a post office, but a gas pump for automobiles and not one, but two general stores. There were also two saloons but due to prohibition, they were closed. According to my seat companion, the erstwhile operators were now back in the brush distilling and purveying a kind of alcoholic beverage that would, "either blind you or kill you outright. Take your choice." He was some kind of salesman on his tedious way to Butte and knew all the local merchants well.

After Clinton, where we stopped only about half as long as at Milltown, came Bonita, approximately ten more miles away. After the "Bawwding" call at Clinton, the conductor came aboard and stopped at my seat to warn me that I was to exit at the next stop. The train, he said—looking at his gold timepiece out of his blue uniform vest pocket—was trying to make up lost time and I should be ready to disembark promptly on arrival.

The conductor and the engineer of this train apparently had poor communication as we eased out of

Clinton very slowly and oddly without a single jerk. Only a couple of short blasts on the whistle were heard. The top speed could not have exceeded twenty-five miles per hour and as we approached the confluence of Rock Creek with the Clark Fork about six miles this side of Bonita, the train slowed to an even slower pace so the engineer might better assess the fishing possibilities of the entering flow. Rock Creek was flooding: fishing doubtfully good. As we came to this fascinating land-mark, the talkative Butte-bound drummer helpfully pointed it out. This was where I gathered up my telescoped fish pole and packsack and made my move from the seat to outside the coach door. I awaited, with plenty of time to spare until the Bonita landing and braced my feet well against the usual jolt of the sudden halt.

Descending the several steps from platform to cinders along the track, I saw no buildings or other indicators of a community to go with the sign "Bonita" anywhere in sight. I looked up toward the engine, a Model T truck backed up to the open door of an express car, with two men, one big and one small, standing in the back, loading and unloading mail sacks and boxes. I was the only passenger to get off. Nobody was there to get on.

Making my way along the cinders toward the truck, I had the uneasy feeling of maybe being in the wrong place at the wrong time and a thousand miles from nowhere. As I wandered slowly and uncertainly ahead, the big part of the mail exchange crew climbed care-fully down over the tailgate of the truck and headed slowly in my direction as though walking on eggs. As we drew together, he stopped and bent forward strangely grabbing himself. After which he straightened up and just stood and waited. On coming up to him, he pulled the worn leather glove off his right hand and reached out a big brown paw.

"Howdy," he greeted, "You must be Hessel. I'm Lou Nichols." Whatever might be painful in his midsection was not reflected in the steel grip of his hand.

"Joe Hessel," I affirmed. "Sure happy to be here."
Then again, Lou grimaced in agony and involuntarily
bent forward hugging his belly. "Oh," he groaned.
"Anything at all I can do?" I asked, now deeply concerned. "Nothin'. Just lifted one mail sack too many
right after the darn hospital. Had a horse fall on me an'
get the saddle horn in my gut." He straightened up his
big frame to his full six feet and more, then took a few
tentative steps just testing. After this, while pulling the
glove back on his hand, he emitted a most surprising
and unusual sound.

Lou had rather peculiarly pursed lips and I am not
sure that without this feature, he could have produced
this sound. I tried to do it time and time again, but
could never quite bring it off. It was the sound of liquid
burbling out of a small-mouth bottle. It was a perfect
imitation, always with one slightly delayed last-gasp
burp that was very comical. But amusing as it was,
when you got to know him, you discovered that Lou only
gave out with this counterfeit sound of a bottle pouring
at crucial moments when it might be okay to laugh
silently, but never aloud. It denoted pain, frustration,
disgust, exhaustion, and disenchantment in general.
Very occasionally, it might indicate acceptance of the
inevitable or biting the bullet. The first time I heard it
there along the train on first arrival, it left me dumbfounded and wondering, "What in heck kind of forest
ranger is this?"

The locomotive shot out a blast of steam from the
drivewheel cylinder, or somewhere up front. The conductor at the steps to the day coach hollered "Baw," just
exercising his lungs. Lou motioned for me to follow and
headed back toward the truck and the train hesitantly
started rolling past the sign saying "Bonita" toward the
next stop sign about ten miles distant that read "Bear-
mouth," and hopefully, eventually all the way to Butte.
It was to be my last contact with what father would
refer to as "civilization" for some time to come. From
there on, "civilization" was to consist of all "savages."

As I knew them, Rocky Mountain savages are the most delightful, self-sufficient, work-hard-play-hard, independent and carefree people on the face of the globe. Not entirely facetiously, they even referred to themselves as savages.

Probably the most savage of all the various "savages" I was to encounter in the Rockies were the Salmon River savages of whom I am sure Old Uncle Bill would have proudly considered himself one. By comparison, the Rock Creek "savage" of that time was what might be called "relatively advanced," exposed as they were to weekend fishermen from the big city of Missoula, and sometimes even the bigger city of Butte. As to the Rock Creek variety, I was about to meet the first.

On arriving at the truck, the small man I had distantly detected turned out to be no man, but a woman dressed in Levis and a man-type Stetson hat. To me, it was a new departure. Never had I seen a woman dressed in anything but a skirt, much less a cowboy hat. The lithe figure jumped nimbly over the tailgate of the truck to an easy landing directly facing me.

"Joe," said Lou, "meet Miss Maud Hauswirth, Em Hauswirth's better half and our postmistress. Maud, this is our new cawn country recruit, Joe Hessel."

Pulling a leather glove off her right hand as Lou had done, and enthusiastically extending the bared little paw with a warm, friendly smile from under the hat, Miss Maud looked to me anything but savage. "Hello, Joe," she greeted softly. "Welcome to Bonita and Montana." Surprised as I was, I juggled my fish pole from right hand to left, grabbed off my hat and crushed it under my left arm, barely in time to meet her handshake which was pleasantly cool and firm. "Thank you," I returned more than a little flustered. "I'm mighty glad to be here—and to meet you." I guessed the trim, most attractive Miss Maud might be in her late twenties or maybe thirty. When Lou told me later she was closer to forty than thirty, I couldn't believe it.

Now apparently fully recovered from his bout, Lou lit

up a big, long cigar. While he continued to hold the flaming kitchen match, Miss Maud hastily extracted a cigarette from a pack of Lucky Strikes out of the left hand pocket of her snap-button cowboy-type shirt and lit up, too. Maybe I had seen a woman smoke sometime previously, but I couldn't remember where.

At that time, I avoided all forms of the weed like poison, but I certainly had no objections to others smoking if they wanted to smoke, be it male or female. Uncle Bill smoked a big bent-stem briar pipe almost constantly. I thought if I ever took to smoking, I would smoke a pipe, too. Father smoked an occasional cigar, like after Sunday dinner while he read the *Chicago Herald Examiner*. His favorite brand was San Felice. Bernie O'Neill, a friend of mine, and I sneaked off deep in a cornfield now and then to smoke dried corn silk or ragweed seed wrapped in newspaper, an indulgence definitely not habit forming. Once, Bernie showed up with a full pack of Camels that he had come on to somewhere so we had a chance to sample the real article. After puffing a few of these, our consensus was that fancy cigarettes were worse than cornsilk or even rolled ragweed seed.

Before replacing the Luckies in her pocket, Miss Maud hospitably held out the pack with a questioning look in my direction. Not wanting her to think I was a sissy purist but had a good reason for declining, I gave her a quick appreciative smile and said, "Thanks, but I'm training for track. Running and smoking don't mix."

Lou grunted. "One guy I won't worry about startin' fires."

"Is that a fly rod you have there?" asked Miss Maud. "I don't think I've ever seen one like that."

I held up the rod for closer inspection. "It telescopes from long to short and vice versa." I demonstrated by pulling out and pushing back the tip.

"Interesting," she said. "Does it catch fish?"

"That," I laughed, "remains to be seen."

"Put it in back with your pack. There's room for all three of us to ride in front."

"That would be crowded. Let me ride in the back along with the pack."

"You heard what the lady said," Lou put in. "Throw your outfit in back and ride up front."

The Model T, of about 1924 vintage I estimated, had some hard miles on it and since he was standing on the driver's side, I assumed it belonged either to Lou personally or to the Forest Service, and that he was about to drive it. Wrong on both accounts. The reason the Texas gentleman was standing on the driver's side was to hold the door open for the driver and close it after she got in. The truck belonged to the Hauswirths and the driver was Miss Maud. I thought I had now seen everything. Like with smoking, I might have previously seen a female behind the wheel, but I couldn't say where or when—positively never a female *truck* driver.

Standing with crank in hand in front of the vehicle, Lou looked at the driver, and after she turned the key and shouted "Ready," he gave the crank a quick turn. The motor popped, quivered, and died. "Give it a little more gas and less spark," called the crank turner. Miss Maud moved the spark and gas levers and nodded. Adjusting the crank, Lou gave it another turn. This time the motor coughed, popped, and with Miss Maud making hasty adjustments in spark and gas, finally settled down to an "in business" sound. With me next to Miss Maud in the middle, Lou came and squeezed in.

From the Bonita sign along the NP tracks to Hauswirth Mercantile, a long, low, false-fronted structure facing on U.S. Highway 10, was about half a mile. In 1928, U.S. Highway 10 was nothing but a graveled, washboard, dusty, crooked arterial from east to west, across the northernmost tier of states. Although a motorist mainline, the traffic it carried was anything but continuous or deafening and every now and then, sometimes with long intervals in between, a gas burner would come bumping and rattling along kicking up dust, but that was the extent of it.

Out in front of the Hauswirth establishment was a

tall, transparent-topped ten gallon gasoline hand pump. During the summer, when her husband Em was out in the woods working for the Forest Service, Miss Maud operated the pump and sold a fair amount of gas. When Miss Maud was gone to get the mail, or for some other emergency reason, she put a sign in the window that said, "Back in a Few Minutes," locked the door and left. This meant any length of time from a quarter hour to an hour and a half. For anyone caught short of gas, beans, or bolts, nothing was to be done but wait. For ten miles or more in either direction, it was the only place you might buy gas, tacks, or a can of peas. This was Bonita, the whole of it. Em and Miss Maud maintained living quarters in the back of the store. They had no children. Total population of Bonita: two.

In summer when Em was mostly away, except now and then on weekends, Miss Maud was alone. When once I mentioned to Lou that this looked to me like a little risky, he said, "Huh! Don't fret about Miss Maud. She talks soft and looks kind of puny, but she's tough as a boot. She can shoot the eye out of a deer fly at twenty paces, and has loaded guns stashed all over the place." At the time Lou told me this, I thought Miss Maud must really be some special kind of female, and she was. But there in that country at that time and elsewhere I traveled up and down the Rockies, she was far and away from being the only one.

After Miss Maud sorted out the official Forest Service mail, a short time chore, Lou and I took off for the Rock Creek Ranger Station in his personal car. Lou's car, a spotless and shiny 1927 blue Buick coupe, was a surprisingly up-to-date and sporty vehicle. It was the one extravagance Lou allowed himself and he was inordinately proud of it. When he stepped on the starter, the motor came to life with an instant smooth purr. I was impressed. "Boy," I exclaimed appreciatively, "this is one fine automobile." With a faint pleased smile, he replied, "Beats heck outa the old grey mah." Cruising comparatively quietly and easily over the rough and washboarded gravel of U.S. 10, I was in full agreement.

Far more surprising and interesting to me than the rapidity and automotive elegance with which we were negotiating the bumps and stirring up dust, was the owner and driver, my new boss man, the forest ranger, himself. With his big, weather-beaten and soiled, once bell-grey hat pushed back on his balding head, tan moleskin shirt comfortably open at the collar, Levis no different than mine, and well-worn high-heeled, cowboy work boots, this caretaker of the great public woods and range was anything but the smartly uniformed and romantic official I had visualized. The thought that age could creep up on a mountain man as on anyone else never crossed my mind. The type I had expected was young, tough, and quick on the draw. Of all things, certainly *never* susceptible to injury from any horse. Sneaking another close sidewise look at Lou, I suspected from the set of his jaw and the sun wrinkles running out from his eyes that he could be tough as any occasion might call for, but he could also easily be even older than my father. Thinking of Father, I thought this big, slow-spoken, apparently easy-going Texan was "savage" no way.

Hearing Lou chuckle, I took my eyes off the passing scene of scattered pine and turned to discover what was funny. With a faint smile and without taking his eyes off the road, he put the question, "You mind me callin' you Squirtah?"

"Mister Nichols," I laughed, "you call me anything you want to. I can take it." And Lou said, "Good. You ah big enough, but it's a name stuck with me evah since I read yo' lettah. From here on, yoah Squirtah and I ain't *Mistah* Nichols. I'm Lou. That cleah?"

"Yessir—I mean yes. All clear." That's how, though no one but no one else ever called me that, I answered to "Squirtah" to Lou.

Without a doubt, Lou had the greatest stock of stories of any story-teller I ever knew. Never a meal went by without him telling at least one and he never repeated, day after day, time after time. Where he got them and from whom in that lonesome land, I could never imagine, but certainly not from Miss Maud whom he saw most frequently when he went for the mail. To Lou, exchanging earthy stories with Miss Maud or any other female, would have been as improper, unpardonable, and unthinkable as a slap in the face. It was entirely contrary to his strict Texas gentleman code. Certainly not all his stories came from Em, Miss Maud's husband nor from other itinerant males. There were simply not that many story-tellers with whom he came in contact. As far as I could discover, his well of hilarious accounts, after two years of working for him, remained an unsolved puzzle. A few of his stories I have heard repeated since, but on arriving at Bonita, I had never heard any of them before.

Lou was the kind of story teller who could wring honest laughter out of a wooden Indian with a story as old as the hills. Listeners would involuntarily start chuckling in anticipation the minute he opened his peculiar puckery mouth. Usually his manner was straight-faced, in fact, almost sour. He would chuckle appreciatively and even give a little laugh if someone else's story amused him and was well-told, but he never ever joined in laughing at one of his own. Sometimes there would be a faint smile, but mostly he would grimace and shortly shake his head negatively as if the tale he had told was simply too ridiculous to relate.

In my first two years, Lou taught me most of the basic mountain man tricks of the trade. He taught me how to use, guard against, and maintain essential tools such as the double-bitted axe, one man and two man cross cut saws, pick, shovel, hoe-dag, and Pulaski tool. He taught me to cook with and without sourdough and to manti a pack and hitch a pack on a mule, so buck as he might, the pack would not come off. I learned to read a compass and maps, plus a thousand and one other things. He taught me to make do, one way or another, with whatever might be on hand and to cuss but not actually complain about whatever might not be available. The same with the weather: whether fair or foul, I learned to make the most of it and let it be. I learned to plan and prepare for the worst that might happen in any situation and to give due thanks if the worst never materialized. Above all, I found that if the worst does happen, or if it doesn't, to cultivate and maintain and never lose a sense of humor. The realization and understanding that human beings, including females, are clowns relegated to the most humorously frustrating and painful rotating stage imaginable, will get you over many an otherwise impossible impediment. By example and with his inexhaustible reservoir of applicable anecdotes, this most important fact, Lou taught me. On untold occasions in the mountains and especially in the insufferable big city, this outlook has eased and made possible many crisis crossings.

Lou shook his head sadly. "I hope you didn't have trouble with fleas. We got enough trouble without fleas."

"No," I answered, "I haven't any fleas. Lewis and Clark had some trouble with fleas, but that was way down on the Columbia River."

Suddenly serious, Lou asked, "What do you know about Lewis and Clark?"

"I've read their journal and know they were somewhere here close. The river was named for Clark when they went through."

"Lotsa argument about theh exact route. They had a heck of a time getting through the mountains with no game and little to eat. How they got unshod hawses over the rocks and down timber was a feat to end all. And how they rounded up all them wild Indian ponies in the mawnin', tied packs on them flimsy Indian pack saddles so they'd stay, and get strung out on the trail befoah noon, beats me. The way they tell it, the little business of rollin' a haws ovah tea kettle down a steep sidehill was nothin' otha 'n all in a day's work."

"When I read the book I never thought of that."

"You will when you get to packin' hawses an' mules."

And on several memorable occasions thereafter, I did. And on each occasion, like Lou, I marveled at how Lewis and Clark got their rag tag remuda through "these mountains" and more.

Shortly following this historical commentary, we made a right turn off the road on a lane leading to several buildings about a quarter mile back to the base of a steep pine-covered slope. Apparently, this was the Rock Creek Ranger set-up. If so, I was very confused and not a little let down. Lou pulled up at one end of the long low building and said, "What theah is of it, this is home."

"But where's the creek?"

"What creek?"

"Rock Creek!"

"Oh," Lou chuckled, "The mouth of the creek is about two miles up the road on the othah side from the NP tracks an' the rivah. A road takes off 'bout a mile up wheh theh's a bridge across the rivah an' the road runs up the creek. Milwaukee tracks ah across the river.

"This side of the flat to the othah. Half, three-quarters mile, I guess. Bring youah pack and we'll have Barry bed you down. This here is the bahn, garage, an' wayhouse building. That theh is the root cellah next to the cookshack and beyond is the tent wheh we bunk the road crew. That white building is the office in paht an' where I live in the othah paht."

An open door beyond the barn and garage parts of the long low building led to a large room filled in a well-ordered way with tents, steel cots, blankets, axes, shovels, and other tools of many kinds. Near a window opposite the door, a young muscular individual dressed in plaid wool shirt, Levis and logging boots, sat pedaling a large grindstone sharpening an axe.

"Hey Barry," Lou called. "Heh's yoah new help."

Stopping his pedaling and quickly running his thumb over the edge of the axe, the man Barry rose from his steel seat, placed the tool in a rack and sauntered over to the door. "Barry," said Lou, "this is the Joe Hessel we been expectin'. Joe, this is Earl Barry—my bull smoke, recently graduated from the University of Montana Forestry School and one heck of a football playah. Whether he learned any forestry remains to be seen."

Grinning hospitably and putting out his hand, Barry greeted me with, "Hi, Joe. Pay no attention to what the man says. He's never won a bet on a football game yet. Glad you're here. Plenty to do. Can you cook?"

"Cook?" My surprise must have been obvious. Recovering somewhat, I offered dubiously, "I can boil and egg and make bacon grease gravy."

Lou and Barry looked and each other solemnly and nodded their heads. "You'll do," said Barry. "God knows some around here can't even do half that!"

That is where and how I first came to be a kind of camp cook learning by the seat of my pants. As was the case on many ranger districts with small crews at that time, the district budget did not provide for any kind of cook.

Employees either cooked the food provided or failed to eat. A few could and would cook. Others simply could or would not. And, since the cooking had to be done often before and after working a full day, the cooking business was one of the most sensitive bones of contention and dissention in the ranks. Bread had to be baked from scratch or there was no bread. And generally there was no bread. Many a man carried hot cake sandwiches or filled in with hard tack. Pies and cakes were seldom, if ever, heard of.

With no refrigeration, fresh meat would not keep and seldom got on the menu. There was bacon and ham and ham and bacon, eggs (of various degrees of freshness), and butter canned in brine, a liberal variety of canned goods, plenty of salt, pepper, sugar, flour, baking powder, oatmeal and cream of wheat and that was about it. We had sourdough, coffee and tea, of course, and though limited, even a supply of condensed milk. So what more could you need or want?

As to cooking, much more can be said, but for now I

add only this: According to an unwritten but ironclad law of the woods, he who cooks does not ever, never, wash the pots, pans, dishes or whatever unless for some unknown or emergency reason he may volunteer to do so or unless he happens to be the only one around to cook for. In case he is also left to clean up, there will certainly come a terminal rupture in sociability of the camp society. Further, if any complaints derive from the nature or palatability of the cooking, the complainer must immediately take over as cook, profusely apologize and seek forgiveness, or take a walk.

It was possible at first taste to break out in honest startled surprise with, "My God, that gravy is salty," and quickly add, "But it sure is good," and get away with it, without the cook yanking off his dirty makeshift apron and handing it along with the job to the complainer. With an especially sensitive and frustrated cook, even a little complaint like that might well earn the complainer the can opener.

As Lou turned to leave me with Barry, his parting remark was, "Fix him up with a bed, Barry, an' put him to work."

Barry looked me over, cocked his head sidewise to make sure of what he saw and said, "Joe, you want the bedroom next to the bath or the one with the window looking out at the rose garden?" Faintly smelling a mouse, I cautiously answered, "Being a sucker for roses, give me the one by the window." Barry chuckled. "Good. You picked right. There's not a bath this side of Missoula. Let alone a rose garden."

Leading the way around some shelves filled with assorted pots and pans and other hardware, we came to a pile of WWI folding steel cots. "Grab yourself one of those cots that will work. And over here are a bunch of cotton mattresses. Over there in that locker are Army wool blankets. The grey ones are not quite as scratchy as the khaki and best next to the human hide. Uncle don't furnish any sheets or pillow slips or pillows. So, you'll need one more blanket to fold up for a pillow. I'd take about five or six blankets. It gets darn chilly around here at night. Then over there are canvas tarps for bed roll covers. Around here you won't need one, but if you go out on trail maintenance, you need one for making a bed roll and to keep dry. Yard up what you need over by the door and we'll figure out a place for you to bed down."

While I picked and chose, Barry returned to his grinding stone. Finally, finding a cot on which all the hinges functioned and the steel spring was not rump-sprung, I horsed it to the door and returned for inspection of the cotton mattresses. To find a pad without torn or mouse-eaten ticking took some time. Though recently cleaned and heavily scented with moth balls, the stacks of blankets were far from new. Some were frayed and torn at the edges, looking like they had not only been through a war, but barely survived.

Bed and bedding selection chore completed, I went over to the axe sharpening operation, noting the technique employed with much interest.

"Ever see one of these?" asked Barry without stopping his pedaling or taking his eyes off his work. "My uncle had a big grindstone like that, but the double-bitted axe is different from any in Illinois. All we have there are single-bitted pole axes like a hatchet."

"Um . . . ever try to put an edge on one?"

"Nope. But I see how it's done."

"Some of these are so beat up, the only way to get the nicks out is to use a file to start. Always need a stone to finish. Got your sleep plunder all collected?"

"Yes, sir."

Barry stopped pedaling, put the axe down and got up from his seat. "I been thinkin' about where to put you. There's room for another bunk over in the tent with the road crew, but I tried that once and it didn't work. Old Alphonse Gratton snores loud enough to wake the dead. I moved over here to the barn and made room for myself in the tack room. Bucky Harris, our packer, has a bunk he uses just now and then up under the rafters in the loft. There's room for another cot up there. How would you like that? Kind of unhandy crawling up and down the ladder, but it beats listenin' to Alphonse."

"Sounds okay to me."

"The ladder is right over beyond those stacks of fire rations. You get on up there and I'll hoist your plunder up to you. There is a window to look out of and let in plenty of fresh air. Of course, you need to watch out you don't break your neck getting up and down the ladder if you have to go out in the middle of the night."

"You mean there's no electric lights?"

"One of these days you'll get electricity out here, but not yet. It's Coleman lantern or candle, at best."

Not only did Barry hoist up my plunder, but helped me set up and make my bed. The shallow sloping roof did not provide room enough to stand erect except under the ridge pole. After making the bed, Barry sat down to rest his back.

"Bucky is kind of cranky. Better not sit on his bed or leave anything lyin' on it. But he isn't around more than about one night a week and sometimes not that often." Taking a brief survey of the set-up as though he hadn't seen the place for some time, he added, "It's not much, but it's clean and the roof don't leak. There may be a packrat or two to rattle things around, but mostly they live on the lower level."

"You say there's not a bathroom this side of Missoula. What do you do for a bath?"

Barry looked at me with a half-knowing grin. "You needing a bath?"

"Well, no. Not now, but sooner or later, I might."

"Tell you. This is a real up-to-the-minute place. Up on the hill aways, there's a spring. The spring is piped down so we've got cold running water in the cook shack. You need a bath, you take the water bucket and run some water out of the cold water faucet and pack it outside to a couple of No. 12 galvanized washtubs provided. You heat this water over a wood fire and take a bath. If it's too chilly outside, you heat water on the cookstove and wash in the cook shack. There's that and then there's the river about half a mile or more walk across the flat. I personally go for the river, ice cold, as that may be."

"What about washing clothes?"

"You use the same tubs and a washboard. Same process on the water-haul and heating. Alphonse uses the same water he takes a bath in for his laundry. Hates to see any warm water go to waste."

"No flush toilets?" The answer to this, by that time, I knew full well.

"Ho," Barry snorted, "not by a darn sight. One three-holer out back of the road crew tent for us peons and one two-holer over by the office. Except for emergencies, that's Lou's private property and for any company that comes by and gets caught short." Barry got up from the bed, whacking his head on a low rafter. "Um, goldarn. I should have known better. Bring your gloves and I'll introduce you to a double-bitted axe."

Descending from the loft, I followed Barry out through the warehouse door to a tremendous pile of unsplit logs sawed into about one foot or sixteen inch lengths. A double-bitted axe with a badly beat up handle next to the bit was sticking in one of the unsplit logs. Barry pulled the axe out of the log and examined the damage. "Been intendin' to put a new handle on that one since I came back here.

"First off, this is where you start with the cookin' detail. To cook, you have to have heat and to have heat, you need wood split small enough to fit in that darn wood range. This is yellow pine, good firewood, and splits fairly easy. Only trouble is we never seem to get enough split. Split it to the size of those few pieces you see there in that little pile. Number two, always watch out when you're cuttin' with a double-bitted axe. It's a good tool, but damn dangerous. Dull as this one is, it could bounce or slip and cut your leg off. Here you've got plenty of room, but in the brush, always look up and behind you to make sure you're in the clear before you take a swing. A sharp axe cuts like a razor. Never forget."

"I'll not forget. How much of this pile you want me to split?"

Barry grinned an evil grin. "You just stay here and make little pieces out of big ones till I tell you 'enough'. Not much wood in the woodbox in the cook shack, so before time for lunch, you better fill that. I cook lunch and supper. Lou makes breakfast. Breakfast is at 6:30. Lunch at noon. Supper at six." Handing me the beat-up splitting axe, he added, "Have at it," and returned to his warehousing.

That was about 11 a.m. of a Wednesday morning. I "had at it" the rest of that day and the following morning awoke at sunup with aching muscles I never knew I had in my back and shoulders. I thought and hoped at breakfast Barry would pronounce "enough" and change the detail, especially in view of the respectably large pile of "little ones" that I had amassed out of big ones. No such luck. He said not a word. At 7:30 a.m., chilly as it was, with a coating of white frosting covering all, I was right back where I had left off the previous evening brushing the white stuff off the axe handle and setting another big one on the chopping block for reduction to stove-size pieces. By noon, the day had warmed up to where I was stripped down to my undershirt and had sweat streaming down into my eyes from under my hatband. My pile of "little" ones had grown to almost where I couldn't see over it and I thought I had made enough stove wood to last not only all of one summer, but through the next winter and summer as well.

When lunch the second day came around, I was much encouraged. Barry allowed he would come and see how I was making out.

"By gosh," he said, "That is the best showing I ever saw anybody make in such a short time on that wood-pile. Tell you what, why don't you knock off about a quarter to five, fill the woodbox, wash up and help me make supper. Julius Cairn will be here in the morning and I want you to help him set a few replacement telephone poles along the road between where it takes off from the highway to the river."

"Sure," I answered enthusiastically.

Apparently there was an end now in sight to the wood splitting, when I had begun gloomily thinking there might be no end at all. But the way Barry took off with that little knowing smile on his face, I might have guessed that compared to setting telephone poles, splitting wood was a lark.

While I had volunteered after my first lunch to help wash and dry the "dishes," this was the first offering I had to help with the "cooking." I accepted it for better or worse as a kind of compliment, even with a strong suspicion of what I might be letting myself in for. As to the post-feast cleanup, I had already learned that at the Rock Creek Station, at least, there was one way, and only one way, that this was accomplished. After putting the meal on the table, the cook, himself, never sat down to eat prior to putting two large dishpans of water on the stove to provide hot water at meal's end. If need be, he put another piece of wood in the stove to hasten and assure the heating process. Also, he made sure the large teakettle was full of water. Two cardinal rules applied: use plenty of soap to get the grease off the dishes and use plenty of scalding hot rinse water to remove the soap. You might conceivably get the "runs" from something you ate, but never from too much residual grease or soap.

Three items never subjected to soap were a large cast iron griddle, a tremendous cast iron skillet, and the coffee pot. The first two were scraped clean with a hotcake turner and possibly occasionally wiped off and out with a clean rag. The big enameled coffee pot, when about half full of grounds and eggshells, was emptied out, possibly rinsed with cold water to get the last old grounds shaken loose, recharged with new coffee and set back on the stove.

Though I never touched the black brew, everyone else consumed it in large quantities, steaming hot. At Rock Creek, the standard recipe was one small handful or a large heaping tablespoon of coffee per cup of water, plus one more tablespoon "for the pot." On being brought to a boil, the pot was moved to a less hot part of the stove and a cup of cold water added "to settle the grounds," after which it was ready to drink. When the last trickle had been poured, new grounds were added to the old "up to a point." At breakfast with the frying of eggs, you would throw in a couple of eggshells. What this did to or for the concoction I never knew, except that without doing it, the coffee was never "made right."

Once after twelve hours on a fire line with nothing to eat, I arrived back at the fire camp with my crew, badly beat and hungry enough to eat a skunk. As usual, there was plenty of hot coffee for all comers, steaming away over the fire, not in a pot but in a deep oval copper washtub. Ready to drink anything for a pickup, even the blackest of black coffee, I ladeled a cupful out of the tub and poured it down my empty gut. I have never been so nauseous, pukey poisonous sick—except once after a shot of Herman Gerber's White Lightning up at Lolo Hot Springs. Not until years later, could I be prevailed upon to try another cup. Poured from a shiny electric percolator, rather than a copper washtub, and liberally laced with cream, sugar and scotch whiskey after a long day of pheasant hunting, I opted for another cup. On the other hand, I am a suspicious, infrequent imbiber of the stuff to this day.

Second only to initiation in the coffee-making rite, I was introduced in the kitchen of men without women to the mysteries, marvels, hazards, do's and taboos of sourdough. According to Lou, contrary to what is popularly pictured, the West was won not romantically with a gun, but with plain stinkin' old sourdough. Without sourdough, said Lou, the mountain man and gunslinger would never have found the strength to pull a trigger.

A man's sourdough crockpot was sacrosanct. Messing

around with it could get you shot as certainly as messing around with his water rights, or if he happened by any chance to have one, his woman. This despite the fact that manufacturing the stuff required only a couple of cheap and plentiful ingredients and an earthenware crock or pot in which to contain and preserve the precious simple mixture.

For the making of sourdough, if you might be somewhere accessible to a cake of Fleischman's or Red Star yeast, well and good and lucky. Given yeast, the end result could be achieved somewhat easier and much faster.

Into your crock, simply throw in a cup of water, a cup of flour, a tablespoon of sugar, a cake of yeast and, practically presto, sourdough. Given no yeast, no sweat. With a day or more additional waiting time, and a little potato water, you can make out just the same.

Boil up a big enough batch of potatoes to leave you with four cups of boiled potato water. To this add four cups of flour and two tablespoons of sugar. Let this mixture stand in the open crock in a warm place for a couple of days till it starts to work or "smells right." If you cannot smell, just let it stand and watch it "work" till it looks "right." Cover the crock with a flour sack to keep the flies and yellow jackets out and keep it at comfortable room temperature. Whatever you do, do not screw the lid down air tight. This is sourdough and it *can be* combustible. Take no chances.

Whatever you remove from this basic mixture for making hotcake batter, bread, or whatever, always replace a like amount. For instance, take out one cup and return one cup of warm water, one cup of flour and one teaspoon of sugar. This was Chef Nichols' prescription as passed on to me and was found to be infallible. According to the master, some people might add salt to the potato water starter, but he personally would not recommend any salt in any basic mixture.

Lou's hotcakes were a "must" as much as bacon and eggs every morning for breakfast. It was never exact as to the amount of ingredients and always variable depending on the number of empty bellies to be filled and probably capacities of each. Lou's recipe was approximately as follows: one cup of basic sourdough, one cup of flour, one egg, two tablespoons of sugar. Lou firmly believed that mixing this batter too much was not only a waste of time and effort but knocked out the gases needed to make the cakes light and fluffy. He would let the batter bubble and foam while he greased the griddle with a fatty piece of bacon rind and then carefully ladle on to the sizzling griddle the exact amount for each cake. Generally, this was a considerable amount, as Lou did not fool around with making small cakes.

Since I never had much of an appetite for breakfast anyway, just one of his cakes was far more than I could ever eat. On the other hand, somebody like big Alphonse Gratton would put away as many as half a dozen. Watching him do it was astonishing to me and almost made me sick. Lou took Alphonse's appetite for his hotcakes as a great compliment and kept urging him to have just one more.

If ever there was a surplus of cakes, as was sometimes the case, they went to Dugan, the nondescript hound that wandered in off the highway one day and was allowed to make the place home. The rest went to the several cats kept around for catching rats and mice, and occasionally to Ranger, Lou's saddle horse. Ranger was a real sucker for hotcakes. With a hotcake, you could catch him every time—quicker than with a washpan full of oats.

Naturally, with having hotcakes day in and day out, every blessed day for breakfast, it was not expectable that anyone, no matter how famished, could look one in the eye for supper . . . sometimes a cold one wrapped around a piece of ham maybe for lunch, but never one for supper. The menu for supper was as iron cast as for breakfast, but different. For supper, you always had meat (other than slab bacon), potatoes and gravy, either separately or together, like slumgullion stew which was a fabulous combination of everything left over from pork and beans and spinach to the last of the ham and hambone.

The big surprise at supper was generally the potatoes, and the question was whether they would be fried, boiled with skins on or off, mashed or mixed with sauerkraut. They never were served baked because to bake a potato at that altitude in the up and down heat of a wood range oven would have taken the full time of a man a full day. It took long enough to get potatoes done enough just by boiling. The extra time required for mashed potatoes made them come just sometimes on Sundays when the cook might finish his laundry in time to have a few minutes to spare. Sometimes the way they tasted you might wonder if he hadn't used this laundry water to boil them or dropped in a shot of toothpaste during the mashing. Notwithstanding, you ate what you took from the serving dish, licked your chops, and never, never complained in the presence or possible earshot of the cook, unless ready and willing to take on his thankless job. Sometimes it got even that bad.

At Rock Creek when I was there, those who cooked were darned good cooks. They might come direct to the cook shack from the corral, from off the hill with plenty of pitch on their pants, or from whatever else they might have been doing, but they invariably washed their hands and face and combed their hair prior to peeling a spud or opening a can. Maybe they didn't get quite all the dirt out from under their fingernails, but, by gosh, they were clean and neat. As Ben Rice, the packer, used to say, a little dirt in the gravy was not noticed and never hurt anybody, anyway.

That first Thursday night I was asked to help Barry with supper after eight full hours (7:45 a.m. to 4:45 p.m.) on the woodpile with no "coffee breaks," an hour for lunch, and washing dishes in between. I found Barry in the cook shack with sleeves rolled up and a fire in the range, peeling a few potatoes.

Not taking his eyes off his work, the minute I opened the door, he said, "Joe, go out to the root cellar and get us a can of peas, corn, or some kind of vegetable other than hominy or carrots or spinach and a can of fruit, peaches, or apricots or something. We had pineapple last night, so don't bring pineapple. And one good-sized onion."

The root cellar was located right next to the cook shack, between the cook shack and the barn and peeled pole corral. On the other side was the board-floor, framed nine by twelve tent, reserved for the road crew. There were no sidewalks between here and there, anywhere. Just river-run gravel, common to the whole narrow valley except here and there some alluvial soil had been patchily deposited.

It was my first time in the root cellar and I found it very interesting. Cases of canned goods were stacked on shelves under the mounded dirt roof. Bins and sacks of potatoes and onions sat on the floor. Slabs of bacon and cured hams string were suspended from spikes in the log rafters. The cellar was remarkably and pleasantly cool. Compared to outside temperatures, it was cooler in summer and warmer in winter. Without knowing that root cellars were old as the hills and that practically everybody roundabout on the ranches had one, I thought it was a great invention. Also, for the first time, I discovered that our butter came canned, according to the label, "canned in brine." That was also a great invention.

The butter with which I was familiar came out of a churn.

Returning with a can of creamed corn, a can of apricots, and a large white onion, I found that Barry had finished the peeling operation and progressed to reducing the spuds to fairly thin and fairly uniform slices in a large skillet other than the cast-iron skillet in which Lou fried breakfast bacon and eggs. All the cooking utensils were handily hung on a number of spikes driven in the wall behind the stove. There was also a spike for the dishrag and dish towel. The dishes, which were white enamel with a thin blue border, were neatly stacked on a wide unpainted shelf above the pots and pans.

"Don't just stand there doin' nothin'," said Barry, "get a can opener out of the drawer under the table and open the corn. Put the corn in a pan on the back of the stove to warm it up. Open the apricots and put them in a dish on the table. Then go out in the cooler in back and bring in what's left of that ham and see if you can cut me off about five or six slices. When you get the ham, bring in the butter."

The cooler was a large screened box hung on a couple of small pine trees in the shade behind the cook shack. Everything needing to be kept cooler than the cool of the root cellar went into the chilly night and cool-breeze-conditioned cooler. The way that screened, shaded, open air contraption kept things cool was surprising. The only thing wrong with it was that it wouldn't keep fresh meat cool enough for long enough and it wasn't bear proof. Occasionally at night, a wandering bruin would meander down off the mountain, get a whiff of the ham and other contents, and tear it all to smithereens. Not often, just now and then.

Axes weren't the only things Barry put an edge on around that place. The kitchen knives were always sharp as razors.

"You know how to slice that ham the same thickness top and bottom?" He asked.

"You bet," I said. "I didn't work in a meat market for nothing."

"Okay. Cut 'em about a quarter inch thick and scatter the slices over the top of the spuds in the skillet, *after* you slice that onion and add the onion to the spuds. While you get with that, I'll see if I can whip a batch of baking powder biscuits out of that no-good oven."

When I had the onions sliced and mixed with the sliced potatoes, with the slices of ham arranged on top in the big deep skillet, as directed, I thought it was a work of art.

"Okay on the ham and spuds. Now what?"

Barry, with hands full of dough and flour coating his big hairy arms half-way to the elbows, paused for a critical look.

"Looks good. Now pour some cold water in the skillet, enough to about cover the spuds. Then put the skillet on the hot part of the stove, put that lid on the skillet and we'll see what we got."

"What do you call it?"

"First time I ever saw potatoes fried that way, I thought fried potatoes were fried with grease."

"That's 'everyday fried'. These here are healthier and faster."

"Don't you need any salt and pepper?"

"Not with all the salt in that ham. Maybe a little pepper later. Go set the table. There'll be just you and me and Lou. Put a bottle of honey out. Lou is wild for honey and biscuits—if they don't burn."

That was the night Lou told the sad story of grandpa and the outhouse. What brought it on was my appreciative remark to Barry that his biscuits turned out great and hadn't burned even a little bit. The mention of "burning" did it. While helping himself to about his seventh or eighth biscuit and honey, Lou said that down in the Arkansas Ozarks there was a family of hillbillies way back up a gulch: ma, pa, three boys in their late teens, and grandpa. Grandpa was almost blind, but with his cane, he could feel his way around pretty good including finding his way down the path to the outhouse. One day, without remembering to say anything to grandpa, the old man and his three boys went to work and dug a new outhouse hold on account of the old hole getting full almost to the brim, and they moved the outhouse over the new hole. After his grits and corn pones that night about dark, grandpa set out down the outhouse path as usual, feeling his way along and walked right off in the old unfilled outhouse hole. Floundering around and unable to get out, the poor old boy started hollering. "Fire! Fire! Fire!" One and all, this brought the whole family on a high lope. When they got him hauled out of the hole and were scraping him off as best they could, one of the boys said, "Good gosh, Grandpa, how come you holler, 'fire', and scare us like that?" "Heck, boy," grandpa said, "you never see'd anybody get help by hollerin' 'outhouse', did ye?"

Putting butter and honey on the last remaining biscuit Lou soberly shook his head saying, "I hope you get the picture. Poor old man, but he was smart."

Since there was no daily, weekly, or any kind of news sheet to read, or for that matter little else, and no decent light to read by even given reading matter available, people mostly went to bed at sundown and started the day right after sunup. At six, when I left my roost to splash some icy water on my hands and face and brush my teeth, I saw this strange, ramshackle Model T truck parked next to the corral and wondered who it belonged to. In the cook shack visiting with Lou and drinking a hot cup of coffee was Julius, who had arrived from his digging up Welcome Creek off Rock Creek about twenty miles distant.

Busy with his sourdough batter, Lou turned and said, "Squirtah, this is Julius Cairn from up the creek. Julius, this is Joe Hessel from Illinois. He's your help on the telephone line." Rising from the seating bench at the table with the quickness and ease of a cat, Julius grinned broadly behind his scraggly growth of whiskers and reached out a gnarled, crusty hand. "She's a long way jus' for telephone." The way he gripped my hand, I thought it was broken. Grinning back in spite of this, I answered affirmatively, "A long ways."

Julius and I were friends from that first, early morning meeting. Though wiry and much smaller in stature, somehow he always reminded me of old Uncle Bill. But unlike Uncle Bill, Julius was outgoing and enthusiastic in manner, with darting black eyes under his greying, bushy eyebrows. Barry told me he was a fast man with either a gun or a knife and mostly liked his own company.

After breakfast, we loaded the rear of the government Model T truck with a couple of long-handled, pointed digging shovels, a heavy steel digging bar, and a couple of double-bitted axes with the bits protected by black leather sheaths, two quart canteens of drinking water wire clamps and cutters, glass insulators, lineman's climbing spikes and belt, and lunch (three fried ham hotcake sandwiches and a can of sliced pineapple). Even though our work would take us less than two miles from the station, wasting time and gasoline just to come in for lunch was out.

Turning off the highway toward the river, where the narrow gravel road (one-way with turnouts for on-coming traffic) took off up Rock Creek with Julius at the wheel, we shortly arrived at the spot where a new peeled and creosote-treated lodge pole pine pole had been dropped off. The single wire grounded line from the station up the creek thirty-five miles to the Rock Creek Guard Station had spur lines off the main stem to Sliderock and Quigg Peak Lookouts, the Grizzly Guard Station and six or seven small stump ranches.

A primitive and rickety communication system at best, the line was hung over most of the distance on trees with plenty of slack. If a tree came down across the line, as frequently happened, the wire running free through split insulators would usually not break but simply use some of the provided slack up or down the line from the windfall. A downed tree might or might not ground out the line from the point of fall to all points above, necessitating a foot patrol to discover the point of trouble and cut the tree off the line. There were also other deficiencies and problems.

Every time a receiver was lifted along tne battery-powered line, a drag was placed on the whole system and it was almost impossible for anybody to hear anybody. Starved for information as the clients up and down the line always were, a ring on the line would result in all of the receivers being lifted so people could listen in on whatever might be going on. This practice of everybody on the line trying to listen in so nobody could hear anything would drive Lou up the wall.

"Gosh darn it! Hang up the phone and get off the line! This is an official call and none of youh business," he would roar. And maybe so and maybe not, you would hear receivers being softly bung back in place. If not, he would continue to roar with ever-increasing volume and colorful profanity till the line finally cleared and he could get on and transmit his message. The ranchers on the line, of course, paid nothing for being connected. Service to ranchers and homesteaders on the government line was provided primarily so they could report fire starts and emergencies.

Since the few trees along the line between the station and the river were far enough back so as to miss the line along the road if they fell, the wire along this distance was stretched tight and fastened to standard type rather than free running insulators. The poles to be replaced were spindly originals barely topping the heavy growth of willows common to the entire river wash flat. Before doing anything else, it was necessary to clear the willows from around the old poles entailing use of the razor-edged axes we had brought along. I very nearly terminated my summer's work at the outset.

Clearing willows with a sharp, double-bitted axe is somewhat hazardous even for an expert. The ease and quickness with which a sharp axe works against the limber and evasive stems of willows for the beginner is unbelievable, especially when attacked with enthusiasm and unnecessary vigor. The axe can slip and bounce and cut a man's foot off. It can also slip and bounce just enough to slice through the moccasin welt of an expensive Russell boot so as to practically wreck the boot and miss drawing blood by the width of a pair of heavy wool sock. That's the same miss margin as when that old .22

rifle suddenly fired and missed taking my right big toe off. Suddenly, a ringing started in my ears when Barry said as he handed me my first double-bitted axe, "It's a dangerous tool. It can bounce or slip and cut your leg off."

At lunch when we sat down together, Julius did not miss seeing the slice in my boot anymore than Uncle Bill had missed seeing the bullet hole. Julius just smiled a thin little smile and said not a word. Nor did I. After a vital lesson is learned, nothing whatever is left to be said. We ate out hotcake ham sandwiches and talked sparingly of other things. Julius opened the can of pineapple with his pocket knife which I had never seen done. I said it looked like it might be hard on the edge of a knife. He said, "Not if it is a good knife." Once opened, we forked the pineapple slices out of the can with a willow stick and shared the juice.

The one and only other close miss I ever had with a double-bitted axe happened one night after supper under a dark stand of great western red cedars in a camp at the junction of the Papoose Creek and Locksa River trails in 1930, two years later. In the dim light of a small warming fire, I picked up an axe and took a swing at a block of wood to add more fuel. On the downswing, somehow I managed to hit a taut, unseen tent rope with the handle of the axe just below the bit. Like a bowstring firing an arrow, the rope bounced the bit back at me and by the margin of a hatband and thickness of the felt in the crown of a western hat, I missed splitting my foreskull and spilling out my few poor brains on the ground.

Again, numb with surprise and realization of what might have been, I heard ringing in my ears, the voice of Barry saying, "Always look ahead of you, above you, and behind you, to make sure you are in the clear before ever swinging an axe." Of course, by a quarter inch, I might have cut the rope so it did not throw the axe back at me By the same token, no less, in that instant I might have been flukily deceased.

Excuses come a dime a dozen—a life or limb, but once. In the mountain wilderness where hazards especially proliferate, a belated or lack of learning, the lesson of looking at least once before swinging or stepping is frequently either seriously crippling or fatal. Vividly, I remember that twice by the narrowest of margins, I lucked out.

Between splitting wood and digging post holes in the river-run gravel, I would take work on the woodpile at least ten to one. The pile of split wood can be seen to get higher. The gravel hole gets wider and wider but little deeper with grunts, blisters and sweat thrice as many and much. "Take a five" every so often but no such thing as a coffee break was ever heard of. While taking five and catching our breath, Julius examined the unearthed gravel with more than casual interest, more especially the deeper the hole and the finer and sandier the gravel.

"Humph," he would say to no one in particular examining the finer particles of sand in the palm of his hand. "No good. No goshdarn good." And I agreed. Of course, it was "no good." It was the most frustrating digging I had ever put a hand to. I got to wondering why he kept looking and kept looking at the gravel. Finally when we would sit down for a blow, I got to picking up handfuls of gravel and looking at it also. As far as I could see, it still looked like just so much more gravel.

Finally, once after I had examined and brushed off my handful of gravel, and Julius was about to do the same with his, he looked at me as though for some kind of confirmation and said directly to me rather than to nobody in particular, "Heh? No good." I came right out and asked: "Julius what the heck in this darn gravel are we looking for?" He was surprised. You might say astonished.

"You don't know?" I shook my head. "Sure don't."

Quietly, as though he might understand and forgive my ignorance, he answered, "Color. Gold. You never see color?" "Never—ever." He grinned a pleased grin, nodding his head.

"Tomorrow, I will bring a pan and you will see."

"You mean there actually is gold in this gravel?" I asked incredulously.

Waving an arm up and down the Clark Fork Valley, he said, "All along. Not much. But color. Tomorrow, we will see."

The next morning, Saturday, when we reached the four-foot bottom for the last of our four poles at about 10:30 a.m., Julius went back to the truck and returned with a pan somewhat larger than the big bacon and egg skillet and no handle. This was my introduction to a standard gold pan. With the long-handled ladle-like shovel, he lifted out enough sand from the bottom of the hole to fill the pan a couple of times. This he placed in a large gunny sack, well back from the hole, so as not to be disturbed while we set the pole, filled the hole, and rehung the wire.

At noon, I carried our ham and hotcake sandwiches and a can of plums in the gold pan while Julius lugged his take of sand in the sack a couple of hundred feet over to the river.

As we were eating, Julius reached in his pants pocket and brought out a small rough piece of white rock. Handing it to me, he said, "You have never seen gold. That is wire gold in quartz." Inlaid in the piece of rock could be seen wires and threads of pure yellow metal.

"Wow. Where did this come from?" Julius grinned his thin grin. "Ore from my mine."

"Judas Priest! Do you have a lot of this? It must be worth a lot of money! A fortune!"

The old French-Canadian prospector shrugged and spread his hands, palms up, disparagingly. "What's money. She's no good—money! Bacon and beans!"

"Umm, Humm!" I said thoughtfully rolling the rock around in my hand. "Uncle Bill used to say the same thing."

"Uncle Billy?" Julius asked dubiously and somewhat perplexed. Then waving his arm at the universe, "Uncle Billy up there. In sky. In air. In water. Rocks, trees, and all round. Sometimes good. Sometimes bad."

Since this was the first time I had ever heard the Great Spirit referred to as "Uncle Billy", it was my turn to be momentarily perplexed. "I think," I said slowly, "your Uncle Billy and my Uncle Bill were a little different. My Uncle Bill was a prospector like you." Julius pointed a horny finger at himself and laughed heartily. "Like me? One no-good bum." I shook my head. "Huh uh. Uncle Bill was no bum, Julius. And I don't think you are, either. A little different, maybe, the way he lived and you live. But he was no bum. And you are no bum." "Ah ha!", pointing that same horny finger at me, "You don't think Julius is a bum, you ask somebody. Lou, Barry, somebody. By golly, you ask somebody." I smiled at him and shook my head. "I won't ask anybody. I make up my own mind. I think you are no bum."

Julius set the can of plums firmly on a rock and opened it with his pocket knife. Extending the jagged edged tin container to me for the first pick of a plum with my sharpened stick, he said, "You come see me at my mine?" "Gosh!" I said. "Yes. The first chance I get. I've never seen a gold mine. I'd like nothing better. Before I get to the plums, here's your rock back. Don't want to lose it."

When I held the hy-grade piece out to him, he shook both his head and the can of plums negatively. "Hah ah! I give it to you. Your first time gold." Pausing with his eyes lighting up conspiratorially, "Somebody ask you. You find right here in post hole in river gravel. Okay?"

"Julius," I remonstrated, "you can't give me this rock. It's too much—too valuable. I can't." "Poof," he disgustedly ejaculated. "Not worth nothing. Besides you find heem. Right here in digging post hole."

I looked at the laced gold quartz and thought it was the most beautiful, most exciting keepsake ever. "You're sure you want . . ."

"Sure, sure. You find heem. You keep heem." And Julius laughed uproariously. "She's beeg, beeg joke. Everybody know no rock like heem in river gravel, but everybody go looking." He laughed so hard he almost spilled the plums. "Everybody know you beeg, beeg liar—just like Julius, just like Uncle Bill—but everybody go looking up and down river."

I laughed with him. I tossed the nugget in the air, caught it and put it in my pocket. "Okay. If that's the way you want it—a big, big liar just like you and Uncle Bill." Then seriously, I said, "Thank you, Julius. I can't thank you enough. I'll keep it always and always remember where I found it. And how." He said, "Poof." And again, "Poof." And again, "Poof." We ate the whole can of plums and shared the syrupy juice out of the can.

Pouring about half a panful of sand out of the sack, Julius squatted close to a riffle and with a shaking, half circle motion, washed the sand back and forth and around, spilling a little sand and water over the pan's outer edge with each move. Shortly, nothing but some very fine black sand and a little water remained. Carefully examining this with a forefinger, Julius shook his head and grunted disgustedly. Digging with his finger to the bottom of the pan and pushing the residue out of the water off to the side, he took a pinch of what was there and spread it in his palm up to the light. "See?" He asked. "Fine flour color." Sure enough faintly, but distinctly, I could see the fine yellow flecks against the dark brown skin of his hand. "Ahh!" I exclaimed breathlessly. "I see it." But no darn good. Not a thimble full. You work all day."

I picked up the pan, spilled out the remaining water and poked at the small amount of remaining fine blackish sand with my own fingers. "Look," I said excited. "More color." Julius chuckled. While I held the pan, he poured more sand out of the sack. "You try. Maybe next panful be better. Plenty wash. Always next pan. Always chance."

Quickly, I learned that squatting, holding the heavy pan, and maneuvering it as Julius had done was not nearly as simple and easy as it looked. First off, I almost pitched forward and landed in the riffle itself. Julius thought it was funny. Tolerantly, he came up behind me, reached down over my shoulders, and putting his hands over mine, guided my moves of the pan. "You see?" "I see, but it's not as easy as it looks."

Getting the gravel sand washed out to what really counted, seemed to take forever. In the awkward squatting and reaching position required, my legs, arms, and back were aching long before I ever got there. Finally, gratefully with the much lightened pan, I was able to stand up. In the finds held to the light, I suddenly saw a color unlike anything Julius had produced. Then it was gone. Then again, it was there. "Julius," I cried excitedly, "Look!" Julius looked and unexcitedly said, "Um." Carefully poking a finger at what we were looking at, he brought it out and adhered to his digit. "Little flake. Better color, but not much. Another panful maybe pinhead nugget." There were a few more flakes, but not a "pinhead" nugget in all of the remaining sand.

After lunch and the impromptu prospecting, we went back to swamping out the willows under the line all along the road to the one-lane steel bridge over the river. We still had several hundred yards to go when we heard a car coming from off the highway and shortly saw that it was Lou in his blue Buick. Pulling up along the road near where we were working, he turned off the motor and walked over to our clearing. After testing the stability of the last post we had planted, and inspected how the line had been rehung on the new post, he followed up the swath under the line to our present stand. Taking off his hat and mopping his brow and balding head with a red bandanna, he pronounced, "You boys been doing a good job." Julius grinned appreciatively. "She's hot, but we get heem." As for me, I felt good all over even including a couple of blisters on my hands; to think that the ranger, himself, would take note of such a small project. I beamed, too.

Lou sat down on a handy, large rounded boulder. "Julius," he queried, "You think you can finish brushin' out this line on your own? I need your helpah for anothah chaw." This came as a big surprise to Julius and especially to me. Quickly recovering, Julius said, "Sure. Sure. You need my helper—you take heem. I finish this job." "Good. It's kind of an emergency. I need to get word to Alphonse and the Mad Russian to come down off the hill to help Hauswirth with some road work on Monday." "Ah hah," said Julius knowingly. "Squirtah," said Lou, "put your axe and shovel in the back of the truck and come on with me."

After I got into the blue Buick and we were heading back to the station, Lou put a question to me with both exciting and frightening implications. "Squirtah," he asked, "you know anything at all about hawses?" "Yessir. But not too much. My grandfather had a driving horse for his buggy that I used to drive a long time ago when I was pretty small. I helped him harness the horse to the buggy. My cousins had a saddle horse that I rode a few times—never any distance. I can cinch up a saddle." "That's more than I expected. You think you can ride about seven miles up the Kitchen Gulch Trail and back without gettin' pitched off or lost?" I swallowed something stuck in my windpipe and breathlessly said, "Yessir. On your horse? On Ranger?" "On 'Rainjah'," Lou affirmed. "I wouldn't send you if theh was anybody else to go." "I can do it. I'll make it." "Always a first time. Might as well be now, as later."

Lou's mount, "Rainjah" was a beautiful, strangely dappled grey; powerfully built with a big barrel and strong legs well adapted to carrying the owner's 200-plus pounds uphill and down all day and day after day. Standing sixteen or seventeen hands with clean-cut, well-proportioned neck and head, inquisitive eyes, and alert, sensitive ears he was recognizable as a mountain man's mount even to a novice like me. That I should be trusted to venture into the vastness of this strange, wild land alone and aboard the forest ranger's very own, personal saddle horse was beyond my wildest expectations. I accepted the fact as both a challenge and a test, with no little trepidation. If the truth be know, the ranger probably had more faith in his horse than his rider and would have trusted me with no other.

After leading Ranger out of the corral, Lou wrapped the reins around the hitching pole and ran both a curry comb and brush over the animal's sleek hide, causing him to step from side to side probably in sheer ecstasy from the treatment. "Rainjah!," Lou commanded impatiently. "Stand still!" I laughed. "I think that curry comb tickles his belly. He likes it." Ranger nodded his head and vigorously shook himself end to end. Lou reached up with his left hand and administered a sharp tug on the reins while continuing the belly scratching. "Stand still." Ceasing his side stepping, but continuing to nod and shake his head, the horse submitted and stood still. "Too much oats and not enough work," Lou muttered in mock disgust. "Fetch that saddle and pad from over by the tack room door." The saddle was encumbered with strange leather covered stirrups and a kind of harness like I had never seen before. Altogether, it was about as much as I could lift with one hand and the weight surprised me.

"That's Barry's outfit. It'll fit you better than mine. We won't have to shorten the stirrups so much." Carefully fitting the pad on Ranger's back and giving it a couple of solid thumps as though to glue it in place, Lou picked up the heavy saddle, paused momentarily while he said, "Ho, Rainjah" and with a single flowing movement, set the outfit topside the horse. To me, it looked like a real trick. "When you put a saddle on a haws, always get it up close against the withers before you set the cinch. That way, you won't be ridin' back on his kidneys, an' keep a reasonably tight cinch." "What the heck are those leather toes over the stirrups?" Lou snorted. "Darned taps—tapaderos. To help keep your feet dry in wet weather and warmer in cold weather. First came from Mexico. Cowboys used 'em down in Texas and the southeast to ward off wear and tear on boots by brush and thawns. Don't see 'em so much up this way. I never weh 'em." "And what's all that harness hooked to the saddle? I never saw that before." "As a flatlandah, you wouldn't," Lou answered. "This country stands on end—steeper'n a cow's face. This breechin' goes under a hawse's tail to keep the saddle from workin' forwahd goin' downhill. And this is a breast strap to keep the saddle from slidin' back climbin' uphill. Some use this riggin' an' some don't, but it's easiah on a horse an' ridah as well."

As Lou put the said items in place, I watched every move carefully so next time, if there might be a next time, I would make no mistakes. Taking a final hitch on the cinch, Lou put the left stirrup in place. "Now put yoah foot in here and climb aboard so we can see how much to shawten the stirrups." As I went to put my foot up, as directed, he suddenly reached out a big hand to my shoulder. "Wait a second. Where'd you get that cut in yoah boot?" With both of us looking down at the incriminating evidence, I almost whispered, "Yesterday, cutting willows." "Damn. You cut yoah foot?" "No sir. Not a scratch. Just the boot and a little sock." Lou shook his head. "I'm not suah whethah yoah safe alone or with somebody. Go ahead. Put yoah foot up heah. You lucked out once. We'll find out if you can do it twice. Ho Rainjah."

It was all I could do to stretch my leg up as high as the stirrup, and awkwardly grabbing the saddlehorn with both hands, I barely managed to haul myself aboard. Atop the tall horse with the new feel of hard leather under my butt, I had plenty of misgiving.

Stirrups shortened to the place where I could stand up and just barely clear the saddle, I slid out of the seat and went into a conference with Lou over a map. "Evah see a map like this?" my mentor inquired. "Not exactly. But I can read a road map." "Well, this heh is a road and this broken line heh is a trail. You see that?" "I get it." "Now, you take out the station heh an' go up the highway heh an' turn off heh like on the telephone line with Julius and cross the bridge heh. Rainjah won't bothah none crossin' the bridge. He's like me, puttin' on a few yeahs, an' knows what it's all about.

"Aftah crossin' the rivah, you follow up the Rock Creek Road heh. Can't get lost as they ain't no othah roads othah than into a couple ranches to get off on. Up the road a piece, thehs a sign says, 'Old Man Mine 4 Miles' and a arrow pointin' in that direction. Understand?" "I understand." "You take off from theh up this trail. Fehly steep trail. An' you just keep goin' 'till you get to this old mine. Alphonse and the Russian are camped right theh in a tent. You'll see theh camp and time you get theh, they'll probably be theh. If not, you get off, make yo'self comfortable an' wait 'till they come. Then you give 'em this note. Alphonse can read some, but it makes no difference. He knows Rainjah an' will know fur suah I sent you. Tell Alphonse to come on down to the road an' wait theh at Kitchen Gulch wheh the trail takes off and someone will pick them up in the truck an' take 'em on up to Grizzly Guard Station to Hauswirth's camp. The note says the same thing, but you tell 'em anyway so thehs no doubt. You understand that?" "Sure, I've got the message." "Maybe you can get a bite to eat when you get up theh. It'll be gettin' a little dahk time you get back to the road, but Rainjah will bring you home. He knows wheh the oats is."

The thought that I might be riding in the dark had not occurred to me. Uneasily, I considered that this mission was assuming some of the aspects and risks of Paul Revere's Midnight Ride. But come what may, the die was cast and I was about to uncast it no way.

Unwinding the long reins from the hitching pole, I patted Ranger on the neck, put the right rein up and over and stepped back to put my foot in the stirrup as before. Lou, standing nearby, said gently, "No, Squirtah. Not that way. Turn the stirrup out and get up from the front. Let the pony know you're about to hit his back. Hold his reins right on the hawn with youh right hand and get purchase on the hawn to pull yohself up and astride. Talk to the haws and let him know what goes on."

Taking the directed new stance and stretching

mightily for both stirrup and horn, I said, "Ho Ranger. E-e-asy, ba-boy." Surprisingly quick and easy, I was aboard—tall, indeed, in the saddle. Lou gave Ranger an affectionate slap on the rump and chuckled. "No worry about this old boy. To get him goin' an' keep him on the move, kick him in the belly a little with your heels." Ranger and I started to move out when suddenly Lou shouted, "Hold evahthing. Somethin' I forgot." Hauling in the reins, I stopped Ranger in his tracks, but he impatiently hauled back at the reins and pranced around no doubt wondering "What now?" just as I was.

Walking up and putting a hand on the reins just below the bit to settle Ranger down, Lou said, "You know how to steer this crittah?" I said, "Sure. Left turn pull on the left rein. Right turn, pull right." "An' wind up still goin' straight ahead. These ponies don't drive like back East. Theh taught to neck rein. You keep both reins in one hand all the time. Turn left, you move your hand left so the right rein tightens against the right side of the pony's neck. Turn right, vice versa. Let's see you try it. Turn him in a circle left an' then right." I tried it and I was amazed at how easy and how well it worked. "Hey." I hollered enthusiastically to Lou. "That's great." Kicking Ranger in the belly into a fast running walk, we were off out the lane to the highway.

By the time I got back to where I had left Julius, I was getting the feel of the saddle and the stirrups and all, and thinking very cocky that here I was at long last just as I had dreamed it might happen, really a cowboy on the ranger's very own horse.

Julius, down off the road out of easy hearing, cutting willows, stopped his cutting and waved most encouragingly. Taking my hand off the saddle horn, I most enthusiastically waved back. Getting a glimpse of the waved hand, my trustworthy steed mistaking the move for an impending slap with the reins, took off in a full gallop like a shot. Just in time, I caught hold of the lifesaving horn or would have been left sitting on the road, rather than in the saddle, in the dust. Shortly, emerging from my surprise and hanging on for all I was worth, I hollered, "Whoa, Ranger! Whoa!" Seeing that we were on the way to crossing the steel river bridge at full gallop, in near panic I hauled back mightily on the reins again hollering, "Whoa! Whoa! Ranger! Stop!"

As suddenly as he had taken off, Ranger obeyed, throwing up a cloud of dust and gravel ahead of me in the process. Had it not been for the frozen iron grip I had maintained on the blessed horn, I would have been over his head, out of the saddle mingling with the gravel and dust.

With Ranger trembling and me petrified, we paused there, greenhorn flatlander and western mountain horse getting a new bearing. Reaching forward and patting Ranger reassuringly on the neck with a shaky hand, I soothingly, brokenly, got out, "Easy, Ranger. Sorry boy. I wasn't about to hit you. All my fault." After he stopped trembling and settled down, I felt like I was again back in the saddle. I loosened the reins, kicked him tentatively very gently in the belly with both heels at once and said softly in his ear, but never letting go my grip on the horn, "Let's go boy. Let's walk across the bridge. And find out what's up the road." Ranger shook his head, snorted, and moved across the bridge. I thought to myself of Julius back there swamping out willows and laughing his fool head off and the story he would have to tell.

Beyond the bridge, we came suddenly to Rock Creek, and the size of the stream with its wild flooding water was something to see. I had not imagined it was so big, so fast, deep and dangerous. The narrow road skirting the water was almost awash. That this torrent sheltered those magnificent trout I had seen in Gate's sidewalk showcase was easily believable, but how in God's name, had Norman Means worked his Bunyan Bug magic to catch them? Fascinated by the sight, express train sound, and overwhelming exuberance of the rushing mountain water, a slight turn in the road away from the creek arrived as a mild disappointment.

Just beyond the turn was a good-sized flat, forested with big, beautiful, orange-barked pine trees, the same kind of pines that had supplied the Station woodpile. Barry had said western yellow or Ponderosa. Among the trees were rings of smoke-blackened rocks and remnants of campfires. Unpopulated at the time by campers, I concluded this to be what was called Kitchen Gulch campground. At the upper end of the flat was the trail turnoff sign I was looking for—Old Man Mine 4.

Though it did not say so, the figure "4" meant miles from here. Said sign consisted of one by four board nailed, shoulder high, to a handy tree. The message was routed out on the board and both board and message were so weathered as to be practically indistinguishable at any distance, one from another.

A National Forest road, denoted on maps by a black line, could be anything from a brushed-out wagon track to a one lane graded gravel-surfaced thoroughfare with turnouts, such as what Ranger and I had traveled on a water grade up Rock Creek. As opposed to roads, trails were shown on the same maps as broken or hyphenated lighter black lines and where they were shown on the map to be, might actually be only approximately along the true line of travel. Most were unsurveyed and the location drawn in from best estimates.

A trail might switch-back all over, up and down the face of the mountain, or it might pitch off in a literal chute. For the uninformed, first-time traveler, the map concealed infinite wondrous as well as frustrating surprises. The wonder was why and how the trail locator picked the given route as opposed to a way obviously better, and the frustration was because the traveler had no choice other than that of relocating the trail with no funds or manpower to do the job.

Crow-flight distances were one thing and trail distances distinctly another. Trail routes as much as possible generally followed water drainage routes, but if the locator happened to get tired of following a watercourse, he might take off straight cross country come what may.

Of the thousand plus miles of these national forest trails I have traveled through the remote back country of the Rockies, one I especially remember for being most appropriately designated was the "Goat Roost" trail in the Selway Wilderness of Idaho. Nothing short of a mountain goat could get up this trail to roost, let alone get back down, and why, unless looking for thrills and strenuous exercise, any human might want to, always seemed to me an unanswerable question. Even so, the original Forest Service Trail system up and down, around and about the Rockies passed through and gave foot and horse access to the most spectacular, exciting, unpopulated, virtually untouched, and soul-satisfying scenery on God's green earth.

On that magnificent day in June, 1928, at the turnoff to the first of many, many subsequent trails, I was drinking in and absorbing to the bone every enthralling detail. Like most, the Old Man Mine trail was grubbed and shoveled out wider still to allow passage of a loaded pack horse or mule.

On the tree where the sign was nailed appeared what I had been told by Barry was the Forest Service identifying trail blaze: a horizontal dash over a vertical slash, more or less resembling an inverted exclamation point. The blaze, cut deeply through the bark into the trunk of the tree at this point appeared on two sides of the tree, one facing toward the road, one facing the trail above the sign. Along the trail, the blazes were easily visible both going or coming along the route. Wherever you came on this blaze, according to Barry, you would find yourself on a designated Forest Service trail that one way or another would lead you to an occupied or unoccupied Forest Service cabin, a sign affording certainty of present location and distance to another point, or junction with a road.

It was the one and only dependable blaze to be encountered in the whole wild woods. Any other blazes on trees could lead to maybe somewhere or most likely absolutely nowhere. They might be made by miners, prospectors, trappers, or a hunter simply marking the way back to a deer, elk or some other kind of game kill. Never, Barry had cautioned, get suckered in to following any of these without first knowing or definitely determining where or what it might lead to.

Old Man Mine Trail headed up the dry creek bottom that ended in the flat of Kitchen Gulch, but shortly veered to the left following the steep grade of an ascending pine-covered ridge. About halfway to where I could see the ridge top leveled off, my mount automatically came to a halt. "Okay," I told him with an encouraging pat on his sweat-wet neck. "Take a break." After catching his breath, without any urging Ranger dug in and continued the climb all the way to where the ridge top ran out of trees and natural blazes as well.

The flatlander tenderfoot had not been briefed on how to proceed where the markers petered out and considered in a trepidacious development. The horse he rode thought nothing of it and happy to be at the top of the steep grade, kept confidently proceeding straight up the line of the rounded grass covered ridge. Since he acted as though he had been there before, I slacked the reins and let him go. In the near distance appeared a handmade pile of rocks which I managed to recognize as the equivalent of a blaze where no trees grew to blaze. Much relieved, I again patted the sweaty neck encouragingly and said, "Good boy, Ranger, you figure it out. Take it easy boy. We'll get there," Ranger shook his head and let go with a loud barrage of hot air to our rear. And, shortly up ahead, the timber started in again and when we got there so did the blazes. I estimated we were maybe a mile off the road. Maybe, at the steady, fairly rapid walk Ranger maintained, a little more. Though the upgrade was constant, it was much easier and Ranger seemed to have his head set to get the work over and done with as quickly as possible.

Almost an hour of solid travel went by through the pines which had changed from Ponderosa at higher altitude to another unknown type. Between the trees, I caught glimpses of a big bird with spread wings circling and circling in the blue, blue sky. I wished I could see what he might see.

By now, the first good feel of the hard saddle was feeling less good and uneasily I was thinking the "4" on the sign was wrong or the miles were as big as the sky. "Ranger?" I asked, simply by way of hearing my own voice in the great pervading quiet, broken only by the clop, clop of horseshoes pounding the trail. "Where the hell is that camp? Have we gone too far? You think we're on the right trail? It's getting late, and we gotta get there and get back." Clop, clop, clop, clop.

Then, almost at that instant, I smelled the answer: wood smoke. Emerging from the trees into a little open park I saw the white tent with a black protruding stove pipe putting out white smoke; it was pitched by a little pool of water at the foot of the rubble dump from a long abandoned mine.

Alerted by the sound of our approach, a grizzled head poked out of the tent and looked, and disappeared momentarily, to be joined by a head wearing a big black hat. Coming into full view of the inhabitants of the tent, I saw that the one with the grizzled bare head was built like a great hairy-headed bull, dressed shirtless in grey long underwear with wide black suspenders holding up dark shapeless wool pants stagged off at the eight-inch top of heavy logging boots. Tall, skinnier, and clean-shaven, the one under the wide-brimmed black hat wore a red and black paid wool shirt with the shirttail hanging out.

Riding up abreast these residents of the wild, I pulled on the reins and said, "Whoa, Ranger." Ranger, rather than whoaing, pulled back impatiently on the reins, and kept dead ahead for the water hole without breaking pace. Grinning an embarrassed grin and nodding a greeting, we passed briskly by with me still hauling on the reins and my steed with the bit in his teeth. We whoaed shortly where Ranger chose to whoa. He eagerly put his nose in the crystal clear pool.

Wearily and stiffly, I lifted my right leg out of the stirrup up over the horn and slid down out of my perch. As I came to earth, I was momentarily unsure whether my knees were broken or simply paralyzed, and leaned against my mount's stout side for temporary support. Not wanting to appear inexpert in the saddle, however, I gathered my forces as quickly as possible, dropped the reins to leave Ranger to his own devices and stiff-leggedly made my way back to the tent.

"Howdy," I greeted, "Ranger Nichols sent me. One of you must be Alphonse." The grizzled bull nodded enthusiastically, grinning broadly. "Me. Who you?" with the circulation gradually returning to my knees and beginning to feel that I might not be crippled for life after all, I was able to laugh. "Name's Joe—Joe Hessel. I'm new." Alphonse extended a big, dirty, calloused paw and laughed uproariously. "Ah ha! Ranger he don't stop, does he? He knows this place there's water." With the grip put on my hand, I forgot all about my pain in the knees. The strength of Alphonse's welcome was calculated to crush all the fingers of my right hand and almost did. Trying desperately not to indicate any pain or discomfort whatever, I got off another half-broken laugh. "I'm finding out he's got a head of his own." "Ah ha. Good head all right. He think fill his belly. Good water. Good grass." Then, with a brief jerk of his mop toward the completely deadpan man in the black hat, Alphonse introduced, "Rusky. He don't talk much except cuss like heck in Cossack." Otherwise, I thought quickly, the Mad Russian. Holding out my hand with another friendly howdy, the black hat took it and released it quickly without a nod and without a change of expression. Then he turned almost furtively back into the tent.

Alphonse threw the tent flap back. "Come in, come in," he invited. "We get this fire heated up and have some tea. Tell us what's doing down at the station. Ten days already and only ten miles trail cut out. Sonuva-gun. Plenty windfalls. You tell Lou another week at least."

Rusky put another stick of wood in the little box-like sheepherder stove and opened the draft as far as it would go. I took the note in the unsealed official envelope out of my shirt pocket and handed it to Alphonse. "I think maybe there's a change of plans." Alphonse looked at the envelope without removing the note and passed it right back to me. "Ah ha. So you read heem to us. My eyes she's not so good to read."

His eyes, I would bet, were sharp as an eagle's. What he was saying was that he could not easily decipher the written word. I sat down on a handy block on unsplit firewood like Rusky had settled on and which was the only thing in sight for a seat, removed and unfolded the longhand message.

"Alphonse. You and Rusky leave your tools and bed-rolls and close up camp tomorrow, Sunday. Bring your personal gear and hike out to the road at Kitchen Gulch. Somebody will meet you there about two in the afternoon with the truck and take you up to Grizzly Guard Station. Hauswirth has some road work he wants you to help with for about a week. Signed, Lou Nichols, Forest Ranger."

Rusky sat with his shaved chin in hands, elbows planted on knees like he was deaf and heard nothing at all. Alphonse appeared stunned. "But this trail," he said finally, "she's not finish!" "Well, anyway," I answered, "that's the written word. Can I tell Lou you'll be there? At the road at two tomorrow afternoon?" Alphonse first shook his head as though in unbelief, and then reluctantly, affirmatively, "Sure, sure," he agreed sadly. "But this job she's not done."

It was big news when I announced that Julius Cairn and I had been working on the telephone line between the highway and the bridge. Over one more cup of tea, loaded with sugar, after some fried ham and a couple of cans of warmed up pork and beans, Alphonse rolled a Bull Durham cigarette and Rusky lit up a very large and well-used pipe.

"That no good Cairn," Alphonse fondly reminisced,

"that old dog! He don't know a post from a hole about telephone lines. All he knows or cares about is finding the gold. And when he finds it, poof! Off he go looking for more!" I affirmed that in my book and in the short time I had known him, he was a very nice and helpful old guy. Although Rusky kept uncomfortably eyeing the cut in my boot, he said nothing at all.

Also, uncomfortably, I kept watching the sun sinking lower and lower toward the horizon and shadows of the trees growing longer and longer. When I felt that I could not possibly sit and visit another minute, I went out in the little green opening in the timber where Ranger was grazing the rich growth of grass and gratefully found that he had not stepped on or broken the trailing reins, as I was sure he would do when Alphonse had told me to just turn him loose.

Leading him over to a nearby rock that seemed heavensent for standing on to mount his tall frame, I put my foot in the stirrup in the approved manner and climbed aboard while Ranger stood solid as the stepup rock. It was not until I rode up to the tent to bid adieu to my new found summer crew mates that I found I had committed one more cardinal sin ever so tell-tale of the greenhorn horseman.

Head cocked a little to one side and half quizzical grin on his bewhiskered visage, Alphonse put the question: "You always get on horse that way?" "Only when I can find a rock or something to stand on." "From right side? Some horse he pitch you sky high. Kick your lights out."

I was mortified. Thoughts flashing back, I realized it was true the rock had been on the wrong side. Then remembering his lie about his poor eyes, I brushed it off. "Not Ranger. Ranger will let you get on from either side."

"Ah hah. Ranger, maybe. Ranger one darn smart horse." Fleetingly, I thought I detected a flicker of a grin even on Rusky's impassive face and had the feeling at least that he must have sensed the humor in the complete novice.

With a last grin and wave, I kicked Ranger in the flanks and took off down the trail in the twilight as embarrassed on leaving as on arrival. What stories Rusky might tell, I had no worries. About Alphonse, I was not so sure. "Darn, oh darn," I thought, "how stupid can I be?" It was one more lesson learned and never ever forgotten. Before arriving back at the Rock Creek Station, I was to learn several more.

The first, shortly brought to light, was that by comparison with the relatively easy progression of a saddle horse, uphill or on the level, his foreleg bracing descent is anything but easy. For the rider, unlearned about standing in the stirrups, it can be agony to the spine, butt, inner side of legs, knees—especially when the horse is in a hurry to get back to the barn. By the time Ranger had put the trail from the camp to the road behind us—which seemed to me, in my shaken saddle-sore and shattered state, twice the time it had taken to go up, though actually much less—the twilight in which we had started had changed to moonlit night.

I recall over the years a number of wilderness rides extending into the dark of night. On several occasions, though I had complete confidence in my mountain-wise horse, I took out my flashlight, dismounted, and for safety sake, proceeded afoot and led the horse. This was not comfortable nor enjoyable. This, with Ranger, was only my first wilderness night ride.

Where the trail met the road at Kitchen Gulch, though still four miles or more distant, Ranger smelled oats and accelerated out of his easy running walk into a spine-jarring trot. "Darn it, Ranger," I chattered through clenched teeth, simultaneously hauling back on the reins. "Slow down!" Ranger dropped back as ordered to his steady fast walk. As we reached the stretch of road along the charging creek, I was swept with an exciting exuberance and thrilling sense of fulfilled high adventure. Freed of the dark pine and willow shadows, the rock-torn current flashed in the surprisingly bright light of the near full moon like a silver ribbon sprayed at odd intervals with spilling diamonds. The express train rumble of the flood seemed mysteriously muted as if the vast implacable forces of nature were restfully coasting and getting impetus for the morrow.

Where the narrow graveled motorway shortcut east-wardly to the river bridge from the west bending creek, the shoulder was widened by the width of an unsurfaced trail frequented by livestock and horsebackers. Also, unbeknownst to me, it was occasionally tunneled under by resident burrowing gophers.

Instantly, as he was pacing along, Ranger's right foot came down over one of these treacherous shallow tun-nels, the tunnel collapsed, my mount was abruptly brought to his knees and still in the dreamlike trance engendered by the trip along the creek, I was somer-saulted out of the saddle and landed flat on my back in the dust seeing stars other than those of the firmament and wondering how lightning had struck out of such a clear, clear sky. When my blurred vision cleared and I finally caught my breath, the reins were still in my hand and I looked up to see a trembling Ranger looking apologetically down at me. For a minute, I just thought, "to heck with it" and laid there.

The horrible possibility then suddenly struck me that Ranger might have broken his leg. Getting frantically to my knees expecting the very worst, I reached out and ran my hand cautiously and gently over his right foreleg. Feeling no shattered bones, I rose shakily to my feet, threw an arm around my friend's neck, and stood there looking up at the Milky Way giving silent, but heartfelt thanks.

On this Saturday night in June, there had been no takers at the impromptu Kitchen Gulch campground. The road and the night were ever so gratefully Ranger's and mine alone. "Ranger," I said aloud, bawdily break-ing the quiet of the tremendous surrounding void, "Let's me stay off your back awhile and just walk." And leading the way for half a mile or more to the bridge, we walked. Then, coming to a step-up rock on the *left* side of the road and *left* side of horse, I reluctantly remounted.

As we came down the lane off the highway to the station, the Coleman lantern in the office building was lighted and I knew Lou was waiting for me. I wondered how many of the adventures of the evening I should relate to him and decided the less said the better. When we went by on the way to the barn, the back door of the office opened and Lou hollered, "Squirtah, you had any suppah?" Not stopping, I called back affirmatively. "Yeah. I ate up at camp."

At the corral, I wearily dropped the reins, eased myself out of the saddle and wondered if either physically or mentally I would ever be the same. The saddle and harness when I pulled them off Ranger's high back and lugged same to the rack in the tack room seemed to have picked up another forty or more pounds in the course of the ride. When I slipped the bit out of his mouth and replaced the bridle with his halter, Ranger, rubbed his wet nose against my face and softly nickered his relief. Rubbing his back, behind his ears and down his neck and nose, I told him he could count on getting his coffee can full of oats and get it, he did. Then I climbed the ladder to my loft and without even bothering to look for ticks, fell into bed half asleep before I hit the blankets. The next day was Sunday. I didn't have to rise and shine till 6:30 because breakfast would not be served till 7.

After Julius and I washed the breakfast dishes, I cleaned the accumulated grease off the wood range which was very much like the cob and coal cookstove that Mother used at home. Having gone this far with the cleanup, I decided that in lieu of Sunday School, I would launder the darkened dish towels and make use of the laundry water to scrub the cook house floor. These chores behind me, I took the towel and soap and headed down the long lane, across the highway and the "half mile or more" across the gravel and rock stream cottonwood flat to the river.

Here, after some searching, I found the likely flat rock at river's edge I was looking for and peeled off my clothes. Julius had warned me about the willows as being "darn good place for tick." Standing there on the warm surface on the rock in my birthday suit like a monkey looking for fleas, I examined my hide by eye and by feel for ticks and sure enough in my left armpit, I found one—fortunately not yet much dug in. With the help of my pocket knife, he came loose and off without leaving even so much as a bite mark. Transferring this hardshelled, deadly parasite to the rock, I struck a kitchen match and before he could crawl away, applied the flame that made him curl, blow up like a minute balloon and explode with a barely audible pop.

Then, just testing, I put my bare right foot in the little backwater below my rock; and retrieved it like from a hot electric connection. Staggering backwards in shock, I almost lost my balance and fell off the platform. "Good gosh," I shuddered silently, "No need to have wasted a good kitchen match on the darned tick. I could have thrown him in the water and frozen him to death."

Many times, I have debated with myself and others— notably Mother and my wife—the desirability, yet the miserable necessity, of subjecting myself to soap and water. Being innately a confirmed believer in preserving the body oils like the Eskimo and convinced that all bodily cleansing agents are the scourge of modern man, my position in such debates has always been negative, but never without an impartial consideration of all arguments and pleas that might conceivably be justly advanced by the affirmative. In this case, given the petrifying temperature of the water and the fact that barely a week had elapsed since my last hot bath in the big city, I really did not need a bath. I should have won the argument hands down. On the other hand, there was here a new and unusual point of challenge and personal pride involved. If Barry could do it, I could do it, even though death in the process might well take me.

Then entered my considerations, the *modus operandi:* to subject myself to the sure torture little by little or get in, get wet all over, get out, apply soap all over and get back in and rinse all over? Either way, the outlook was formidable. Clenching my teeth and fists, I chose the latter, let go all holds and landed in the shallow sand bottomed back water beside the rock. I gasped for breath and, wet from head to toe, came flashing back. Shuddering, shivering, and teeth chattering, I frantically soaped torso, limbs, head, and between the toes.

So vigorously and busily as I engaged with all this, that the sound of an approaching train on the down-grade Milwaukee tracks across the two hundred feet of river bottom failed to register. Whether a freight or passenger made little difference. There I was in plain view not only caught with my pants down, but, except for a thin lather of soap, stripped stark naked. To slip off my rock and immerse in the icy confines of my inadequate bathtub or to kick modesty and just crouch there on my perch in the raw and wave gaily at all and sundry as the thing thundered by was one of those great spur of the moment decisions.

I could see now it was one of the long, long freights for which the electrified Milwaukee Road was famous and I made up my mind in a hurry. To heck with the engineer and the male train crew! I pulled up my knees and continued to sun bathe and let the soap lather cake in place. I heard the earth whistle for the Rock Creek road crossing; the engineer leaned out and spotted the nude apparition. The zany nude cheerily waved greetings with a bar of white Ivory soap; the engineer gave a quick extra answering toot, and, far to the rear, came the crew in the caboose.

In the interval, to the accompaniment of clattering rail rolling stock, I took the gosh-awful paralyzing plunge into the backwater to rid myself of soap, sizzled

out like a leaping sailfish, grabbed the towel from where
it had been too far from the bath, briskly wiped the near
solidifying ice from legs and lower torso while trying to
prevent my chattering teeth from chipping on each
other. I shivered quickly into my shorts and Levi's, and
returned to my seat on the rock to dry the rest of me.
When the caboose finally passed by, I triumphantly
waved the towel.

Three hands poked out the open windows waving
back. I thought to myself, "That makes their day. The
only darn thing that would have given them more to
talk about would have been a bare female. By the time
the story is all told, I will have been a mermaid, at least
bare-bosomed." Certainly it is from such mundane
material that the lurid and tantalizing tales told around
bunkhouses and campfires are derived.

This one would go something like: "Had a friend once
who was a Milwaukee freight engineer and some of the
wild things they come across along the right-of-way
everyday, people wouldn't believe. He was tellin' me,
there was this day on the Clark Fork when he comes
around a turn somewhere east of Missoula and sure as
hell sees this gorgeous blond standin' there on the bank
of the river naked as a jaybird's butt. She was wavin' a
bar of soap invitin' him to come on over an' have some
fun. Well, you know how much time and distance it
takes to stop one a them mile long Milwaukee freights
highballin' above thirty, forty, or more miles an hour.
He sure wanted to get next to that babe, but right then
it just wasn't possible. So what he did, he . . ." The sky's
the limit and they're a dime a dozen, so pick your own
ending. Any old conclusion, as long as it is juicy and
unbelievable. I've heard them all around camps and
campfires the Rockies over. The only real trick is in the
telling of the tale. Wandering back across the flat, I had
time to cook up and round out a brand new version that
I might pawn off on Barry, or even Lou.

Coming down the lane, I saw smoke leaving the cook
shack stove pipe and directed my steps in that direction

to discover what exotic concoction might be on the fire for lunch. When I opened the door, the unusual, delicious aroma was almost too much. Lou stood there with one of the cleaner, if not much whiter dish towels aproned around his slightly paunchy midriff with shirt sleeves rolled up and dusting of flour up his bare forearms.

"Goldarn, Squirtah," he greeted, over his shoulder. "You swamped out this boah's nest so I had to bake us up a batch of fresh bread." That was as close as Lou ever came to a compliment or out and out expression of appreciation for a job well done. "Aw, I'm sorry," I replied contritely. And then brightly, "But it sure smells good. Just like when my mother baked cinnamon rolls on Saturday afternoon for Sunday breakfast."

Lou opened the oven door of the range just enough for a quick check on what was happening in the interior, and made with his famous fascinating imitation of liquid burbling out of a narrow necked bottle. "Sonsaguns, don't burn, we might even have a couple a them. What you got in mind for this afternoon?" "If it's okay, thought I might get my outfit together, hike up to Kitchen Gulch and try to catch a fish." "You know how to herd a Model I truck?" "Forwards and backwards. I been driving a Model T ten miles a day and back to high school for four years. You mean I can take the truck fishing?" "Not by a darn sight! That truck don't move except on official business. Had in mind you might take Julius a barrel of gas, couple bales a hay and a sack of oats, pick up Alphonse and the Russian and go on up to Grizzling Station. Give you a chance to get acquainted with a little more country." "You bet," I said eagerly. "Right after lunch?" "Get hold of Julius out of the road crew tent and get him to help you. Lunch'll be ready time you get loaded. After that, the two of you can get goin' anytime."

Excitedly, I was on my way without more ado. "Put some gas in the truck outa that barrel with the hand pump opposite the tie rack," Lou called.

The first trip up the Rock Creek road past and beyond Kitchen Gulch, me behind the wheel of the laboring "official" Model T pickup truck with Julius, my up-front tour guide and Alphonse and Rusky riding the bales of hay, along with the oats and barrel of gas in the rear, though uneventful, opened up new landscapes as thrilling to me as they must have been to the first mountain man who pushed his horse up the exciting narrow drainage over nothing but a game trail. The cascading creek must have been just as noisy at spring flood time. The great towering orange-barked ponderosas a hundred years previously, though somewhat smaller in girth and height, must still have been an imposing and inviting forest, free of tangling undergrowth. Back from the road the few deteriorating weathered structures of what had lately been a miner's wayside known as Quigley made the route that much more interesting.

According to my most knowledgeable guide, the Mother Lode was still certainly there only awaiting the lucky man to come along and turn the right rock. Somewhere up the creek there above Quigley was a mountain known as Sliderock. This mountain, "she's broke all up, big and little pieces" but down underneath somewhere, "somewhere sure as heck, one big rich vein," only waiting to be discovered.

Once, suddenly, as we rounded one of innumerable turns, I jammed on the brakes and excitedly pointed up in the timber. Alphonse hollered from the back, "Log across road?" Laughing loudly, Julius poked his head out from in front and hollered back. "Nothing. Big dry doe. Getting fat. Ready to eat." He turned back quizzically and incredulous to me. "First deer? You never before see deer?" "Never running wild. Once in a zoo." "Ho. Around here thick as tick. Maybe we see bear. You never see bear?" "Only in that same zoo—a long time ago." "Ho. Long time me, not you." And poking his head out again, he hollered, "Alphonse. Look for bear. He never see bear."

A couple of more turns up the road we did not see a bear, but almost ran head on into a little bunch of white face cows and calves. As I again pressed hard on the brakes, Julius leaned out the window simultaneously pounding on the side of the truck door and shouting, "Yee hah, yee hah!" This not only gave the cows a start, but me, too. "Goldarn Ham Riddle cows. Never in fence. Always in road." "Who's Ham Riddle?" I asked as we eased past a couple of salves slow to leave the road. Looking straight ahead, Julius replied, too quietly, "You ask Lou."

The route straightened out for a short distance across a small, partly cultivated, flat featured by a rough log cabin, log barn with sagging roof, a couple of other smaller ramshackle log buildings, pole corral, and several pieces of rusting farm machinery, all back from the road against the timber down a poorly pole-fenced lane. "Riddle ranch." "You mean that's a ranch—the whole thing? How can anyone make a living off that?" Julius shrugged. "Little deer. Little trap. Little fish. Little flour. Little salt. Get by."

If you were allergic to close neighbors and seeking a reasonably remote hideout, the lower thirty-five or forty miles of Rock Creek that were on the Rock Creek Ranger District was a fairly likely place to look. As a place to practice agriculture with any expectation of digging out even a meager livelihood, it was not. With the possible exception of one barely adequate homestead at the mouth of the creek and the Half Moon Ranch across the creek from the road about three miles above Kitchen Gulch, the no-possible-way Riddle set-up was typical.

Due to steep rocky topography with only here and there a small flat and opening that might conceivably grow a few potatoes and scant pasture for a milk cow in the short summer, the total resident population over the entire length of the slender lower valley numbered not more than a dozen rugged individuals plus a like number of very unfriendly, lean and half-starved dogs. Only by poaching a few deer, fishing the creek when fishable and not frozen, and trapping a few available mink, muskrat, marten, and coyotes for cash enough to buy flour, salt, and beans, could the residents "get by."

Around another turn or two, the road up Rock Creek went straight ahead across a one-lane log bridge over a sparkling, lively stream about a third the size of Rock Creek, crossing from the left. Just before the stream an unsurfaced spur road even narrower, turned off upstream to the left. A sign nailed on a tree at the intersection notified the traveler that this was "Grizzly Creek" and an arrow pointing up the spur road indicated "Grizzly G.S." Julius said, "Turn here." Off on the unsurfaced narrow winding spur road through the timber we went.

On arrival at the several acre clearing in the great ponderosas beside singing Grizzly Creek, I thought the big, peeled log, one room structure with a tremendous stone fireplace at one end was undoubtedly the most beautiful and appealing place of habitation I had ever seen. Literally, a dream house come true.

Off next to the timber at one side of the Grizzly Creek Station set-up was a large log corral six feet high occupied by a couple of saddle horses and eight or ten big, well-fed mules. Nearby another exquisitely fit-together log building with a loading dock and hitching rack was where we unloaded the gas, grain, and hay.

Alerted by the clattering sound of our coming, the two current inhabitants of the premises stood on the small unroofed porch of the living quarters awaiting our arrival. "Mr. Em and Bucky Harris. They be glad to see us. Have Rusky to cook." "You mean that Rusky is a cook?" "Great cook. Bake bread. Makes pies. Cook, like crazy!" The way Julius said it made me know that having the silent, so-called Mad Russian "to cook" was as pleasing to him as it might be to Mr. Em and Bucky.

According to my informant, the taller of the two, in the wool shirt, stagged-off Levis, and "not so big hat" was Mr. Em, and the somewhat shorter in "Levi" shirt, wearing leather chaps, who on nearer approach was also distinguished by a short burned-out remnant of a roll-your-own cigarette dangling down from the corner of his mouth, was Bucky Harris, the packer.

Emory Hauswirth was a strong, handsome man looking younger than his years, easy to meet, with a quick disarming smile, but also commanding respect and capable of being hard as nails. He could do anything, and anything he did was done right. For example, Julius said proudly, with him and Alphonse to help, Mr. Em had built that fire guard station, the corral, and warehouse right there at Grizzly. He had built all the log bridges across the creeks up the Rock Creek Road and most of the road itself. Best log and road construction anywhere in the mountains. "Lots of people try hire him, lots more money, but he like it better right here. With Lou. He like Lou. And fish. Fish just like he work."

When we pulled up and stopped, Julius and Alphonse quickly piled out and it was like a family reunion. "Julius, you old powder monkey. I haven't seen you all winter." "Hah. Mister Em. Glad to see you. Shoot rock, plenty." "Alphonse, your belly is bigger than ever. How the hell you going to run that grader." "Ho. Grader, she's no problem." Even Rusky, though holding back, was grinning happily. "Rusky! Am I glad to see you! Get on in there to that cookstove and take over. That darn Harris can't even boil eggs." Nodding and shaking hands bashfully, the Black Hat mumbled something or other in Russian and lugging his pack, moved on toward the door.

Taciturn and reserved, Harris nonetheless cordially shook hands with the three old timers, a little sardonic smile playing around his mouth. Then, as if in need of support, leaned against the building, hauled out a sack of Bull Durham and papers from his left shirt pocket and slowly proceeded to roll a new cigarette. "Julius," he drawled, from under the brim of his big battered and weathered grey hat, "You ever get any good outa that little mule you bought from Hawkins?" "Jeannette? You bet. Darn good for mine. She don't go nowhere. She's home."

Disembarked from the driver's seat, watching and listening and just more or less waiting, enviously wishing to be a member of this family, also, and wondering vaguely if I ever would or could be, I just stood there feeling somewhat left out, a conspicuous stranger.

Use of the word "family," apropos Forest Service employees most of the many years I put in with the outfit, was no misnomer. From bottom to top, they were people with a common, proud, tough mission, and newcomers were not only very cautiously scrutinized and tested, but not always accepted. The word most used by "outsiders," descriptive of the nature of those in the organization is "clannish." This questionably accurate adjective has been applied to mountain men, mountain dwellers, and those who follow the woods and wildlands, since Year One. The criticism or accolade or whatever was gradually cheerfully accepted with a carefree, "What the heck. If the shoe fits, we'll wear it." The truth is, it was not only worn but worn well, and God help those who did not measure up. For the misfits, there was a time to get out. It was not sometime in the future, but now! No one was left long in doubt. Mistakes, if not fatal were permissible once, sometimes twice; but a third time hardly ever.

Since the way from bottom to top in the organization was not beset with partisan politics, but based strictly on merit and experience, the general feeling was of working "with," rather than "for," old dependable friends with whom, in case of arriving at decisions it was possible to place a strong dissent without suffering recriminative marks, if overruled. Actually dissent was at a minimum and decisions, once rendered, were stoutly defended. Loyalty to the organization and to leaders therein was nothing short of that in the famed French Foreign Legion with its root beginnings in the likes of that of Mister Em or Ranger Lou. There were other reasons, such as the handy fabulous fishing in Rock Creek and his small business in Bonita that kept Mr. Em from selling his much sought-after skills at a higher price somewhere else. In large part, it was plain downright loyalty to a cause, associates, and leaders that he believed in.

At the moment Julius was bringing Mister Em around the front of the truck and I went forward to meet them. "Joe, this is Mister Em. Mister Em, meet Joe. Darn good dig post holes."

Mister Em shook hands warmly with a direct searching look. "So you're Joe!" "Joe Hessel, Mister Hauswirth." "Forget the 'Mister'. Just Em. Maud said you'd be along driving the truck when I talked to her awhile ago on the telephone." Up and down Rock Creek, that's how fast word traveled about even the slightest inconsequential detail. Everybody on the line, you can be sure, now knew a new body called Joe Hessel had come to Rock Creek and was driving the government truck. Big news.

"Yessir. She sent you up some mail and a couple of *Saturday Evening Posts* by way of Lou before I left."

Em laughed. "Darn little time of light to read by, but I'm glad to have it. Maud also said you were a fisherman. I hope you brought your outfit. We can go catch a mess out of the creek here for you boys down at the station and maybe a couple for Maud."

"Oh no. I have to get back with the truck."

"Not that fast, you don't. This is Sunday. I talked to Lou and we've got time to catch a few fish. Get your outfit together and we'll get going."

The first-time feel of a wild trout in a wild mountain stream hitting and taking an artificial fly cast out on the swirling, sparkling water with a practically weightless split bamboo fly rod, is a sensation originally conceived only for the deities, but one day slipped through divine fingers, and like a lucky falling star, landed within the province of earth's mortal mountain men.

When the hook in the pretty fly unexpectedly came loose from the rainbow's mouth and was whipped just out of mortal man's reach into the branches of a dead willow where it stuck and stayed, all heck was to pay because it was the very last of a supply of three carefully hoarded *borrowed* flies.

"Don't jerk so darn hard! It just takes a little flick of the wrist to set the hook. If you miss, there's the fly still in the water—not up in the willows—you darn Illinois Sucker fisherman." "Sucker fisherman is right. You think I'll *ever* learn?" "Sure you'll learn. Here's three more flies. I tie 'em myself so we've got plenty and they're cheap. How many fish you got?" "Three. Little ones. How many have you caught?" "A few. Go on ahead of me. There's a good hold up ahead. And fewer willows." "Can I see what you've caught?" Em lifted the top of his creel. "Take a look." "Jeez! And you think I can ever catch fish like that." "You bet. A few more flies, I'll make a trout fisherman out of you yet." Em laughed and slapped me on the back. "Go on up to that next hole and get with it. This is barely half a mess." Half a mess was better than half a creel full of about ten-inch beauties. No little ones like mine at all. Shaking my head dubiously, I made a way through the willows "on up ahead."

That hole up ahead was a pure beaut, one of the few places where Grizzly Creek was forced to slow its mad steep dash down to Rock Creek due to a rocky uplift in the channel. The sunlighted water churned between and over big boulders that blocked the watercourse as far as I could see. The spilling torrent came to rest around one last room size rock and leveled out in a deep, long, extended and slow-moving slick before again racing on over a shallow gravel bar. Willows were almost entirely replaced by grass and sedge and the water level was virtually bank full. It was a precious, hidden, un-trampled glade fulfilling in every respect one of every trout fisherman's dreams.

"Don't lose him. Get him under the gills and hit his head on a rock. That's a good one."

Em had come up through the willows so quietly and I was so preoccupied with landing one more fabulous fish, I had not heard him come. Glancing up with a start from where I was down on my knees at the water's edge struggling to subdue a slick wriggling trout just un-ceremoniously hauled out on the bank, I relaxed, broke down with uncontrollable laughter in surprise and sheer ecstatic happiness and almost lost the fish, free of the hook, back in the water. How long Em had been standing there observing the awkward antics of the learning pupil in action, I never knew. All I know was that it was the most unforgettable, Heaven-sent Sunday afternoon of a lifetime and that if I never had another like it, I had them all.

"Well," Em said quietly, as we sat there, with him rolling a cigarette, "It beats heck out of going to church. But now that we got all these fish, we have to clean 'em."

The revolting manner in which I have seen some supposed-to-be trout fishermen go about cleaning a trout, you wouldn't believe. Of course, before Em showed me, there on the bank of Grizzly Creek that day, I was as ignorant as any other ignorant butcher and would probably have gone about it the same way.

Holding the fish belly up in the palm of the hand, Em inserted the point of his big sharp pocket knife in the anal opening and with a quick forward swipe slit the belly open not quite to the mouth. He made another quick swipe with the knife just below the lower jaw, severing the junction of the gills with the jaw. Then laying aside the knife, he got hold of the gill fastening, pulled downward and out came gills, guts and all but the elongated veinlike heart at the top of the rib-cage. Finally with a quick upward thumbnail along the backbone, he wiped out the dark bloody circulation system, rinsed the fish in the creek, and there it was, quick as you might say "scat"—slick and clean as a whistle.

"Never cut the head off till you're ready to cook. Some people like to cook 'em, head and all, if they're little. Me, I take the head off just before I cook. Trouble with most of mine out of Rock Creek, they won't fit in a fry pan even with the heads off. These ten-to-twelve inchers are just right. Put some of that grass around 'em to keep 'em cool and put 'em all in your sack." In lieu of an extra creel, I had been supplied with a washed out flour sack for carrying my catch. With what the two of us wound up with, the sack, bulging with cleaned fish and grass, contained what Em very conservatively estimated as a "fairly good mess."

"There's a way to fillet a trout with all the bones out and with hardly using a knife," Em told me. "I've seen it done and I've eaten the fish. Laid out flat, they cook through better and faster. With no bones to bother, they can't be beat. Somehow, I never learned to do it."

A few years later, I came one-up on even the great Mr. Em. After a lot of teaching and tattering of fish, I finally did learn from Ann, Brad's fish-wise Scandinavian wife.

If you really want to know this tricky little-known technique that I have passed on to my sons as Mama Ann instructed me to do it, here is the way to proceed. It is not easy at best and especially not with trout fresh taken from a cold mountain stream or lake. It is much easier with trout hung out of reach of wandering cats, bears, and other fish fanciers, overnight in crisp mountain air, or trout that have been frozen and thawed.

Sever the head from the cleaned fish with a good stout blade, thereby exposing the upstanding backbone and curved rib structure of the trout. Next, slit downward from anal opening to tail. Put the knife aside. With the left hand, take firm grip on the fish with slit belly pointing at your belt buckle. With thumb and forefinger (or middle finger) pinch against the upstanding backbone and push toward the tail of fish forcing flesh away from same with thumb and finger downward and outward along ribs on both sides of fish from head to tail. Pull peeled backbone and ribs from skin along the top as you move down. Finally, give flesh freed bone structure of fish (backbone and ribs) a quick hard twist at junction with tail. What you have left in the palm of right hand will (or should be) the flat, boneless fillets of both sides of the trout held together in the middle by the skin, with tail remaining attached.

Now, if you can perform this feat from these few written instructions without personally being shown and without leaving the fine, pink or white flesh of the fish torn, tattered, or shredded into a pulpy mess, take a bow. You are one of the chosen few. Among all the accomplished fishermen with whom I have been associated over all my years, I have never met another familiar with and capable of accomplishing this sleight of hand.

Proceed to plop your lovely firm, double fillet in flour mixed with salt and pepper (or corn meal) and drop it in a very hot skillet containing a small amount of bacon grease and watch it sizzle. When crisp and golden brown on one side, use a pancake turner and flop it over exposing that side to the skillet until the same color. Remove from the skillet and serve piping hot. With or without a splash of lemon juice or smear of Durkee's sauce, at the end of your fork is a bite for the gods. Eat it, crisp skin and all, or pick the meat off the skin, and throw the skin away. As an exotic hors d'oeuvre or the filling for a hot cake sandwich, it is delicious cold as when still sizzling off the stove.

The biggest trout I ever manhandled in this manner was a thirty-inch rainbow taken from Alaska's Newhalen

River in 1941. University of Michigan's Doc Baxter and his two helpers, Walker and I, feasted on that fabulous fillet most of two days. The smallest was a seven-inch brookie from a beaver pond in Colorado, consumed with a good number of similar sized others at one sitting with no leftovers. One was as difficult as the other. Easiest to handle are those from ten to twelve inches like those that Sunday afternoon from Grizzly Creek.

I told Em I had met a friend of his while purchasing some plunder in a haberdashery on my way through Missoula and that this friend had said to tell him he would be up to tangle lines with him sometime during the summer. Though obviously happy to have the message, his reaction was typically the reverse. "That buttons and bows peddler is so busy featherin' his nest, he don't have a minute to call his own. I won't believe it till I see the whites of his eyes."

When I tried to thank him for all he'd done for me, he was just as obviously pleased but gruffly brushed me off. "Aw heck," he said with a kind of embarrassed little laugh. "Don't thank me. Thank Maud. She knows I'm darn choosy who I fish with, but she put me up to it. Someday you might be able to do her a good turn." That day would come when I could and did, but in so doing, the pleasure was to be far more mine than hers.

I was anxious to get back to the station with the precious fish for a fish fry and the first fresh meat I had in a week! I needed to ask Barry a couple of questions—one having to do with horses and the other regarding dental health that Lou had put me up to.

Turning off the highway down the station lane, I could see smoke curling out of the kitchen chimney and knew that Barry or Lou or both must be cooking Sunday supper. Hoisting my sack laden with grass packed trout to the supposedly waiting hot skillet, I opened the cook shack door and came face to face with the tantalizing aroma of frying steak and the kitchen smoggy with smoke. Lou, with his back to the door, a flour sack, as usual, aproned around his middle, and a big two-tined fork in hand was at the stove. Barry sat at the table set for three, drinking coffee.

"Wahoo. What you got in the sack?" he greeted as though he didn't know.

"Fish from Grizzly Creek for supper."

"Supper, hell. Look what's on the griddle. Lou's treat, fresh from the big city."

Moving over and looking around the hefty bulk of Lou, I beheld the three biggest, thickest T-bones I had seen since working last year in Buhler Bros. St. Paul butcher shop for Uncle Paul, sizzling on the hot cake griddle.

"How you like it cooked, Squirtah? Raw, medium or well?"

"Just beyond raw this side of medium. Mmm Um," I breathed.

"And fresh store-bought bread to go with," Barry exulted.

"Wash up, Squirtah. We're about to get with it. After suppah, hang your fish in the coolah. You know what the blind man said when he got to the fish market?"

"What'd he say?"

"He said: 'Hello, girls! Git outa heh an' go wash yeah hands."

"Yeah, I'm goin' but before I go, I gotta know: When you were in the big city, Barry, did you manage to get your teeth fixed?"

Barry slowly set his coffee cup on the table. "Whadda you know about teeth?" Then in a mock, very hurt, quiet and threatening tone of voice: "Lou, you put him up to that! Believe me, Joe, all the girls I know live way over across the river from West Front Street. They have nothin' to do with fixin' teeth."

"Yeah, Squirtah, but he has to go by West Front on his way across the rivah. Heck of a note if he's home without his teeth fixed."

"Aw," Barry exploded in laughter, "go ump, both of you."

Big joke. A toothache was always a surefire excuse for going to town, but a toothache was nevertheless always suspect as being an excuse.

When Barry and I went out and sat on the cookhouse steps, he smoked his pipe before hunting the covers. After doing up the dishes and cleaning up the kitchen was the right time to put my second question: "Barry, I know it's none of my business, but I wonder if you can tell me about that horse, the one that fell backwards on Lou and has him crippled up. Was it, by any chance, Ranger? I can't believe it was Ranger."

Barry tamped the tobacco down a little tighter in the bowl of his pipe and lit another kitchen match.

"Lou said you took a little ride on Ranger and used my saddle. How'd you like it?" "We had to shorten the stirrups a couple of notches. Darn. I forgot to let those out for you again. I'll do that first thing in the morning. I got a lot to learn about horses and riding, but I had no trouble with Ranger. He never reared or bucked like he might hurt somebody." "Huh uh. He's a darn good mountain horse—got some Tennessee Walker in him somewhere."

Barry was no way in a hurry to answer the question. He paused, taking another long pull on his pipe. "Lou's a top hand with a horse. He once could rodeo with the best of them. But he won't admit he's gettin' along in years and that so-and-so Thompson, that owns the 2-Bar, set him up. Just hearsay, but that's what I hear. The 2-Bar runs a lot of cows and has a grazing permit on the Forest, but Thompson has been overstockin' his permit and a couple of times Lou caught up with it and got into Thompson for trespass. Lou went down there to make a ride with him and a couple of his hands. Tried to show him why he couldn't have a bigger permit because his range is overgrazed by what the permit calls for already.

"Word has it that Thompson fixed Lou up with a wild ringy horse that had already half killed a couple of riders. Lou knew what he was up against, but wouldn't say anything, naturally, because he figured he'd stay with the bronc just to show Thompson he could do it. Got up on a steep hillside in a patch of timber. A little windfall, the maverick didn't want to get over. Lou put the spurs to him. He reared and lost his footing and on account of the timber, Lou wasn't able to fall clear of the saddle and got the horn in his belly with the horse on top of him. The wonder is, it didn't kill him.

"At least, that's the story passed along by one of the hands along on the ride. He said he quit the outfit on account of it. I went to see Lou when he was in the hospital and asked him what happened. All he did was to make that cockeyed sound of water burbling out of a bottle and tell me he'd let a darn cayuse fall on him when he wasn't lookin'. Far as I know, he's never said much more than that to anybody. One thing for sure, Thompson never got an increase in his permit and he'll be thinkin' twice before he tried to run anymore in trespass. Lou's been around here long enough, Thompson well knows a little trick like that is not soon forgot." Barry knocked the ashes out of his pipe on the heel of his boot. "Been a hard two days in town. Think I'll hit the covers."

It had been a doubly hard and full two days for me right there on the District and I readily tagged along. Though unaware of it on retiring to my attic, tomorrow was to be one of the most momentous in the shaping of my life.

Sliderock

It was about eleven o'clock in the morning, when Lou returned from his daily run to meet the train and get the mail. Barry and I were in the warehouse putting together what were known as emergency smokechaser packs—thirty-five pounds of provisions like pork and beans, canned tomatoes, blanket, file, whetstone, canteen, et cetera, that a man carried on his back, calculated to sustain him for two or three days, when he went looking for and putting out a fire afoot and far from homebase.

Coming in the door and making his way over and around this paraphernalia, Lou took a seat on a case of canned plums, dejectedly removed his sombrero and wiped the sweat off his forehead. "Barry, you won't believe this." "What?" "You know that goldarn Gawjah-cracker forestry student, University of Gawjah, we was gonna put up on Sliderock?" "Yeah—he's not comin'?"

"How'd you guess?" "Well, somehow it just figures." Barry, with a couple of hand compasses in hand, took a seat on a case of sliced pineapple. I picked a seat on a stack of surplus army blankets. Lou picked up a lady shovel and automatically sighted down the short handle checking to see if it was straight or warped. "At this late date, he lets us know! What d'uh we do?" "Darn good question." Lou put down the shovel and was looking intently at me as though maybe I had just arrived on the scene. "Squirtah," he said slowly, "you ain't no forestry student, but you don't wear spectacles. How's yoah eyes?" Just beginning to catch up with the situation and the portents of the conversation, I shrugged and said off-handedly, "Heck, Lou, I see fine." Long pause. "What d'uh think Barry?" Barry was grinning a little cynically and skeptically at me. "Lou, he's not even dry behind the ears and wouldn't know smoke if he had a noseful. But you want to know? I got a feeling if Joe wants to do it, he'll take teachin', and can handle the job okay." With barely an inkling of what the job of lookout might entail, I nonetheless sensed that it was of some little consequence in the scheme of things and could hear opportunity knocking on my door. "Gosh, Barry," I said eagerly. "Thanks. If you *think* so, I *know* I can."

Lou reflectively and a little sadly shook his head and burbled some water out of the bottle. "Darn brass in fire control ain't gonna like it much—a greenhorn kid up on that peak. How come I'm always gettin' myself in a bind like this?" Barry laughed. "As long as he can see and can stand his own company . . . You think you could take that, Joe? All alone on a peak miles from nowhere for two months or more?" "Sure," I said positively.

Lou looked at me once more and painfully got to his feet. "Squirtah, with no raise in pay, you just been promoted from whistle punk to lookout. An' heaven help us all if you don't pan out. Barry's runnin' a fire trainin' session over on Seely Lake District startin' day after tomorrow an' you're goin'!"

I got up off the stack of blankets so excited I could

hardly contain myself. "Don't worry. I'll be here at the finish." Lou and Barry both laughed and Lou reached over and gave me a whack on the back. "That's what I like. You got the spirit an' that's half the battle. If nothin' more the experience'll be good for you."

As Lou departed, Barry sat there with his hands full of hand compasses and again looked me up and down. "Darn boy, you let yourself in for something. I've known grown men who just can't cut it with no company for two months and more." "Aw heck, Barry," I grinned at him confidently, "I'm a born loner. You wait and see." "I'll be waitin'," he answered seriously and a little grimly, "I been there."

Fire training schools for smoke chasers, lookouts, rangers, and practically all Forest administrative personnel from the regional forester down, were as much a part of the spring scene as the snow melt. Fire control to all intents at that time was what the Forest Service was all about—prevention, detection, suppression, transportation, communication, supply, strategy, total war on fire. In its infancy, the Forest Service had basic hand tools—no air reconnaissance, no power pumps or saws, no smoke-jumpers, virtually no nothing except a few dedicated men, mules, main strength, and awkwardness. There was no Smokey Bear prevention program, no hairy flag-waving "environmentalists." The word "environment" like the word "conservation" had hardly been shelled out. The public and the politicians for the most part could have cared less. Any fire of less than a thousand acres seldom made the papers.

In the vast sweeps of inaccessible, sparsely populated Rocky Mountain wilderness, largely in National Forests, Parks and Public Domain, most of the raging conflagrations were touched off by lightning strikes, but where men entered, Nature was a piker. Railroads, logging and lumbering, constantly proliferating mobile recreationists created a nightmare for the undermanned, meagerly financed, poorly equipped national forest fire protection organization. Where pure cussed carelessness with fire left off, the arsonist (set on clearing the land of snakes and insects or for just plain spite) frequently took over. Millions of acres of fine virgin timber and precious watershed cover, not to mention quite a few human lives of civilians and firefighters, went up in smoke each year. The battle, uphill and against all odds all the way, at the outset appeared hopeless and to lesser men certainly would have been. Some effective new weapons and methods have been brought to bear, but the war is far from being won to this too-late day.

The fire school that Barry ramrodded at Seeley Lake registered only six students and was conducted without aid of any textbook. The group was made up of first, second, and third year young, vigorous employees aspiring to careers in forestry or just out to make a stake during the summer. Two men were from the University of Montana School of Forestry at Missoula, one from the Idaho Forestry School at Moscow, one a drifting, sometime logger from up in Washington, one native with no particular attachment or calling, and me—obviously the youngest, smallest, and greenest of the lot. Luckily there were no prerequisites for the course and no awards for outstanding brilliance given out at the end.

Barry, the instructor, opened the first session promptly at 7:45, Friday morning, with an appropriate hilarious dirty story. From there on he enjoyed the undivided attention of one and all, along with their high regard.

Following a free-for-all discussion of the use of a file versus use of a whet-stone for sharpening an axe, we progressed to proper techniques for filing and setting the teeth of a two-man crosscut saw. When the saw was sharpened, a sawing contest between a Seeley Lake team made up of the some-time logger and one of the Montana U students and a Rock Creek team made up of Barry and me was held. (I happened to be the only sorry

Rock Creek participant Barry had to work with.) With Barry hollering at me all the time in desperation, "For C-sake, pull! And stop dragging your feet!" Rock Creek lost by a good two inches. Which, just because Barry and I had won all the kitchen matches in the seven-card stud poker game of the evening before, everybody said served us right. Both the winning and losing didn't hurt our standing in that foreign community.

That afternoon, we made it up when it came to splicing the two ends of a broken No. 9 wire ground telephone line and rehanging same sixteen feet up on a thirty-inch ponderosa pine tree. Putting a good tight splice in the heavy wire was one thing to learn, but with the line in your lap and climbing and nailing it up a thirty-inch diameter tree was something else. Climbing a smooth pole with lineman's spurs and belt was something less difficult than going up a rough barked tree difficult or impossible to reach around. Tree climbing spurs are longer and sharper than pole spurs. They need to be driven in deeper so as not to "kick out." The real trick is with the belt, and keeping the proper tension while hitching it up the trunk. What I had learned from Julius about climbing was not much, but enough to get me up and down the tree with no slips and second fastest in the class. The local roustabout, it developed, had at one time worked for a telephone outfit and he was real catty.

What ticked us all, most, was the futility demonstrated by the Idaho representative who was a kind of loud know-it-all and nobody's favorite. When he finally did spike his way up high enough to hang the insulator, he let his spurs kick out and slid back down like a shot, getting a good burn on both hands and knees—not once, but three times. After that, he was much more toned down without nearly so much palaver.

A good deal of time was spent learning to run lines with a hand compass. The Seeley Lake Ranger had set out a number of red flags hidden in the heavy brush. The trainee was given a compass bearing and approxi-

mate distance and told to go retrieve the flag. Several of
the bearings, of course, went straight across a heavy
alder and willow swamp. The one unlucky enough to
draw these bearings came back wet to the hips much to
his own discomfort and hilarity of the group.

When the first athletic day was done according to the
sun, it was far from done for us. Each man was
equipped with an empty two-pound coffee can with hole
punched in one side about half way back to the bottom.
Through this hole was driven a large white candle. The
can was carried horizontally by means of a haywire
handle. The total upshot, when the candle was lighted,
was a surprisingly good, beamed lantern, which went by
the name of "palooser."

The class was divided into three two-men crews and
each crew was directed to go to three widely separated
given points around the station grounds and given a
compass bearing from that point. Somewhere in the
dark of night, we were advised, along our bearings
would be a "going fire" clearly visible when we got there
and putting out smoke we could smell. What we were
not told was that the amount of smoke would not be
enough smell wafted even downwind for any great
distance at all. The fire was hardly more than a good
comfortable campfire meagerly tended by Barry and the
Seeley ranger who sat there, when we came floundering
through the brush on our various compass bearings with
our makeshift lanterns, chuckling and comfortably
drinking from a big pot of hot coffee.

The distance of the fire from the starting points was
at least a mile or more. The terrain naturally was rough
as a cob, brushy, and mostly straight uphill. The things
the trainee crews had to say about fire schools and
school officials were not fit to print. At last, all crews
came beating their way to the fire and were rewarded
with a cup of stinking black coffee without benefit of
either cream or sugar.

Day Two started promptly at the same early hour.
"How do you put out a fire?" "Pour water on it!" Big

laugh. "All right, wise guy, you're on a ridge with a big lightning struck snag on fire in the top and a bunch of windfall around it two miles from the creek. Now how do you put out a fire?" "Sit down and pray for rain." "Any more smart suggestions?" "Heck, yes," said the logger, "Cut it down with a pulaski tool and put a line around it. Take a shovel and throw some dirt on the hot spots an' try to hold it till it cools off." "What kind of line—how wide, how deep?" "That all depends." "Depends on what?" "Depends on how hot the fire is when you get the snag down. How much axe work it takes. Which way the wind's comin' from; how hard it's blowin' and a lot of things." "In other words, you'd stop and think?" "No, by God, I wouldn't stop whatever I was doin'. I'd be doin' plenty, an' thinkin' in the meantime about how wide an' how deep I'd need to build the line where." "That's good advice. You Idaho, that wanted to pour water an' pray for rain, take your shovel or pulaski and show us how you'd build a fire line twenty or thirty feet up that sidehill." "I've never seen any fire line." "That's obvious. Slim, take him over there and get him started, but let him do all of what's necessary." "That, I'd love!"

Come noon, not only Idaho, but everyone else other than Barry, the trainer, and Slim who was appointed crew boss, had put in so much fire line down to mineral soil and one to three feet wide, around so many imaginary fires under so many imaginary conditions, the whole timber and brush covered hillside was laced with lines. There was no coffee break but just every now and then, we had the opportunity to take a five during a review and discussion session. By comparison, digging post holes, even in frustrating old streambed gravel with Julius had been relatively restful. When the morning finally dragged to a sweaty, exhausted end, I could not imagine anything more that might be worse. Barry had one more short speech to make. "This afternoon we are going to touch off a real, honest-to-gosh fire where it can't get loose and you birds are going to put a line around it and put it dead out. If you don't kill the last smoke by sundown, you can take turns patrolling the line and mop it up before breakfast." I would never have suspected that he had such a malicious streak.

The saving grace of that great educational experience was the fact that in deference to the occasion, Seeley District had been afforded a special grant for hire of a first rate cook and the purchase of plenty fresh red meat and fresh vegetables. The quantities of mashed potatoes, gravy, steak, roast beef, and pie consumed were awesome. The typical logging camp table sagged under a mouth-watering menu.

Notoriously among the world's most capacious feeders, the logger was also one of the most finicky of what he ate and how well it was prepared. Knowledgeable logging operators counted more on their cuisine than wage scale to attract and hold good help. The big trick was to attract and hang onto a good cook, and keep him both happy and reasonably sober. Woods cooks were as independent and finicky in their way as was the logger. They would up and quit at the drop of a hat for no good reason, or some friend would come along and pull a cork in the kitchen and for two or three days at least, the cook would be a goner.

Following the midday repast, after the appetite developed by building segments of fire line all morning was satisfied, Barry's fire fighting contingent was far better tuned up for a relaxed siesta than any afternoon demonstration of proficiency on the actual article—a going fire.

The preselected place for this demonstration was about a half acre tangle of brush hiding a few dead and tangled windfalls and harboring a patch of incipient spruce plus one mean looking old dead snag thirty-five or forty feet high and about a foot and a half through— an uncleared remnant in the Seeley horse pasture that should have been touched off and left to burn to begin with.

Barry waded into the jungle with a can of kerosene

while the crew called him an arsonist at work and suddenly as he came hurrying back, the fire took off with a disheartening shoosh. Not only that, he ordered us to just sit tight till he gave the word "Go."

When at long last, the word was given, with a sharp warning to keep an eye on the snag, the fire was spreading in all directions from the foot of the snag where it was started and getting plenty hot. As flames went up the snag, it started to throw sparks. Slim, who had three years as a smoke chaser, and whom Barry had again appointed crew boss, gave quick directions. "You and you take shovels, get some dirt and knock down the flames on the spruce thicket. You and you take pulaskis and start a line as close to the fire as you can get it on the downwind sides and try to flank it. As soon as they get the spruce cooled off, the two with shovels will help you. You, [indicating me] bring that saw, a couple of wedges, and a pulaski and come with me. We gotta take that pitch snag down or it'll burn all night."

He was himself, armed with a shovel and double-bitted axe. With me on his heels, we ran to where it looked like the shortest distance through the burning brush—mostly dead willows—to the base of the snag. Tossing the axe aside, he started swinging the shovel breaking a way toward the snag and beating out fire as he went. Backing out suffocated by smoke and gasping for breath, he waved me forward. "Get in there with the pulaski and see if you can pull some of that burning brush away from the trunk."

Just in case you have never heard of same, seen one, or enjoyed the dubious pleasure of using one, the pulaski fire fighting tool is a light, well-balanced combination of axe on one face joined to a long narrow-bladed grub hoe on the other. It was named for and supposedly originally designed by the famed hero of the great 1910 holocaust in the Northern Rockies, Ranger Pulaski, no known relation to the famous Count Casimir of the American Revolution. For chopping and trenching, there is nothing quite like it.

With a pulaski, I got "in there" and as long as heat and smoke permitted, used the digging end to pull burning needles and old bark out away from the bottom of the snag, scattering debris and dirt behind me as if without getting a clearing around the snag there would be no tomorrow. When I could take no more, practically blinded and suffocated by smoke and sure the soles of both boots were on fire, I backed off and beat my way out to fresh air over the same route I had come in.

Slim was shoveling and throwing dirt on hot spots in the burning brush like he was killing snakes. "Get your breath. Bring saw and axe," he gasped in passing. I nodded running for fresh air.

On exiting the smoke to the clearing, I came surprisingly face to face with Barry already in hand of the axe and with a big fat grin on his face like the whole show was a Sunday School picnic. Gulping in sweet, clean air, I took the saw in hand. "Give me the axe." Still grinning, he put up his free hand in the slow-down signal. "Let it burn out a little. Hotter than the hubs on the hinges of hell in there. No use killin' yourselves off. It ain't goin' nowhere." "Slim's the boss. He told me to bring him the saw *and* axe."

Barry turned dead serious—no grin. "That," he said, "is exactly the right answer. On a fire, never forget it. Bring the saw and the pulaski. I'll take the axe." The blaze around the snag had cooled down a little and the smoke thinned. Slim was still beating down smoldering brush and throwing dirt making good headway.

"Hey, boss, which way you want to fall this thing?" Slim paused, looked up and saw Barry, wiped the sweat out of his eyes, smearing charcoal and grime across his face in the process and pointed. "The shortest way out to the clearing, to the top lands in that green grass." Licking more embers out of the way and slashing a few remaining branches interfering with his swing of the axe, Barry planted his feet and started putting in the undercut on the side facing the clearing.

As he briefly rested on the shovel handle, Slim

watched the chopping obviously much amused. "Darn old fire horse," he said half to himself and half to me, "he *had* to get his hands dirty. Smell of smoke was just too much."

The way Barry made the chips fly and the size of the chips were a wonder to me and a credit to any pro logger. As the smoke began to get to him and he began to fade a little, Slim handed me the shovel. "Clear out more room to work the saw, while I give him a hand."

When Barry surrendered the axe to Slim and had caught his breath, I had plenty of room cleared for pulling the long two-man saw. Barry picked it up by one handle and motioned me to take the other. As we moved in to begin the cut, Slim stood back and held up his hand in the "not yet" signal. "What's holdin' you?" Barry shouted in mock exasperation above the surrounding sound of crackling brush. "I had that cut over half done when you took over." While getting his wind, Slim put his thumb to his nose and waggled his fingers. In response, Barry grinned an evil grin. I made the mistake of trying to laugh and with the smoke almost choked.

When, after cutting the undercut still higher and deeper, Slim once more stood back and gave the "go ahead" signal, Barry and I aimed the saw on a level just above the bottom of the undercut, made a couple of tentative passes with the saw, and started making saw dust—me doing my level best to pull and not drag my feet.

The expertly sharpened and set big teeth of the saw bit in fast and deep while I pulled and didn't drag my feet till I was sure my lungs would break. Suddenly, with me almost jerking the handle off, the snag settled on the saw and there was no more pull or push. Steel wedge in hand, Slim motioned me to stand clear while he inserted the wedge in the cut and with the side of the pulaski, started driving it home. I learned there was more sign language applied in the woods than words and you had better keep a sharp eye out as well as ear.

Ever so little, the snag leaned toward the undercut and the clearing, relieving the bind on the saw. Slim stood back and in a loud voice hollered, "tim—bur, tim—bur" while nothing happened. Barry motioned me to get back on the saw.

After half a dozen pulls, the snag gave with a creak and ominous cracking sound. Barry motioned frantically for me to do something I didn't understand. Slim pushed me aside and quickly removed my saw handle. "Take the handle off so he can pull the saw out before it does. And stand clear. It might kick back from the stump."

After Barry had pulled the saw out of the cut, Slim again picked up the pulaski, hollered, "tim—burr" once more and took another swing at the steel wedge. Watching the top of the high snag, fascinated, I saw it lean farther toward the clearing, but still it did no more than groan, creak, and crack. "Undercut still wasn't deep enough," Slid said to nobody in particular. Barry moved over warily watching the leaning dead tree.

"Tough old buzzard. You got another wedge?"

"Yeah. But we may have to cut it some more with the saw. Stand back and let me give that wedge one more lick with the pulaski. We should have brought a maul." Slim hit the wedge a square resounding blow. The top of the snag swayed, shuddered and headed slowly, but ever faster exactly in the direction in which it had been aimed. The splintering crash as it hit the ground was both the most fearful and satisfying I had ever heard. The trunk broke clean at the undercut and did not kick back. "Yeeoe-hoo." Now that it was down, the work had only begun.

Slim handed me the pulaski. "Cut that burning dead bark loose. I've got to go see what kind of line those yahoos are building." Taking the axe and shovel, he took off. Barry had already disappeared. Cutting and prying smoldering and burning bark and dead limbs, as I went, I laboriously worked my way from the stump up the blackened trunk of the snag to where the shattered top lay safely smoking in the green grass of the pasture.

From where I stood, it looked to me like the whole blaze was largely burned out and cooled off and all left was what was known as "mop-up," the dirtiest, most tedious and most important part of the whole fire fighting operation. We needed to patrol and "cold-trail," testing suspected hot spots with bare hands all around the fire's perimeter until the last wisp of smoke was gone. We dug out smoldering roots and burned out spark-throwing unburned patches inside the line. We widened and deepened the line at the bottom of steep slopes to catch rolling hot chunks and embers. We took every precaution that the corralled fire did not flare up with a gust of wind, jump the line and again run wild.

At a subsequent, larger fire school where I participated, the cause of the fire was determined to have been wanton careless on the part of the ranger of the district where the school was held. A kangaroo judge and jury were appointed and hard tell-tale evidence introduced in the form of canned pumpkin smeared on a crumpled sheet of official Forest Service notebook paper plus a half-smoked cigar butt—pointing to the indisputable fact that the ranger had taken occasion to relieve his bowels, laid his lighted cigar down and gone off and forgotten it in the process, and thereby started the conflagration. He was found guilty on all counts by the jury and fined five gallons of ice cream with fresh strawberries by the judge. In those days, this was an almost impossible sentence. The nearest ice cream was thirty miles distance and strawberries in Montana at the time were not yet in season. He somehow managed to produce the ice cream in the short time before the school ended, and the topping came fresh from his wife's stock of the previous year's canning, equally delicious and appreciated.

In the case of the Seeley Lake school fire, it was agreed by Barry that no all night patrol was necessary after all, for by nightfall, he could find not a remaining thread of smoke or hidden hot spot. After a frigid, clenched teeth in and out of the lake, and tremendous steak supper, he and I departed in the waning twilight back to Rock Creek, looking forward to heating up some water and hand-laundering some used-up clothes on Sunday morning. As a memento, I also carried away a hole burned in the brim of my hat by a flying ember.

Rattling along over the bumpy road in the Model T truck in the gathering gloom seemed a good time to put my question: "Barry, you know that mess of kittens from that tiger-striped female around the warehouse there at the station?" "Yeah." "Do they belong to anybody?" "Nobody in particular. Alphonse is the cat lover." Barry laughed reminiscently. "He's got a funny peculiar way with cats. Picks one or two or even three at once up by the tail and swings them upside down in the air. They squall and scream and claw the air and each other and he thinks it's hilarious. Most peculiar of all, the minute he puts 'em down, they come right back around his big feet for more." "Umm. That is peculiar." "Yeah. What's with you and the kittens?" "Well, they're old enough to be about weaned, aren't they?" "I guess so." "What would you think if I packed that one tomcat in the litter up on the lookout with me for company this summer?" Barry laughed. "How would you pack it eight miles up that goldarn mountain? And what would it live on?" "I figure maybe I could pack him up there inside the front of my shirt or somehow and feed him on condensed milk and hotcakes and other stuff. He could catch a few mice and rats." "The government sorta frowns on feedin' their condensed milk to cats and a packrat would make mincemeat out of a month old kitten. Besides that, you'd have to bring him back down or he'd sure never get through the winter." "After two or three months I'm up there, I could put a leash on him and lead him down. You know I don't drink coffee and I sure don't drink condensed milk, so I could give him most of whatever ration of milk I might have coming to me."

For the next half hour or more while Barry thought about it, I kept quiet. "Aw heck," he finally said, "if it'd help keep you happy up there on that peak, I guess I

could live with it. But don't do it without checkin' with
Lou." "Sure," I said happily and enthusiastically. "I
wouldn't think of not checking with Lou. I don't care
much for cats, but it would be company." "Yeah," Barry
dubiously agreed, "but I doubt Lou's gonna care much
for the plan, company or no company."

Compared to the breath-taking, awe-inspiring high
rises of the Missions, Bitterroots, and Absarokas of
Montana, Idaho's Salmons, Utah's High Uintas,
Wyoming's Wind Rivers, and Colorado's San Juan's,
Uncompahgres, and Sangre de Cristos, plus a number of
other parts of the Rockies to which I later lost my heart
and came to know intimately, the lowly Sapphires
cradling Rock Creek and the John Long Mountains were
peanuts. In 1928, before the coming of the bulldozer and
the beer can, I thought they were Paradise—Pearly
Gates and the works!

Of the countless rises in the landscape that make up
the Rockies from Canada to Mexico in western U.S.A.,
Sliderock Mountain—from the standpoint of mass and
distinguishing characteristics—is not much. For anyone
who might for some unknown reason, want to pass south
from the headwaters of the East Fork of Brewster
Creek to the headwaters of Harvey or Otter Creeks, it is
just one more rough rockpile to get across.

The one and only reason I can think of forever
pinpointing this inconspicuous, remote home of the
lodgepole pine, eagle, and rock rabbit is that, among all
my innumerable love affairs continuously on-going over
most of a lifetime with segments of the Rockies, homely
Sliderock was my first unforgettable enchantment.

Cutting through the Sapphires south to north, Rock
Creek is the first major watercourse up the Clark Fork
above the Bitterroot River. In between the Bitterroot
and Rock Creek is the Blackfoot River, but the Blackfoot
enters the Clark Fork, not from the south but the north.
Running roughly north and south, abutting the more or
less east to west extending Sapphires are the John Long
Mountains. In the northern reaches of the John Longs,

overlooking the Clark Fork drainage and lower Rock Creek, there is Sliderock, in an area rich in minerals, timber, wildlife, and early Indian and mountain man history.

Humping up barely 4,000 feet above the 3,800 foot level where Rock Creek flows past the ghost town of Quigley, the rounded rocky top of Sliderock is barely above timberline. About half-way up the slope, the open stand of large 200-plus-year-old, orange barked ponderosa pine, proliferating in the lower creek bottom, gives way to dense, higher elevation forests of darker, smaller lodgepole. In summer, the relatively restricted open top of Sliderock is covered with the waving stalks of white-blooming beargrass.

The mass of the mountain is shattered rock, broken and heaved up by untold forces into a sliding pile from which it derives its name. Soil has formed, over the eons—filling the spaces between the broken surface rock, rounding the slopes, stopping the sliding, and providing a nourishing foothold for trees, shrubs, tall grasses and wildflowers. For the most part, in a few places, the sliding rock still lies exposed, from great slabs and chunks to small fragments and particles.

Somewhere at the heart of the mass must lie a vein of gold that surfaced and drifted in the form of flakes and nuggets into the headwaters of several creeks rising from subterranean snow-fed sources near the peak. Under the top in the headwaters of Brewster, Harvey, and Edleman Creeks are the Argo, Hidden Treasure, Jumbo, Edleman, and many other mines, opened and briefly worked by early-day prospectors. Soon abandoned because amongst all the topsy-turvy sliding rock, the mother lode was never found.

By any possible route, the way to the top of Sliderock was a long, steep, exhausting, and seemingly endless climb. It was enough to make a mule stop and blow, groan and grunt, let alone a man. Though not the most direct, the least difficult course was a narrow, winding, switchbacking foot and horse trail located by somebody in the early-day Forest Service who was in a hurry to get there and with no regard to those who followed after. As Forest Service trails went in those days, this was not at all unusual.

Throwing loose rocks out of the trail, as they frequently showed up, was a constant clearing chore for anyone trailing up or down. As to impediments like rolling boulders or wind thrown trees, that could not be removed without help of costly dynamite or a half day's work with axe or crosscut saw, it was up to the frustrated traveler to find a way or make it over or around. By this means, many sections of trails became entirely relocated and sometimes remarkably improved at no cost. Others, unhappily, became almost complete blocked.

The Forest Service trail to Sliderock started at Grizzly Station and, after an optimistically estimated "seven and a half or eight miles," reached the top.

Reopening and manning a lookout point at the start of each fire season after a Montana winter and closing it against said winter at the end of said season was something of an operation itself. Opening dates varied depending on the weather. If spring turned hot and dry, some primary points might be manned as early as June 15 and if the dry weather continued late into fall, the lookout might not be pulled down till after mid-September. Usually the season ran from about late June to September 10 or 15.

With a relatively favorable wet, cool spring in 1928, the date for my launching was set for July 3, which provided time for me to help put up a cutting of wild hay from a part of the Rock Creek Station pasture. I was no stranger to this employment. In Montana, the hay was stacked in the field instead of the haymow of a barn as in Illinois. Blisters given off by the handle of a pitchfork are the same, one place or another.

Following the noon meal and kitchen cleanup on July 2, Barry and I loaded my two-month supply of assorted canned goods, ham, bacon and beans into the back of the truck, along with our personal packs, bedrolls, saddle, a couple more sacks of oats for the pack string and some other plunder. I was not only ready but eager to head for my new home on the hill after packing one more little package. While Barry was getting last minute words from Lou, I hurried into the warehouse and fetched the tiger-striped, month old, he-kitten.

When he saw me coming, cuddling the barely-weaned feline in my arms, Lou burbled some water out of his imaginary bottle and gave with a short, disgusted shake of his head. "Squirtah, all yoah askin' foah is trouble. If it wasn't good riddance, I wouldn't let you do it." "I know and I appreciate it." I grinned back at his scowl. "You got any last words or questions?" "No, sir. I'm just glad for the chance." "Sometime shortly, I'll be up that way and check you out. You be sure to always check in on the telephone morning and night, and don't take any wooden nickels."

Barry climbed in behind the wheel. Putting the kitten beside him, I went and turned the crank. After we got going up across the river bridge, I said: "Lou's the kind of guy that makes you want to go to hell and back for him, like my high school track coach." Barry smiled tightly, waited a minute and said: "He's one of the real old timers. But don't let him fool you. He can be tough as shoe leather."

With the road crew occupying the cabin at Grizzly and Harris bunking in the small warehouse, Barry and I located a place free of rocks by the creek and rolled out our bedrolls in the open. "Don't think it's gonna rain," Barry said. "But it'll be a little frosty in the morning." I had slept out on the ground under the apple and plum tree in Illinois, but never under a ponderosa pine and bright Montana stars.

Bucky Harris was waiting for us when we got there, ready to "manti up" the packs. At that time in District 1

of the Forest Service, sawbuck pack saddles and pan-
niers called "panyards" were largely out and "Decker"
saddles and "manties" were in. While the diamond hitch
was still occasionally employed where heavy or awkward top packs might be encountered, the sling hitch
with the Decker saddle was the basic hitch used for
fastening the load to the saddle. Rather than sacking
whatever was to be packed in twin leather or canvas
sacks to be hung on the prongs of a sawbuck pack
saddle, each side pack was wrapped with rope in a six-
foot square of heavy canvas, called a "manti." This
allowed for more versatility in the shape, the size and
balance of a load. Big, strong mules were the rule,
capable of carrying big, heavy loads sometimes up to as
much as 400 pounds.

Forest Service packers generally were experienced
professionals, expert in packaging as well as tying on
the loads so they would ride most easily over rough
mountain terrain and through the timber without
slipping one side to the other or coming undone. Tough,
taciturn, highly independent, and not about to take any
sass from anybody, the professional Forest Service
packers performed an indispensable yeoman service.
Sadly, with the advent of roads and air transport, like
the grizzly bear, they have almost vanished from the
present day scene. Much that I learned from them, I
could never have learned from books or any other
source.

"Bucky," Barry said, "I think we've got about three
light mule loads to go up. I tried to box and balance 'em
out ready to manti, but see what you think." Bucky
tentatively lifted a few of the boxes with an "Um" here
and "Um" there, rearranged several loose items, and
started setting a pack on a spread manti ready to pack.
I was all eyes and closely watching every fold of the
canvas, loop of the rope, and knot. Bucky moved too fast
and dexterously for me to take it all in, but I got most
and decided against asking any questions right then.
Not greatly different, I thought, from tearing a piece of

wrapping paper off the roll at the meat market and using it to package a piece of meat for a customer with string. Later, when Barry and Bucky went over to the corral, I got a couple of empty boxes, a manti, and a manti rope, and tried it. It was not all that simple.

After abortively wrapping and tying my pseudo pack several times and finally managing to come up with a fair likeness of the six samples stacked on the dock, I went over to the corral and looked between the heavy poles of the six foot enclosure to see what activity was going on in these parts. I counted six mules and two saddle horses.

One of the horses turned out to be Barry's mount, and he was hitched to the snubbing post in the center of the circle. Bucky was bent over the lifted bottom of the horse's right hind hoof using a rasp with Barry standing by holding a new shoe. I climbed up and sat on the top pole to watch. When the shoe was fitted and nailed in place, Bucky lifted and looked at the horse's other three feet, patted him on the rump and turned him loose. Then he rolled and lighted a Bull Durham cigarette. "You ever try to work that wall-eyed mule, you want to watch. He's a ringy sonofagun." Barry went over to take a closer look at the indicated animal and the mule shied and went racing to the other side of the corral. "His back don't look too good, either." "Whoever bought him got took. We got took when they sent 'im out here as a replacement. Somebody outa shoot him before they get hurt." "Yeah, and if somebody did they'd spend a year on paper work explainin' why. If he's that dangerous, don't try to use 'im." "Umm."

It was approaching quitting time, so I washed my hands in the creek and went to see if anything might be done to help the cook. The beautiful long cabin with the magnificent stone fireplace at one end, the kitchen at the other, the table and benches in between, and a steel folding cot, with blanketed bed neatly made along one side, smelled heavenly.

The chef in black hat and ripped-out flour sack apron,

was busy with something in the oven. "Gosh, Rusky, what smells so good?" The silent, stone-faced Russian looked around and almost beamed. He held up a beautifully browned double crust pie. "Raisin. You like raisin?" I went over to get a closer look and whiff and saw not only one, but two pies, one done and one ready to go in the oven. "Um humm. My favorite pie. What can I do to help?"

It was the first time I learned that he could speak, much less use the English language. It was a strange linguistic mixture of his native Russian, but by putting two and two together, you could fathom the gist of it. The thing was that he could understand more than he could speak and if you didn't know this, you could be in trouble. Rusky was plenty big, tough, proud, and sensitive to any aspersions cast on his character. He was a refugee of the Czar's military, ready, willing, and able to put a hand to most anything, but not one to cross.

When I asked if I might help, he somberly glanced at the wood box. It was almost empty. "Okay. I'll fill the box." After doing that, I filled his two water buckets out of a watercress spring back of the cabin and set the coverless, wood plank table. Amenities like tablecloths and napkins in those days in the Forest Service were considered frivolous. If you needed to wipe your hands, you wiped them on your pants.

When Em Hauswirth and his crew of Alphonse and Julius arrived about 5:30, I was filling the Coleman lantern that hung from a loft beam on a length of No. 9 telephone wire over the table. Outside of big one by six camp candles set in saucers next to bunks, it was the only type of illumination.

"Golly," said Em alighting from the mud-splattered Model T road crew pickup. "We've got us some new camp help. How's my fishin' pardner?" "Hi, Em." I grinned warmly. "You want to go catch a few before supper? I'm ready." "Let's wait till after supper." Julius came over and slapped me on the back, almost making me miss the funnel and spill the gasoline. "I hear you go up," he pointed tentatively in the direction of Sliderock lookout, much as to say, "congratulations, now you are really one of us." Alphonse, his portly French Canuck buddy, confidentially said, "we hear you take up kitty. Smart. He be good for company." Then demonstrating with an upward and back and forth movement of a grease and dirt-marked fist, he said, "You take by tail, swing like this, by gar, make happy and no leave." "How did you know all this?" "Ha. Ha. She's no secret on nobody—nobody!" The two of them went off to wash in water especially heated for the occasion on the back of Rusky's range, chuckling with glee.

Heating water for the crew to wash with after a hard day's work was a courtesy indulged in by a few considerate camp cooks. Usually if you wanted hot water, you heated it yourself and if on his stove, only with the cook's permission. With a cook, the kitchen and his stove were sacred. Any intrusion without permission, and he might take your heating water and pitch it out, container and all. By the same thoughtful token, Rusky had warmed a pan of condensed milk for me to feed my infant, four-legged summer company, now confined near my bed by the creek in an empty egg crate.

At supper that night, Em wanted to know if I had taken my fly outfit along to the lookout. "Where would I catch any fish on top of a mountain?" I had stashed my outfit at the Station. "You ninny! You never want to go *anywhere* without your fishing outfit. You got to come down a mile or more to a spring at the head of Harvey Creek to get your drinking water. Just a little way down the creek, half a mile, more or less—there's some pretty good water with some natives. Not very big but mighty good for a change of diet when all you've got to eat is ham, bacon, and canned beef. After supper, we'll rig you up with a length of line and leader and a few flies to carry in your hat band. You can cut yourself a willow stick for a pole and you'll be in business."

"Em," said Barry, "don't go puttin' ideas in his head. He's up there to keep his eyes out for fire—not fishin'."

Ed laughed disparagingly. "He can get up early, can't he? Besides that, it's startin' out to be a wet season. He can't see nothin' when it's rainin' or he's all fogged in. What better'n to go catch himself a mess of fresh fish? Saves the government on his grub an' keeps him from gettin' scurvy."

I was all ears. Bucky agreed with Em that it looked like a light fire season. So did Julius who said he'd been around for over twenty-five years and had that feeling. Even Barry admitted it was certainly starting out that way, but late July and August and early September could be something else. Then about the time for raisin pie, he brought up another subject.

This might be a good time for a little game of "put and take." It wasn't often on the Rock Creek District that we got five people who could play poker together all at once and we ought to celebrate. If nobody had any pennies, we could play for matches. Barry was as hooked on cards as I was on Rusky's raisin pie. Em said it was fine with him as long as we had lights out by nine o'clock.

So Barry broke out a practically new deck he had "just happened" to bring along, lighted the lantern, spread a well-used khaki-colored, war surplus blanket on the table and divided a box of kitchen matches into five equal piles. Rusky didn't savvy American games of chance so was counted out. Julius and Alphonse helped clean up the pots and pans. Bucky went out to see something or other with his livestock, while Em and I put together my make-do fish line.

Shortly, everyone reconvened at the table and the dealer started to deal. His favorite game was seven-card stud and that is what he dealt.

It was one of those games for me, like every card player gets into at one time or another, where every card wanted or needed falls exactly in place at exactly the right time. I simply could not lose. My pile of matches grew and grew in embarrassing proportion. It was a penny ante, ten cent limit, limit three raises, kind of game, or the outcome might have been even more awkward. As I gathered in the loot, Julius suspiciously eyed me like a thief; Alphonse thought it was hilarious; Bucky, Em and Barry swore mighty oaths and changed the game from one sort to another every time it came their deal. My phenomenal luck changed not one iota. I was called everything from a shyster card shark to a downright crook. It was a game long remembered by all participants.

"Goldarnit Hessel," said Barry as we groped our way to our hard, open-air bedrolls, "it's not possible to be that lucky."

"Yeah," I chuckled, "it's possible, but I don't believe it, either."

Next morning after breakfast at 6:30, Barry told me to head on up the trail and he and Bucky would catch up with me "somewhere up the line" with the pack train. Packers, rangers, and sometimes, if an extra saddle horse happened to be available, the bull smoke went horseback. As much by personal preference as by necessity, all other peons like lookouts traveled afoot. Being free of worry about feeding, shoeing, catching, and sometimes losing a mount, hiking had its good points.

About 7:15 a.m., with my he-kitten against my belly in the loosened front of my wool shirt, I lit out upward to Sliderock. In the early morning chill, both the heavy shirt and the warmth of my furred burden, were welcome. In top physical condition, sucking in great drafts of the sweet bracing air, I set a pace calculated to get me there as fast or faster than anyone had ever covered the distance before. It became a race against the mountain. It did not take me long to recognize the mountain for a rough and tough opponent. Hardly even well underway, sweat began to form under my hatband, trickled down the bridge of my nose, down my cheeks, and off my chin. Though sweet, the air seemed to be of little substance and in remarkably short supply. The exciting race turned into a grind like the last fifty years of a quarter mile dash, and virtually before it was well underway, brought me to a grinding gasping halt.

Easing down on an inviting rock for a second wind, I looked up the steep unremitting trail climbing the timbered sidehill for as far as I could see ahead of me, and gained a new respect. Obviously, this race called for a new and different strategy. Absently stroking the fuzzy, tiny head poked questioningly out between a couple of buttons on my shirt, I quickly recuperated, rose from my resting place, and started anew at a somewhat slower pace calculated to feel the mountain out. There was no more reckless do or die mad attack for me. Mountain climbing, I decided, demanded more downright determination than enthusiasm and desire. It was the right decision.

As I progressed upward, I was able to stretch the distance between rest spots farther and farther. Continuous challenge, I came to recognize, was the name of the game. Consciously coordinating every step, sweating out of every pore, lungs straining, and so thirsty I was spitting cotton, I loved every minute. This man against mountain was a kind of competition, the likes of which I had never dreamed. Rather than ribbons and medals, the rewards were wondrous: ever changing and mysteriously refreshing new vistas of wild unpopulated, richly forested mountain terrain at every ascending level. Anticipation of sighting the whole vast panorama spread out in all directions below on attaining the top seemed in itself a source of continuously renewed strength and determination for pressing ahead.

With no mile post markers, the first-time traveler had no idea how far he had progressed nor how far what might lie ahead. With a timepiece like a watch, distance might have been estimated by length of time on the march, but I had no watch. After what seemed like half the morning had passed, I finally heard somewhere below me what I had been listening for—the faint sound of steel shod hoofs striking rocks in the trail. With a switch back across a grass covered opening ahead of me, I pushed up to where the timber set in again and I could look back and watch the riders and pack string come up across the open sidehill.

Since sounds do not travel far before being absorbed by the intense, prevailing quiet of the great outdoors, I did not have long to wait. First emerging from the lower timber, came Bucky slouched easily in the saddle on his big bay saddlehorse, reins held in right gloved hand and the lead rope of the first loaded pack mule in the other. Lead ropes of the second and third mules were tied to the saddles of those ahead. Barry came bringing up the rear.

Pulling up abreast of where I stood to one side of a slight leveling of the incline, Bucky's horse, wet with sweat, stopped with urging as did the mules behind. Resting forward on his saddlehorn, Bucky allowed himself the faintest flicker of a smile. "How's it goin?" "No complaints," I answered, thickly grinning through caked lips. Reaching back on his saddle, Bucky produced a canteen. "Want a swig a water?" "Thanks." I could have drunk the canteen dry, but I knew better than to do that. I drank a little, rinsed out my mouth, poured a little in my hat for my cat and passed the canteen back. "'Nother mile or so you'll hit the head of Harvey Creek. I'll fill a five gallon sack at the spring and pack it up to the top for you." Packing water in a "sack," much less five gallons at a time, was a new one on me, but it sounded like he was doing me some kind of favor, so I let it go at that. "Okay. Much obliged." With a touch of spurs to his horse and a jerk of the lead rope on the first mule, Bucky moved out.

Barry on his mount moved up. "Hey, Lucky, you been comin' up this mountain like a cat shot in the rear with tacks. Thought we'd catch up with you way back there somewhere." "The way your horses and mules are sweating, you haven't been losing any time yourselves." Barry leaned forward and patted the sweat-slick neck of his horse. "Stock have been taking it easy all winter. Just eating. They're not in condition yet." "About how far have I come? How far to the top?" "Aw, I'd say, we're a little over halfway. Keep going like you have been, you'll be there in plenty of time for lunch. You want me to pack that darn cat? I can put him in one of those saddle bags." I looked down at the small head of the kitten poked up, looking out of my shirt front. "Naw, he's no trouble. He's riding all right. We'll get there." "Okay. See you up there." As Barry tapped his heaving belly with the spurs, his horse grunted and lurched forward up the trail.

From there to where I finally came to what Bucky had called the head of Harvey Creek, seemed more like two miles than only one to me. The crystal clear, fast flowing stream where it crossed the trail was shallow but wider than I expected—too wide to step or jump across. Taking the kitten out of my shirt and placing him close to the water where he might drink, I sprawled flat out on my belly and plunged my own perspiring face into the icy stream.

The creek bottom below the trail had been cleared of timber. Remnants of the long ago, short time gold rush were everywhere evident. The weathered grey remains of small, dirt-floored log cabins, with doors and windows gone and roofs caved in by the weight of snow over many winters, were loosely scattered along the watercourse on both sides. Mossy, rotting sluice boxes and overturned gravel from the stream bottom cluttered the channel. Rubble dumps of tunnels, hand punched into the sidehills of every little tributary dry gulch, were mute evidence of the exhausting, fruitless search for the mother lode.

Along the trail across the creek on a narrow bench above the stream, I came to an incongruously well-built and large cabin of squared, hand-hewed logs. Panes in the narrow casement window extending almost the entire considerable length of the structure were still unbroken; the sturdy plank door still hung on both hinges and the unlocked latch was still easily operable. Investigating further, I found the spacious one room interior tightly floored with untreated planks. The heavy shake shingle roof neither sagged nor leaked. A small wood burning cook stove occupied space at the far end of the large room and the stove pipe was still in place. Next to the stove was a short, hand made board bench— the only furnishing.

A short distance from the front door of this mysterious structure appeared an open plank-boxed-in catchment of spring water. This, I rightly assumed, must be the water supply for whomever might once have occupied the cabin, as well as who might presently man the peak. Up from the spring, the trail re-entered the thick stand of a black-barked, pole-sized stand of lodge pole pine. Rightly assuming this, I wrongly assumed the end of the trail could not be far. A single charge up the mountain, I thought, should get me there with some to spare.

Eagerly and best foot forward, following the horse tracks, I set forth only to have Charge One come to an ever slower, increasingly lead-footed, weak-kneed, gasping, final halt, with the top nowhere in sight. The only things in sight, in fact, were the mocking horse tracks in the ever onward and upward trail and the silent secretive lodgepole. Sinking down on a windthrown log beside the trail, removing my hat, and wiping sweat from my eyes, I recovered strength and gained a renewed and even greater respect for my mountain and a new concept of the limit of conditioned human endurance set against steep terrain at high elevations as compared to flat midwest levels. It cut a human down to size—the size of an ant. Not only was I seeing the mountain, but feeling it, and the feeling, like the sight, was awesome. It was like my first close sight of the wild rushing water of the Clark Fork off the Higgins Avenue bridge in Missoula. It was the feel of a whole new dimension: strange, fascinating, exhilarating, ultimately challenging. I was sensing infinity and eternity.

"Cat," I said wonderingly and somewhat uncertainly to the little four-legged life in my lap, "back in your pouch. Here we go again." Only this time I did not add, as I had on leaving the spring house, "all the way to the top," which I shortly reconfirmed was rightly less-boastful thinking regarding the puny ability of a mere human opposed to natural physical obstacles erected by the Great Spirit in the path of progress.

Despite renewed resolve, Charge Two got me no farther than a beautiful peculiarly lonesome and unoccupied peeled log cabin surrounded by a peeled two-pole fence still in the timber and still not within sight of the top. Obviously of far more recent vintage than the spring house, this fine habitation was double-locked and posted with an official black on yellow metal Forest Service warning sign against trespass or vandalism. It represented even more unanswered questions than the lower-down edifice. There was no spring or visible water supply, nothing but a likewise superbly constructed peeled log, very inviting, two-hole outhouse at the outer edge of the fenced compound. The original trail past this puzzling dwelling was blocked by a fallen tree diverting present travel in a large half circle around the top. I personally shortcut the circle by way of the old trail straight over the toppled trunk, conserving both time and energy.

Shortly after leaving this landmark on my third "go," I abruptly emerged from the timber and there before me across a large open area of grass and broken boulders was revealed the blessed top. It was crowned by a tower somewhat resembling a squared and roofed small midwest-town water tank.

Perched on four substantial forty-foot peeled log legs was a ten foot by ten foot shingle-roofed aerie faced on all sides by winter shutter covered large multiple paned casement windows from roof down to about three feet from the floor. Wide roof eaves, shading the windows, extended approximately half way out over a three foot, pole-railed catwalk all around the elevated lookout roost.

What ingenious methods had been employed and what
problems encountered in getting all necessary materials
horsed into that wild remote location and getting the
structure erected could well be imagined. The big, long
log legs certainly had to be horse skidded long distances
up the steep slope of the mountain. Shorter timbers for
cross bracing, lumber for flooring, siding and the roof,
glass for the windows, cement for setting the legs and
anchors for guy-wires, nuts, bolts, nails and what-have-
you—all somehow were packed in on the backs of horses
or mules. That tower and many another like it were a
monument to the men who built it. Just thinking about
how they got those awkward monster legs set on end
and a platform and cabin put on top was enough to
make me suck in my gut, especially when I was up there
walking around outside on the catwalk and looked down
the forty feet to the jagged rock.

Access from ground to tower was via—not stairs—but
a crude forty foot ladder fashioned from peeled lodge-
poles and spiked to the supporting timbers. The way to
the door of the cabin on top was through an oblong hole
in the platform catwalk, ever inviting a fatal misstep or
stumble. The builders obviously ran out of lumber or
encountered a last minute shortage of some kind for a
protective trap door that should have been but never
was.

Another hazard demanding constant attention was the
fastening of horizontal ladder rungs to the vertical
arms. Spikes holding the rungs had a frightening way of
working loose. What happened on grabbing a loosened
rung at any height up the ladder, but especially near the
top, was Katy-bar-the-door.

One fellow climber of these primitive means of lower
ascension that I heard of got a handful of rung that
came loose at about the twenty-five foot level, fell
backwards and over tea kettle, hit a telephone line that
luckily held and flipped him feet down at about the ten
foot level and managed to break nothing but both legs.
After the second time he missed calling in, a smoke

chaser and packer made fast tracks up to his peak, sounded the alert, gathered him up on a makeshift stretcher on top of a mule and brought him out to the waiting sawbones. The legs were repaired and he lived to tell about not only what happened, but why he had failed (for lack of a new straight spike) to respike the rung long since. This was considered a mighty poor excuse. There was telephone and haywire to tie the rungs lying around all over the place.

Heavily insulated against expectable and actual lightning strikes or near strikes, the cabin atop the tower was nevertheless warned of as probably the most hazardous place on the mountain when the commonplace spine-chilling and petrifying electrical spectaculars were passing by. The recommended haven when heavens were splitting with fire and hell roaring thunder was something else.

Twenty or thirty feet removed from the base of the tower was placed a small, maybe eight by ten feet, weathered log cabin—a dead ringer architecturally for those broken-down prospector bedrooms scattered around the hillside at the head of Harvey Creek down near the spring house. Apparently of about the same vintage and put together by the same breed of cat, this cabin forced a six foot man to stoop or have his hat knocked off and scalp peeled on entering. The door itself was made of two by six inch rough lumber well-hung with new steel hinges. The low ridge roof had been fairly recently reshingled and was leak-proof and tight. Spaces between the logs had been rechinked so the commonplace tornado force zephyrs were turned away.

Past the door, the one-room interior was found to be floored with well-worn rough boards with enough space between to allow for sweeping any accumulated dust or dirt between the cracks.

On the lee side from the wind, was an unscreened sliding wood casement window, two by six feet, through which the swarms of native and visiting flies and yellow jackets freely circulated during the summer months when it was open. Under this window was a small one-legged table, the side opposite the leg being nailed to the wall. In the left rear, where the cook had the least possible light to make out what he was doing, was a dwarf size wood-burning cook stove with an ever more dwarf size oven. Along the interior log walls on both sides of the stove were a few rough board shelves where the occupant might store his provisions. Across the corner at the rear of the stove was stretched a length of telephone wire on which to hand the wash rag, dish towel, wet socks or whatever else might need drying out. In every handy place were nails and spikes for holding ready to the hand a cast iron skillet, pot, hat, coat, towel, or again, what-have-you.

Just to the right of the door on entering, were two of the most prominent and most used spikes spaced exactly the right distance apart and at exactly the right height for hanging an elongated canvas five gallon backpack water sack by the two shoulder straps.

Again, at just the right height under these two spikes was a double wide shelf on which was placed a tin wash pan and bar of soap. When the sack was in place and had water in it, whoever might be entitled or given permission to use the plumbing accommodations had but to push the button of the spigot at the bottom of the sack and thereby let a minimum of the precious liquid dribble into the pan. For hot water, all that was needed was to step outside the door for some kindling and a few pieces of split lodge pole, build a fire in the stove and wait fifteen minutes, finger-testing for the desired degree of "hot" as you watched time idle by and warded off bedeviling insects. Very handy and very simple.

As well as being far lesser of a target for bolts out of the blue than the cabin on the tower, this snug hole above ground was especially well-guarded by grounded metal pipes rising fore and aft of the structure and connected by a third pipe just clearing the low ridge of the roof. During electrical storms, I was told and retold that this rough retreat was the one and only safe place on the mountain to take cover.

The cabin on the tower was big enough to accommodate a steel cot in addition to a handmade chair and the centered mapboard, but it was unsafe in storms. With the stove, table, groceries and all in the cabin on the ground level, there was no place for a cot. The summer inhabitant of Sliderock was short of a place to sleep, so the answer to this small detail was an old nine by twelve wall tent set between the four legs directly under the cabin of the tower. It was in process of erection by the packer and bull smoke at the moment I topped-out and delivered the kitten from my shirt front for the last time on the premises of his and my exotic summer home.

As I stood wiping the dripping perspiration from my face and forehead, the tent builders paused in their wrestling with the canvas and poles. "Had you noticed we got company?" Barry asked Bucky. Turning in mock surprise and looking at me, Bucky exclaimed, "I'll be!" "You horsebackers go ahead and talk." "If that's the way he feels about it, we ought to let him put up his own rag house." "The least he could do would be to build a fire in his stove and heat up a pot of coffee for lunch while we do his work." "Okay, you guys," I grinned. "I can take a hint. Be my guests."

Over next to the open door of the lightning refuge and cook house were piled all my summer rations, bedroll, and packsack. Right next to this was a pile of the neatly folded mantis in which it had been delivered, topped by neatly coiled ropes. Not far removed, the two saddle horses with saddles removed and three mules with saddle clinches loosened stood tied to a hitching rack, drooping heads, heaving sighs, acting like they had traveled the last possible mile.

Entering the cabin and flashing a look at the interior furnishings (which was all the time needed to absorb them in detail), I noted the full water-beaded five gallon water sack hanging on the two spikes over the tin wash pan. The wood box was surprisingly full with shaved kindling placed ready on top of the stove. Opening the closed draft on the stove pipe as well as the one below the fire box, I placed kindling and wood inside, applied the flame of a kitchen match, and shortly had the abbreviated cabin interior filled with a smothering smoke.

Hastily exiting with smoke through the open door, I heard Barry hollering at me and vaguely saw Bucky doubled up over for something very funny. "You dumbhead. Get up on the roof and get that coffee can off the stove pipe." How was I to know an empty coffee can had been inverted over the stove pipe to keep out the winter snow? It was one way to find out, and I never made the mistake of starting a fire in any stove again without looking first for a covering over the smoke outlet. Learning for the uninitiated as I had already well learned can come hard. This was one more little item to add to my list of those with which I needed to even the score with Barry.

Bless that English-language-less old dog, Rusky! Along with homemade bread and fried ham sandwiches, he had sent along three big pieces of his delicious home-made raisin pie for that memorable day's noon repast. As we all sat eating the pie and Bucky and Barry were drinking their coffee and I my precious water, various items of considerable interest to me came to be gradually unfolded.

The spring house from which I had to backpack water all summer had once been a rip-snorting trading post and saloon, and was "*only* maybe" a mile and a quarter down the hill. The fine cabin "just under the top in the timber" had been built to domicile the Sliderock summer incumbent for a few years, until it was discovered said incumbent was spending all his time reading racy magazines in his comfortable headquarters under the hill instead of keeping an eye out for fire in the tower. Now it served as a glaring object example of what not to do if you expected a lookout to keep an eye on his work.

The garbage pit that had been excavated with the help of a couple sticks of dynamite was almost full, but would probably last out one more season. It was supposed to be fly-tight, but far from it. The privy hole, likewise blasted out of solid rock, should make it for at least two more seasons. The one-holer, itself, had the door blown over the hill in a last summer's storm, but, what-the-heck, all the door on an outhouse did was to get in the way of the pretty view, anyway. While he was occupied in the outhouse, the lookout could carry on with his fire detection detail, lucky to have a smooth seat, a practically unused catalogue for paper, three walls and a roof. As a result of the same last year's storm, the whole rickety little log building leaned a mite in the direction of the prevailing wind, but not enough to throw the user off balance. One day, maybe, when I had nothing else to do, I could go down over the hill a mile or more, find the lost door, haul it back and put it up so it would blow off in the next storm. I just couldn't get lost and have to have Barry come looking for me in the process.

After lunch, Barry and I would get the shutters off the windows on the tower cabin while Bucky took off back down the hill with his mules. We would put some new batteries in the telephone and if it was grounded out somewhere by a windthrow and didn't work, Barry would follow the line instead of the trail back to Grizzly and try to cut it out. If he couldn't clear it on the way down, he would go on down and finish clearing it tomorrow. All this was hashed out over lunch.

The first time I climbed the ladder to the tower and looked down from the catwalk around the cabin to the rocks below, the down distance looked more like a long hundred than a short forty feet to me. When I could lift my eyes from the distance down to look at the far horizons across the reaching miles and miles of rising green ridges, rocky mounds and pointed peaks, sheer distance became more breathtakingly awesome than I had ever imagined it might be. Momentary dread of falling instantaneously shifted to an overwhelming desire to spread my arms and fly. "Gosh a mighty," I whispered, already talking to myself. "What a view!"

"Don't just stand there gawking at the scenery," said Barry. "Get the shutters pried off so I'll have some daylight left to get down the hill."

Removing the cumbersome four by six foot heavy board shutters and lowering them with ropes over the catwalk railing to the ground was no mean feat. "Packing water and washing all the panes in these windows inside and out should keep you busy for at least a week," Barry commented. "How many panes are there?" "I wouldn't know, but you'll know well enough by the time you wash 'em."

Centered inside the cabin stood a peeled log upright about four and a half feet tall and a foot in diameter: supporting a one inch by two foot square board on which was glued a map of the surrounding area. On the post under the mapboard was mounted a wall-type, hand-crank telephone. While handy to reading the map, anyone speaking in the horn (mouthpiece) of this thing was forced into a squatting position. Since the walls of the cabin were all windows, there was no other place to put it.

After replacing the two pint-size dry cell batteries, Barry said, "Cross your fingers while we find out if this thing managed to winter through." Turning the crank in what passed for one long ring, he lifted the receiver, squatted and waited. One long ring was the Rock Creek Ranger Station signal. Holding a hand over the mouthpiece, he grinned and winked. "We're through to Grizzly or one of the ranch hookups along the creek. Somebody just snuck a receiver off the hook." Then suddenly taking his hand off the mouthpiece: "Hello, Lou? This is Sliderock. Can you hear me? Well, somebody else is on the line. Gosh darn it, whoever it is, hang up! We're tryin' to check out this line and you're draggin' down the power. There, I heard 'em hang up, Lou. Is that better? Yeah. You're comin' in pretty weak here, too. Okay, yeah. I'll check it out all the way to Grizzly. Can't be too much—maybe only one tree. Yeah, I've got an axe with me. What do you think? Oh, he's fine—standin' right here right next to me. The place came through in good shape. Outhouse door's gone but we lost that last summer. No broken windows. Bucky's already gone down the hill. Will do. Before I leave, he'll know the map from A to lizard. Only the two big drifts left just below the cook shack. Okay. I'll tell him. I'll be in sometime tomorrow afternoon or evening. If not, I'll call in from Grizzly. Yeah, it's passable. A couple of logs to cut out and some rocks to pick, but no real trouble—never busted a egg. Okay. See you tomorrow."

Barry put the receiver back on the hook and stood up from his squat. "Lou wants you to call in again at six o'clock tonight and tomorrow morning at ten. You do that from here on. That's important. You don't call in and we figure something's happened and we have to come looking. You understand?"

"What if that Big Ben alarm clock stops or runs down or something?"

"You call in, anyway. Twice a day. Morning and evening. Far as the clock goes, you'll get to know what time it is clock or no clock. We want you here in the tower from about ten to four especially. Any smoke'll start showing up about ten. There's a couple of smokes that'll always show up and for Christ sake, *don't* report them. You see that smoke over there? And that other one off to the left? Those are sawmills. One of the most important things after a storm is making sure you're spotting smoke and *not* fog. Patches of fog, after a storm, can fool the hell out of you. If it's fog and not smoke and we send a man with a pack ten or fifteen miles across country and he gets there and no smoke, he's pretty darn mad with good reason. And we've lost a day's time when there might be fire somewhere else. How far do you make out that right hand sawmill smoke to be?"

"As the crow flies, maybe five miles," I answered.

"Let's look on the map and see. This pin right here in the middle of the mapboard is right where we're standing. This circle covers most of the country we can see. You know how to read a compass. The circle is just the same. Each one of these squares, you know, represents one section or one mile on a side. These wavy lines are contour lines 100 feet in elevation apart. The closer together they are, the steeper the slope. Now first, take a sight through the alidade and give me a reading on the smoke."

The alidade was a flat ruler-wide piece of steel about sixteen inches long with an upright piece of steel at both ends. One upright was fixed with a narrow slit to look through and the other with a horizontal horse hair center in an open aperture. With the length of steel against the pin, I swung it around to the direction of the distant smoke, looked through the slit and lined up the hair with the smoke. In order to see the reading on the circle, it was necessary to walk around the board to the slot end of the alidade. "The reading is North 32 East."

Without even checking, Barry said, obviously pleased, "You're right on the nose. Now how far is it and what quarter section is it in?" Counting the number of section lines from the pin to where it looked to me the smoke might be, ten in all, and purposely stretching it some, I came up with Section 31, Northeast 1/4, in Township 11 North, Range 16 West.

Giving me an exasperated look, Barry put his finger on the map at least five miles beyond my location. "For gosh sakes, you got to get your eyes stretched for the far look. That sawmill is located right here. Right down on the river close to the road and the railroad. Take another look at the topog lines where you put it. That country's steeper than a cow's face and no roads anywhere. Not even a fool logger'd locate a sawmill in country like that." Barry turned and pointed to a jagged peak on the skyline to the west. "As the crow flies, how far do you make it to that goat roost off there on the horizon?"

"Um. Thirty-five, maybe forty miles."

"That point's clean to the edge and gone off your map. Seventy-five miles if it's an inch."

Incredulously, I exclaimed, "It can't be!"

"Well, it is!"

Barry tore a sheet of paper out of his shirt-pocket-size, official Forest Service notebook. "Now here, I'll give you something to practice up on. Sawmill smoke on river—fifteen miles. Point on horizon seventy-five miles. That rocky hump over there, five miles." Indicating each as he went along, he extended my practice list to a dozen prominent topographic features in all directions from the tower. After this, he tested me on several other ridges, rises, and dips in the terrain and I did much better. The clear, thin air really had me fooled. I was beginning to understand that the lookout business was no Simple Simon look and guess game, as first appeared, after all. Quick and accurate detection and reporting of fire starts was basic to the whole fire suppression system. Barry made this doubly clear and impressed on me the responsibilities of the position to where I came to feeling like the kingpin in salvation of the whole north end of the Rock Creek District.

After all was said and done about my duties, I had one more question. A fraction of the section lines on the map were solid lines, but most of them were broken dashes. "Barry," I asked, "what's the difference?" "Oh heck," he answered, "I was hoping you wouldn't ask that. All the broken dashes mean unsurveyed country. The solid lines mean it's all legally tied together with established section corners from a certified known point. Otherwise, it's more or less by guess. The lines have been projected as best as can be both horizontal and topog, but it's just a good guess at best and variations could be aplenty. But it's better than nothing by a long shot. Plus the fact that in the surveyed a few elevation bench marks have been triangulated in and are established. There's one right over on that point and that's how we know Sliderock's right here. The first thing I did when we got in here was line up the alidade on that point and make sure the reading checked with what it should be. If somebody bumped this mapboard or the tower was blown out of line one way or other, it wouldn't check and the whole shebang would be cockeyed—at a distance maybe a mile or more. Here, I'll show you. This check here on the azimuth circle is the exact right reading. I should have told you to begin with; you need to check that every so often to make sure the map hasn't been bumped or jarred out of line. Slipped my mind. You understand what I'm talking about. I'm sure glad you reminded me."

"I think I get it. Anyway, I will after I study the map some more. I don't quite get 'triangulated in' and that survey business. What does a bench mark look like?"

"A bench mark's a round brass disk with oriented plus mark in the middle and the elevation at the point inscribed on it, about the size of an extra-large silver dollar, set in concrete on a boulder not apt to be moved except maybe by an earthquake. 'Triangulated in' means established with a transit from two other known points. You know how a triangle is formed from geometry? Aw heck, wait till you get to trigonometry and plane survey-ing next year in college. I can't explain it. A transit's about the same thing as a compass only a whole lot more accurate."

When we descended from the tower at about 2 p.m., Barry lost no time throwing the saddle back on his horse for the long, steep return down the telephone line back to Grizzly. "Well, Joe, " he said, removing his right glove and extending his hand. "till the snowballs start hitting you in the butt along in September, she's all yours. I'll be talking to you. Tap it light and you and the cat have fun." And mounting quickly and easily, he started and then once again pulled up his horse, and turning in the saddle, shouted back, "Be sure you get all those gro-ceries inside before dark. You could get a visitor—like a hungry bear. Not likely, but possible." Nodding agree-ment, I waved him down over the hill and watched till his hat disappeared into the timber.

Before doing anything with the groceries, I dug into my packsack for the Woodsman automatic and some shells. I loaded it, replaced it in the holster and hung it on a handy nail inside the cabin door next to the bag of water. Barry never carried a gun, nor did Lou. Bucky went armed with a .30-.30 Winchester carbine carried in a saddle scabbard. When he looked at my automatic, he referred to it disparagingly as a "pretty little pea-shooter" and told me to be careful and not unload it in the direction of anything like a bear. He said it would just sting him and make him mad.

As I was moving supplies indoors, I suddenly heard a startling shrill kind of bark or scream like I had never heard before. Repeated at intervals, the sound seemed centered in the area of the residual snowdrift and large slabs of sliderock just below the tower. Leaving off the orderly storing of canned goods on shelves, I eased over in that direction and shortly spotted the kitten flattened at the edge of the snow, with ears back and ready to pounce. At a very safe distance among the rocks in the direction he was pointed was a strange, smallish grey, awkward-looking dweller of the peaks above timberline variously known, I later found out from Barry, as the rock rabbit, the pika, the coney, and to the Indians as the "little chief." With front legs practically as long as his hind legs, little round ears, and no visible tail, this fellow resident of Sliderock, though a hare family member, resembled a rabbit very faintly. With one more piercing, fearful bark, he flashed back in his niche.

"Hey, Cat," I shouted, "quit bothering the neighbors." Looking up and seeing me, my kitten came bouncing across the talus and followed me back to the cabin where he lapped up another swig from his pan of condensed milk. As he grew larger, cannier, and quicker, Cat spent hours on end lying in wait and making futile attempts to corner the rock rabbit. His creeping and pouncing among the rocks after rabbits was a comical and entertaining performance. To my knowledge, all summer long, he managed to catch and devour only one. Fortunately, he was much better on the thieving packrats that seemingly occupied the cook-shack—top, bottom, sides and near premises—in hordes.

On arrival, this universal bane of all isolated habita-
tions in the Rockies, came in sizes almost as big as Cat
himself. Happily the rat population, though never completely exhausted, diminished, almost in direct proportion to the rate at which Cat grew, and supplemental
rations of evaporated milk became less and less necessary, until Cat drank it only for dessert.

Also, indigenous on the peak as summer progressed
were large numbers of a very large kind of grasshopper.
Surprisingly, after catching and tentatively sampling a
couple of these, Cat apparently found them a delicacy
beyond all, feasting on the unlimited supply throughout
their season. If you have never watched a cat catching
grasshoppers in an alpine patch of big blooming bear
grass, you really will never know how catty a cat can be.
Cat's gymnastics were amazing and his misses and near
misses hilarious.

The farther north you go, the longer the summer days
and the shorter the nights. Continuing to consort with
Morpheus after sunrise in a light-permeable "raghouse"
(as Barry referred to all tents) on an exposed peak is
near impossible. By the ten o'clock reporting in time, I
had a half day's hours and more behind me.

Since the hours from ten to five or six were necessarily confining and sedentary in the tower and since I
had conditioning for running cross-country and playing
soccer come fall much in mind, the "mile and a quarter,
more or less" of alternately plunging and switch-backing
trail between the tower and the springhouse became my
daily workout route. In addition to the five gallon
backpack water bag, which if filled to capacity weighed
forty pounds, my water-packing potential was amplified
by two-gallon handbags, the handles of which consisted
of a piece of quarter inch rope. If the bags were full and
carried for any distance, this hemp rope handle would
cut off circulation to the fingers. At intervals, the
carrier either put down the bag long enough to restore
the blood flow or else.

The hand packs, unlike the five gallon bag with its
push faucet at the bottom, were equipped with cork

stoppers at both sides of the top and could only be filled and emptied from that direction. Very awkward and tricky for pouring or drinking. In new condition, the cork stoppers were attached to the bag by a short length of string. When this flimsy connection broke at an early date, the corks had a way of becoming misplaced or lost entirely and when you were out of corks, you were simply out as there were no replacements short of the Rock Creek Station warehouse and doubtful even there.

Both the five gallon and two gallon bags could best be filled only by process of immersing the bag in the spring or creek. Invariably when filled, it was dripping wet, and one way or another to a certain extent, it leaked. The elongated five gallon bag with the faucet at the bottom had below the faucet a kind of leather fender theoretically to fend any leakage from bag or faucet down the back of the carrier's legs rather than down the back of the carrier. With my bag, the theory was a bust. Whenever I filled the bag with more than three gallons, I was wet from the waist down and arrived at the tower with no more than three gallons anyway. In case of the two-gallon bags, when carried, there was no way to keep them from constantly bumping against the outside of the knee other than holding them straight out from the body at arm's length. Although the spillage and leakage with these, providing you had all necessary corks, was somewhat less, the drainage was down the lower leg into the too-high top of my boots.

The trick in the water transport business, soon learned for more reasons than one, was to carry lesser quantities more often, which worked in with my early rising and athletic conditioning routine first rate. It also reduced the icy washing of my lower appendages to almost nil. By this means, on return from the spring, I arrived at the cookshack with practically the same amount of water in the bag that I started with, and was bathed more comfortably only with sweat from the waist up while remaining mostly dry from the waist down.

At first go, faced with the need for a staggering quantity of water for the window washing, I thought I would go whole hog and pack all nine gallons in all my bags all at once. Emptying what was left of my original supply into the battered tin dishpan, my one stew pan, the coffee pot, and the skillet, I blithely took off at what I considered an easy running pace with empty bags flopping in both hands and on my back down the hill.

With the steepness of the slope and all the braking required, rock dodging, slipping and sliding even in hobnailed boots, it required no more than the relatively short distance from the tower to the pretty unused headquarters under the hill to conclude that an easy pace was anything but that. Very surprisingly, descending a hill was as hard or harder on the human apparatus than the ascent. While the strain on the pulmonary system was much less, the cushioning components in the knee joints were soon quivering with fatigue.

This, I discovered, is why a rider progressing down any precipitously steep slope will be seen to considerately dismount and lead his horse. If the slope is long as well as uncommonly steep and with poor footing and he does not dismount, consider him reckless of injury to both horse and self—as well as cruel or ignorant. While a moderately fast-walking pace is possible over long cross-country distances in the mountains without unreasonable drain on the physical resources of either man or beast, pressing the pace to a run other than in dire emergencies is downright stupid, as any experienced mountain man knows.

I learned several other things, too, that first day. For one thing, a forty pound backpack up a steel trail for an average man in good condition is more or less easily possible, providing he is not additionally burdened with another sixteen pounds in each hand with a small rope handle cutting into his palm or fingers. For a lightweight, seventeen year old in top condition, seventy-two pounds so distributed proved just barely possible, even though he dripped and spilled about eight pounds of water and two pounds of sweat as he humped up the hill promising himself, "never again, never again" in time with his step as he went along.

Next morning after some washing of what seemed an endless number of panes in the casement window walls of the tower cabin, the five gallon pack went to the spring and the two handbags stayed home. One more day with the five gallon bag and the handbags went while it stayed home, and continued to stay home. With the window washing done, three gallons a day everyday, worked out to a more than ample supply for me, even including dishwashing, hand and face washing, cooking, drinking and you name it. What little laundering and bathing considered essential was performed in a washtub discovered under the old trading post and bar.

Building a fire under this capacious container, three-fourths filled with water, I brought the temperature from liquid ice to lukewarm, stripped, splashed, soaped and rinsed my hide. I then rebuilt the fire, reheated the water to hot, and laundered dish towel, handkerchief, and half my wardrobe. I packed fresh shorts, shirt, socks and Levis down and the still wet newly laundered outfit back once, more or less, every week or ten days, depending on how odiferous the exuded body oils became and how much of what I cooked and ate was spilled or wiped on shirt and pants. Twice during the summer, I accumulated enough surplus water to scrub the cook-cabin floor. "Cleanliness," mother continually ground into me, "is next to Godliness." As is eminently evident from the foregoing, I lived strictly by this code, even though dishtowels and handkerchiefs never appeared to launder out that way, exactly.

Yes indeed! Getting the necessary dishpan, vinegar and other paraphernalia, plus water, needed for window washing up the forty-foot ladder to the scene *is* tricky, but possible using the same long rope with which we let the shutters down. For drying and polishing, a ripped-out flour sack dishtowel works, not well, but makes do.

My collapsible steel cot, poorly cushioned by a thin cotton pad, and my several army surplus wool blankets, constituted my place of repose in my rag house under the tower. I opened a well-used egg crate found in the cook cabin on arrival, as a pseudo nightstand at the head of the bed. On the top of this make-do furniture, using a little melted wax, I fastened one of the four chubby white candles included with my supplies. On the shelf under the top, made by the crate divider, I placed one of my two large boxes of kitchen matches just on the off chance that sometime in the darkness of night for some unknown reason, I might need to strike a light. Alongside the matches, conveniently handy, also just in case I put the loaded, holstered "pea shooter."

This innocent and apparently ingenious bedroom arrangement, strangely led to one of the most paralyzing instances of fear I experienced over practically a lifetime in far wild reaches of the Rockies. Though inclined to caution and given to testing the temperature of the water before taking a plunge, I am not of a timid or apprehensive nature in any sense, except possibly to some extent with regard to snakes.

What happened in the dark of a moonless summer night there on Sliderock in 1928 might well have given Julius Caesar a start. A light sleeper, I was first awakened by a rasping sound as if something was converting wood to splinters within inches of my head in the vicinity of the egg crate. Quickly opening both eyes, unfortunately pointed in the opposite direction, catching my breath and not daring to make a move, I laid there and listened to the manufacture of sawdust.

Until I remembered that it was firmly anchored by a heavy log running the full length and back of the tent, I thought I'd make a break under the canvas away from the intruder, whatever horrendous monster it might turn out to be.

Finally, unable to hold my breath or lie quiet any longer, I did the next best thing and sat up suddenly, simultaneously letting go with a screaming, "E-e-e-e-

Yow-e-e, git!" It is not the known that is most fearsome, but what is not known and cannot be seen. With the loud expenditure of air, there came a dull thud like a collision of something relatively soft with something solid. In the little night light there was, filtering through the canvas, I was able to see my nightstand totter and fall. There went my candle, matches, pea shooter and all. I tried to make a quick exit through the open tent flap, but somehow I seemed glued to the bed.

The awful rasping sound had changed to a kind of rattling somewhere between that of a rattlesnake and breaking glass. At that elevation, I knew there were no rattlers or no snakes, period. With all the commotion next to where I sat in bed, the egg crate with the candle-topped end down next to the ground and the bottom end somewhat higher in the air began to move: first forward toward the tent flap, then sideways away from the bed, then back toward the foot of the bed picking up speed as it came, and bang! When the covered and obviously blinded critter caught under the overturned crate hit the bed, the dreaded rattling stopped and the ensuing quiet throbbed like pounding bass drums in my ears.

Without even thinking about donning boots to protect my bare feet from intervening sharp rocks, I leaped from the bed as far from the crate as I could jump and was through the tent flap and behind the closed door of the cook cabin in nothing flat. There in my shorts and undershirt in which I was wont to sleep, I collapsed in my one homemade chair, catching my breath and wondering what next. Should I just sit there till daylight relatively safe or light my cook-cabin-candle, mounted in an empty catsup bottle with melted wax coating the sides, take the axe, and attack without knowing the offensive abilities of whatever I might meet.

The night, like all nights on the peak, was chilly. I got up from the chair and put on my jacket which luckily was in the cabin and not the tent. I found a match and lit the catsup bottle candle. Both the comfort of the coat and the light helped restore my confidence. Opening the door with the candle held aloft, I peered through the still, starlit dark toward the tent. Almost immediately something four-legged flashed between my feet from outside to inside. Exploding a loud, "Wow," I shuddered, jumped outside, and almost dropped the flickering candle. Glancing back at the dim interior, I made out a smallish, long tailed image sitting on the table. "Gosh darn you, Cat. You're a great help."

Cautiously tip-toeing to the woodpile trying to avoid the rocks, I pulled the axe from the chopping block, stood there and thought the situation over a minute while Cat caught up with me and rubbed affectionately around my ankles. "Get away from my feet. Go on over there and see what's in that tent."

Axe gripped in one hand and candle in the other, I slowly, carefully and dubiously advanced myself in that direction. The tent, like the night, was ominously quiet— no sound of any kind of rattling. Approaching the open flap, I saw Cat abruptly shift from his carefree fait to a sudden halt; he became stiff-legged and hump-backed, tail up with hair on end and ears laid back. In this manner, he advanced forward a few tentative stiff-legged steps and suddenly jumped high and sideways spitting viciously, as he jumped. This action produced a brief resumption of the rattling just inside the tent flap. Cat did not back off. Taking a few more stiff-legged steps ahead spitting sporadically, he again jumped defensively high and sideways back in the other direction. What he could see or smell that I could not had me nonplussed. Nervously holding the axe at ready for a defensive swipe at whatever in a sweaty hand, I whispered, "Go get 'im, Cat." Cat turned his lowered head and looked at me, eyes glittering in the candle light, turned back and spat again, but made no further move. There was more rattling from inside.

Taking one more step ahead up even with Cat, I leaned and reached the candle forward almost inside the tent. Very vaguely, I could see the candle wax on the top end of the egg crate, with no candle, pointed in my direction and could make out that the bottom end was held up by something underneath. Whatever it was seemed to be trapped by the crate. Slightly more relaxed, I warily moved in to identify the catch.

"I will be darned." I breathed with relief. "A goldarn porcupine!" With the crate over his head, he could not see to go ahead and with raised quills he could not back out. The crate, I later learned had once been employed as an unlikely cargo container for packing rock salt with which a sheepherder using the high surrounding range, baited his flock to the bad ground. With an insatiable craving for salt surpassing even that of sheep, the porky had followed his nose to my night stand and to satisfy his appetite, was chewing it to shreds. With the door gone and open access provided to one and all, this also accounted for the chewed-up boards and floor holding up the seat in the Sliderock outhouse and the hole in the floor of the spring house trading post. *Now* I knew.

While the night's frightful mystery was harmlessly solved, my troubles were far from it. Under the crate along with the porcupine was the box of matches and much more importantly, my precious pistol, no doubt resting on the intruder's vicious quills. While I thought about this and Cat alternately advanced on the crate, spat, and jumped back, I retrieved and slipped into my boots. Poking gingerly and tentatively at the bottom of the crate got me nowhere except keeping clear of the dangerous swipes of the barbed tail. By pushing up on the opposite end, I might be able to turn the critter loose but what then? He might or might not steer for the tent opening. By sacrificing my flimsy but useful night stand, I might be able to dispose of him with the axe but that would bloody up the bedroom and probably bed and all. I went back to the cook-cabin and brought the broom. At a safer distance from the switching tail and with more leverage, I managed to push the crate and all toward the opened tent flaps. As I pushed and steered , first the box of matches and, Eureka! finally the gun, dropped clear of the quills.

Sweeping the gun clear, I grabbed it up, jacked a shell in the barrel, took aim at where the little head should be and fired with no noticeable effect on the moving tail. Back to the broom and steering and pushing out into the starlight, I moved the crate to a good safe distance from the tent. There happened to be couple of good heavy rocks to hold crate and all in place. I did not want this prowler either coming back or spreading the word that he had discovered a new salt source. Come daylight when I could see, one less porcupine would populate the mountain.

Presently, with chattering teeth, I was back between my scratchy but warm wool army surplus blankets, hopefully to be undisturbed for what little was left of porcupine night.

A couple of days later, July 10, to be exact, and as entered in the official daily diary it was part of my duty to keep, came a violent forerunner of an extended soggy change in the weather.

Keeping a diary was required of all responsible forest officers up to and including supervisors. Only non-responsible laborers did not have to keep a diary. If you happened to be a foreman of a three man trail crew, for instance, you kept a diary. If you were a crew employee under the foreman, you did not. While this daily account might have served some useful purpose such as a record of unusual occurrences, weather conditions, places and dates, for the most part from the keeper of the account's point of view, there was nothing worth reporting beyond the date, itself.

Generally it was considered an unnecessary pain in the neck. Frequently it was written backwards a week or more at a time, particularly on Saturdays when you remembered that you had better do so before falling into bed.

What might not appear in Forest Service diaries was generally far more interesting and important than what got in. Regarding the porcupine night, I did not make mention of the incident in my official diary at all. It was personal and unofficial all the way, a waste of time and paper to put in writing. I once knew a diary-keeping Forest Officer who woke up with a warmth-seeking rattlesnake resting on his chest. That didn't get into the official record anymore than the salt-seeking porky. Purely, obviously unofficial.

Not only was what went into Forest Service diaries peculiarly routine, boring and mostly inconsequential, the makeup of the container itself was peculiar. Known as Form 289, U.S. Department of Agriculture, Forest Service, Washington, Official Business, it was printed in black caps lengthwise, upper left on the semi-hard saddle tan top cover. In the book on the off chance it might be lost and found, was also a mailer. Also, horizontally across the top in especially large caps were the words, CHIEF, FOREST SERVICE, WASHING-TON, D.C., and to the lower right the admonition: "This book is Government property. The finder is requested to deliver it to any officer of the Forest Service, or deposit it in the nearest post office."

Oblong shaped, six and one-half by three and five-eighths inches in size, just right for fitting into a large work shirt button-down pocket, the binding was (take your choice) either at the three and five-eighths inches horizontal left side or the vertical three and five-eighths inches top. Lengthy sentence writers wrote horizontally left to right the six and one-half inches length of the thing. Brief notations were made vertically left to right the narrower width of the book. The sheets were perforated at the bound top (or left side) so the precious entries might be torn out, filed away, and hopefully forever forgotten. Most peculiar and confusing of all, the yellow paper sheets were ruled on one side of the paper with blue horizontal and vertical lines, dividing the page into one-fourth inch squares. For what earthly purpose nobody seemed to know, except to make the scrawled notations that much more difficult to read.

At any odds, lookouts were required to keep this diary and I kept it, never more than a couple of days behind time. As previously stated in addition to the date, entries in the diary, on the lookout at least, had to do with weather conditions which for the most part during the summer months could be and were summed up in these words: "Clear, hot, dry." Often one word was written: "Ditto." In case the writer was wont to tempt a crippling case of writer's cramp, he might enter in his log an item like: "Zephyr blew outhouse door off hinges. Last seen headed South 43 East," or "Good view of northern lights" or "Think lightning hit tower. Rattled stove in cook shack," or "Rained and hailed pitchforks and hoe handles. Darn tent leaked like sieve."

The State of Illinois and the midwest muster some fairly respectable thunder and lightning storms, but few can compare with the explosions and fireworks in the Rockies. The sky-piercing peaks and high forested ridges and valleys are truly the Almighty's bombing range and fire-power testing ground. When the massive, billowing white, bruise-blue, and grey-black ammunition carriers came rolling out of the west, obliterating the sun, and creating a tense breathless quiet before the big guns were turned loose, the Devil himself put in ear plugs and took cover in a deeper cave on the lower reaches of the River Styx. When the full fury of the onslaught struck, fire forked down in random, rapid fire, deadly flashes shattering and setting fire to great trees, splitting rocks, melting telephone lines and striking fear to the very marrow of mortal man's bones. Mysterious fluorescent fireballs floated and bounced around the peak. The constant electrifying claps and rumble of thunder, combined with the howling of hur-

ricane wings and driving, falling sheets of half hail, half
rain was deafening.

Most often there was far more lightning and thunder
than rain. Storms, when they occurred, came and went
in a series of varying intensity with the thunderheads
gathering about noon and fading in the early evening.
The compass bearing of strikes could be noted but fires
usually did not smoke up until the heat and rising wind
brought them to visible life at ten or eleven o'clock the
following morning. Sometimes they might smolder invisible for several days or even a week. Even though the
base of the fire might not be visible, lookouts with fire
fighting experience on the line, could at least approximate the type of fuel and speed of spread by the color,
volume, and drift of smoke. Always there was the
hazard of differentiating smoke from fog. In long hot
and dry periods in some areas, dust devils produced by
whirlwinds occasionally kicked up spiraling dust that
could also be deceptive. Reporting a smoke that was not
smoke, thereby causing suppression forces to be need-
lessly set in motion, was almost as bad as failure to
report the actual article on first appearance. This was
the difference between a dependable lookout and one
who might be suspect due to inexperience, a nervous,
hasty disposition, or other reasons.

Violent and vicious as they were to me, the storms
around the peak were more fascinating and strangely
stimulating than frightening. Curiosity and the challenge involved about midway through summer found me
throwing caution and dire warnings of fatal consequences to the wind. The day came when I watched
Thor's battle wagons gathering on the horizon, dark-
ening the scene and coming at Sliderock like a flame-
throwing steam roller. I thought, "What the heck. This
tower's been standing here and beating these things off
for ten years or more. It will be here for twenty more."

To bolster my vaguely dubious conviction of this brave
and foolhardy reasoning, I one day went out on the
catwalk and leaned against the railing in the direction

and virtual defiance of the rapidly approaching bombardment. A breathless lull almost invariably preceding the first tentative blasts and warning oversize raindrops ended before I had time to rethink my bravado and slide down the ladder to cover even had I wanted to. Out of the ominous overhang ahead of the still distant rumbling heavy artillery, a jagged bolt flashed down at me with blinding, paralyzing suddenness, from which I came to, surprised that I was still actively a resident on the planet Earth. The following, a slightly delayed clap of thunder shook the tower, and without the continuing paralysis I would certainly have had an involuntary bowel movement. Staggering back along the catwalk aided by the fortunately substantial railing, I dashed through the flimsy, half glass door, pushed it shut behind me, and slumped into the homemade chair, thinking I might have made my last mistake. During what ensued in the next thirty minutes or more, there were moments when I was sure of it.

Literally showers of blinding lightning bolts flashed down and around in all directions and how my aerie escaped taking a direct hit was a four star wonder. The thunderclaps shook not only the standing timbers but the rocks in which they were anchored. The bell in the telephone under the mapboard jangled constantly and crazily, and the mouthpiece discharged purple flashes in spasmodic streaks. Why the winds failed to lift the wide-eaved roof off the cabin and carry it into the next county, I will never know, nor why it didn't drill the raindrops straight through the window panes. A peculiar odor of what seemed to be burnt sulphur was in the air and so much electricity I felt strangely charged, myself. I felt like screaming not with fear, but wild excitement.

In total, it was an unforgettable experience filled with "Nearer My God to Thee" sensations—a demonstration of the awesome forces of the universe unleashed and calculated to make a believer out of the most obdurate agnostic.

The storm that day was unusual not only in the fury of

its first attack but in the fact that it cooled off and settled in over the peaks and ridges with rain and fog for most of a week. The evening of the second day of being able to see naught from the tower, when I reported to Barry at six o'clock, I told him that if the fog didn't lift overnight and if it was okay with him, I would skip the morning call and report in again next evening.

What I did not tell him was that I abhorred talking on the telephone in the first place. Having to report in every morning somewhat interfered with my freedom. In the second place, I had discovered an old, still serviceable gold pan under the caved-in roof of one of the Harvey Creek cabins. In the third place, I had in mind some stream gauging with the piece of line, leader, and flies wrapped around my hatband given to me by Hauswirth. Those things I did not divulge to him and there was at least one thing that, being real sneaky, *he* did not tell *me*. As usual at report time, all we indulged in was pass-the-time, small talk.

After discussing the weather, we would get into such things as: "What did you cook for supper?" "Boiled quail brains and fried onion tops. How about you?" "I had a mess of creamed rock rabbit and chipmunk livers on a toasted hotcake." "I hear the stockmarket's going hold wild on Wall Street. How is it on Sliderock?" "Except for a big run in dried prune futures, pretty quiet." "They's about three other people on the line. Goldarnit, this is official business. Get off the line." "You mean me?" "No, darn it, I don't mean you. I mean whoever else is listenin' in. That all you got to report?" "All for tonight. See you in the mornin'." "Okay, so-long." "So-long."

Barry seemed to have the idea that a lookout might be lonesome and enjoyed the sound of another human voice. While I had many a good chuckle over the contents of our "report-in" chit chat, no way was I lonesome. The longer I lived alone in my hard but heavenly domain, the more aloneness appeared to me to be something to be treasured. While not notably inclined to be especially gregarious, neither am I known to be a fulltime committed loner nor anti-social. Only at times, aloneness to think my own thoughts was a condition not only highly prized but essential. Long extended aloneness I discovered on Sliderock can become a grinding bore but also has its moments of ecstatic personal pleasure that few ever have the opportunity to know or appreciate. The search for complete solitude has taken men to all ends of the earth. There on Sliderock I found it, came to appreciate it as a luxury beyond material reckoning, and realized I could never again live completely without it.

Barry said if I could do without hearing his cheery voice the next morning, he could sure as heck do without hearing mine and wherever I was going in the rain, to go ahead and get wet. It'd probably be one of the few baths I'd have all summer.

What there was of daybreak finally dawned. It was plenty miserable wet and cold but not with what might be called rain. A thick, wet cloud had settled in to rest on Sliderock. Fog was so heavy the cook-cabin could not be seen from the tent. Down in the timber, I figured, while cooking and consuming a couple of eggs, things might be a little dark but I would be out from under.

When I arrived at the spring house, my legs and boots were wringing wet from brush along the trail but under the red cruiser, I was warm and dry. Hanging the one two-gallon water bag I had brought along (just for ballast back up the hill) on a spike in the spring box, I dug the gold pan out from under a pile of logs where it was hidden, and hurried to a sandbar down the creek. Along the way at one of the old cabins, I picked up the badly rusted business end of a shovel without a handle, previously spotted. It wasn't much by way of digging equipment but enough for scratching around and filling the pan.

And I struck it! Not rich but the pure quill! I found full yellow flecks and flakes I could pick up with the point of my knife blade. It was not iron pyrite, "fool's gold," that Julius had pointed out in our Clark's Fork dig and warned me about, but the honest-to-gosh pure yellow quill. Somewhere down there, there had to be a nugget and with my sorry shovel I dug, filled my pan and washed sand and gravel till I had blisters. That time I found colors aplenty, but no nugget. (Come the end of summer, I had three—one almost the size of a pea—carefully hoarded in a little medicine bottle picked out of the dump behind the spring house.)

Hands sore from digging and panning, back sore from stooping, knees sore from bending, boots and Levis soaking wet from wading in the water, I finally cached my gold pan and part shovel and turned back up the creek above my water rolling to accomplish Stream Test No. 2. From the ample selection I chose, cut, and trimmed a willow wand as long and limber as possible and attached, at the small end, the piece of line, leader, and fly from around my hatband. Above my prospecting operation and the willows was a long grassy opening through which the cold, clear headwaters of Harvey Creek meandered in a narrow, fairly deep channel. As I skirted this to get to the upper end well back from the water, a half-hearted rain, hardly more than a drizzle, came from the dark, threatening overhead.

There are days when rain seems to activate the appetite of trout to the point where catching them is as easy as shooting them in a rain barrel. Then there are other rainy days in the same places where they apparently fast. On this rainy day, at that time and in that place, if I had three flies on my line everytime I awkwardly flipped my lure on the dark, still running water, I could not have failed to hook three fish simultaneously and before you could say "scat." With my one fly, everytime I flipped it in the water I would see three racing flashes and "bang." The ferocity with which they took my barbed feathers was breath-taking. My wet, cold numbed hands trembled so with excitement and urge to get the fly back in the water. I could hardly free the hook from the mouth of the flopping, slippery take. And what fish they were! Not up to the size of those from Grizzly Creek but the coloring was delightfully different: dark green, almost black, topside with bright orange gills and red bellies. I guessed these full-bodied beauties to be eight to ten inches. I also guessed that in two meals, I might eat a dozen. And heads and bones— what a treat for Cat!

So, I took only that many, and cleaned them and strung them on a forked willow. I left my line on my willow pole for future use, and headed back for the spring house at a brisk clip feeling bouncy and elated. About half way there, I stopped suddenly and sniffed the wet air. I was not mistaken. Assuredly, I smelled wood smoke. Smoldering lightning strike? With all that rain—impossible!

Slowly, following my nose, I came finally out of the timber in sight of the spring house. There was my smoke—emanating from the spring house stove pipe and sinking to ground level where it had been floated in my direction. Smoke was not all that came into view. Tied to the half-collapsed hitching rack stood Ranger and Lou's pack mule, Elmer.

That darn Barry! He could have told me about Lou knocking around Sliderock last night when I had called in, but not a peep! I felt a little like I might have if old Uncle Bill had caught me smoking cornsilk. With some trepidation, I flopped my catch of fish in the cold spring, set my pole beside, and went to face the unannounced inspector.

When I pushed the door open there, sure enough, big as life stood Lou, backside to the warm stove in big hat, chaps, boots, and spurs.

"Well, Squirtah!" Though he acted surprised, I darn well knew Lou had spotted me coming long before I arrived. He was the kind that no one came slipping up on, night or day. "Ain't you got sense enough to come in outtah the rain?" I almost answered, "I might ask you the same question" but thought better of it. I just reached out my hand and said, "Hi, Lou" like I was genuinely very glad to see him, which I was.

With a flicker of a sly little smile, he took my hand in his big paw and, just like he didn't already know, said, "Where the heck you been?" Somewhat slowly and uncertainly, I confessed, "I been out tryin' to improve my time by catchin' a mess of fresh meat." "Well, good. Did you get any?" "You bet, some beauties." "Where are they?" "Down in the spring." "Well, bring 'em in here. I got a right size skillet in my pack and it's past time to eat. A fish fry would suit me just right." There went my planned two meals of fresh caught trout—whoosh, but delicious.

"Squirtah," said Lou, as we were picking morsels off the fish skeletons and wiping greasy fingers on our Levis, "I see you been makin' wood. Looks like you plannin' to spend the winter." "Aw, it's just something to keep me busy—good exercise." "Um. How'd you get the windows so clean?" Lou hadn't just passed by the lookout in my absence. Obviously he'd been looking the place over, plenty. "I used my one bottle of vinegar in the water. Didn't think I'd need it for anything else." "Vinegar? Um. Never heard of that." "Oh sure. It works good. Back in the meat market last summer, we used it all the time washin' counters and the show windows." "I'll be darned. Barry tell you to cut that down tree out of the trail in front of the cabin below the tower and pile the brush?" Suddenly it struck me I might have done something I shouldn't have. "No, sir," I said hesitantly. "Barry didn't tell me to do it. I thought the tree needed cutting so I cleaned it out." "Um. Been ridin' around that darn tree past five summers." The way he said it was more like he was talking to himself than to me. Whether I was right or wrong, I still wasn't sure.

When I told Lou about the night of the porcupine, I thought he would think it very funny, but during the telling he fished a cigar out of his pocket, lit it and never cracked a smile. After I had finished, he sat there on the block of wood he'd scavengered and carried in from somewhere and just relished his smoke like he hadn't heard any of what I'd said. About the time I was sure he hadn't, he finally came out with "You done right to kill the sonofagun. Lucky you didn't get a swipe of his tail on your bare hide. Tree eatin' pest . . . worst pest in the woods. Kill 'em ever chance you get. No use wastin' ammunition. They'll pack more lead than a grizzly bear. Hit 'em in the nose with a club. It's the one exposed weak spot they got."

Shortly after this "down with porcupines" pronouncement, Lou noted that the rain had let up a little and guessed he'd get on down the trail. When he mounted the tall horse and settled into the wet saddle, an involuntary wince of pain caused him to clench his teeth. Sympathetically, I was about to ask him how he felt but quickly decided against. A man's physical health problems were his own personal aches and pains. If he chose to talk about them, that was one thing. If not, it was another. There were times expressions of sympathy were not only unappreciated but entirely out of order. This, I thought, was one of those times.

Tall in the saddle with reins in one hand and Elmer's lead rope in the other, Lou lightly touched spurs to Ranger's sleek belly, started, then suddenly pulled up. Turning in the saddle, he shouted, "Squirtah, left some mail for you on the cook-shack table. You been givin' Miss Maud more business she's had in a month of Sundays." "Great," I shouted back, "Give her my best." There he went and it was probably the only chance I would have to send any mail out the rest of the summer. But mail! I had none since leaving Illinois way back in June. It was better than Christmas. I took off up the mile and a half, more or less, back to my peak at a pace guaranteed to blow a lung before covering half the distance. It was by far the fastest time between spring house and cook shack I clocked all summer.

When Lou said I had been giving Miss Maud some

business, he wasn't just fooling. There on the table was more mail than I had received at one time in a lifetime: eight letters and a mystifying sizeable package. The package was from Mrs. M.I. Bradner—Ann, whom I had yet to meet. Curiously, I opened it first and unbelievably found it filled with homemade cookies and a pound of candy—more delicious than any I'd ever tasted—almond rocca. Above all else, I was craving sweets and the gift could not have been more timely or appreciated. With never having met her, I was sure she must be a lady very special, which in every way, I later found out she was. In every way she was like a second mother, one who shaped my life as much or more than my own. Eagerly, I opened her accompanying letter. It was overflowing with warm welcome to Montana, apology for not having met me on arrival, a promise to meet me at the train when I came in the fall, a slap on the hand for not taking my suit out of the suitcase and hanging it in a closet, hope that I liked the mountains and the work. I read and reread the letter three times, rapidly reducing the supply of cookies the while. More than ever, it left me feeling like I had not departed home, but *come* home.

Second, I opened the two letters from Sally, a willowy blond with bedroom eyes, two years my junior, whom I thought was the likeness of my favorite movie star, Greta Garbo, both in looks and manner—and with whom I was considerably enamored. Sally was disporting herself in Europe with her German mother visiting relatives in Heidelberg. The burden of both letters, no doubt designed to leave me green with jealousy, had to do with being squired around by some enchanting junior of remote royalty. What she had no way of knowing was that I was head over heels gone on a love affair with the Siren of the Rockies. The letters were the beginning of the end of whatever Sally and I had going.

Next came the letter, prim and proper, from Mary. Valedictorian of our class, Mary and I had been closely associated in class activities. Vaguely, after a couple of dates, I tried to picture her in the role of something more than "good brilliant friend" but simply couldn't. But, though cautiously, conservatively worded, it was a good chatty letter covering the doings of classmates and much appreciated.

Next, I opened a short letter from oldest sister, Kay, two and a half years younger, about how scary but exciting it must be associating with Indians and bears and all, and how much work it was washing the cream separator now that she had inherited the job.

Following this, I opened the letter from Mother: Hopefully in that far wild land I was getting enough of the right things to eat. Were there any churches in that heathen land where I might attend services. How did I spend Sundays? Continuing my schooling was a must. Even though I had no desire to become a medical doctor, we would work out something. Father was finishing the house in Urbana next to Carle Park which was to be our new home. I could walk to classes. The campus of the university was less than a mile. A friend of mine had called wanting to get me into his fraternity. The Guernsey cow had finally calved and was giving about three and a half gallons a day in addition to what the calf took. Unfortunately, the cute little calf was a bull. When we moved to the city, it would be the first time that we had ever been without our own milk supply— heaven forbid, how would we survive? Supposedly, I was getting plenty of good fresh milk with all meals. Who does your laundry?

Good friend, Bernie O'Neill, was working six days a week, eight to five and on Saturdays to nine, in the shade and floor covering end of the biggest department store in town. He was making twelve dollars a week and living at home. At sixty-five dollars a month and bed and board in addition, I was making more and I did not envy him his sweltering, hot flatland workshop one iota. However, I learned he had met a real "looker" who worked in the lingerie and who had a sister about the same age, also a "looker." When, if ever, I returned

home to school or something, he would set up a double
date. This was a laugh. The way Bernie went through
girlfriends, by the time I got home the "looker" in
lingerie would be ancient history. Here on my mountain,
females were no way even part of the scene and I did
not miss them a whit.

The last letter opened was the one from my old bow
and arrowmaker and gunlover, Bob Holt. That one I
purposely saved till last because of knowing that whatever the contents, they were of unusual interest. The
letter was especially surprising in that I had never seen
evidence that Bob could, much less did, read or write.
Of all letters received on that memorable day, this one
was the only one I saved:

Philo elll
June 29-28

"Dear Joe,
I will try an answere youre Kind an
welcome letter of 18 well I shuld have ritin
you last sunday But it was so Dam Hot I
could not du nuthin only wipe seat an fight
flies an Juss well we had a little game of
stud last sunday an I made $5.95 to the
good. I sure wish I was out there with you
for we could have a good time too gether
for all I duing here is Keeping from
starving an I gess I could du that thare to
well me an the old man is giting along real
well But I don't know how long it will last
for you Know how he is I gess I have Kind
of Brok him of that Dam singin for a while
I am going to Decater to see my Budey he
was operated on last thursday for a Busted
Kidney and his girl gladis Brand o well
her panse dont fite her so well. I think
thay well get the Hous Dun this week or
the middle of one after that see if I was
out thare we would git some of them deer

or Bust traying woodent we/well, By By Bob."

In my mind's eye, I could see the big muscular man in his cluttered, small, two-room shack beside the railroad tracks laboriously penning this epistle wiping the sweat, fighting flies, and "Kussing" all the while. The fact that he had made the effort and taken the time to "ansere" my note, left me with a warm feeling. That father, "the old man" he referred to, might have done the same which would have been even more appreciated. This, however, as I was painfully aware, would be forever a futile hope.

Father had a penchant for singing loudly, as in church, while he worked. In itself, this to Bob was irritating enough, but Father's constant program of hymnals he considered a kind of personal insult. Bob's animosities to the church ran as deeply entrenched as those of Uncle Bill. Several times, on account of the hymnals, he had almost walked off the job in the middle of a day's work. Father did pay a liberal wage; but with his skills, Bob could have found equal income working for someone else. Why he continued to put up with the "Dam singin'" was always a mystery.

Equally mystifying to me was how Bob's "Budey" in "Decater" had come acropper of "a Busted Kidney." What possible relevancy this might have to the fact that his Budey's girl friend's "panse" didn't "fite her so well" was beyond my relatively meager understanding of the male-female physiological connection. I could only assume that for the male, at least, it was hazardous and best be avoided.

Never one to allow desirable correspondence to wither on the vine for lack of a prompt reply, I felt a great urgency to set me down and answer every letter in detail and with no delay. In the middle of letter one, addressed to Ann and profusely thanking her for cookies, candy, her great thoughtfulness, kindness, and hospitality, it more and more dawned on me that this was an exercise purely in penmanship and utter futility.

With the nearest Post Office at Miss Maud's Bonita General Store, miles distant, and chances that anyone would come wandering by to carry mail to the outside world less than nil, the cause was lost before starting. If there is anything more frustrating than physical inability to express deep felt gratitude to someone, I have yet to meet it. Just for the heck of it, and that one chance in a million that someone might happen by before the first snowfall, I went ahead and answered all the letters, anyway—and lucky I did. Two weeks later, the camp tender for a sheep outfit came packing over the peak looking for the herder and a week later delivered my letters to Lou who delivered them the next day to Miss Maud who put them on the first milk run west and first milk run east, on their bounden ways. For mail, outgoing from a lookout, this was very lucky and rapid transit, indeed.

Of course, with all the mail business, Barry would have to ask who were all these babes I had conned into writing letters, and especially this one, Ann, even sending me presents. A couple letters from this one babe, Sally, he said, smelled like a Saturday night in a whorehouse. As to that, since he had disavowed ever visiting a whorehouse, I asked him how he would know. The package, I told him was full of homemade cookies and candy like he had probably never tasted, and how lucky I was to be on Sliderock rather than at the ranger station where he and Lou would expect me to divvy up with them.

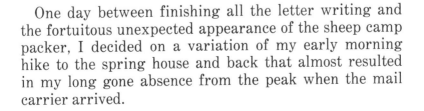

One day between finishing all the letter writing and the fortuitous unexpected appearance of the sheep camp packer, I decided on a variation of my early morning hike to the spring house and back that almost resulted in my long gone absence from the peak when the mail carrier arrived.

After looking at the point on which my mapboard was oriented, day in and day out, I thought it might be instructive to just take out and hike over there and see for myself what a surveyor's "bench mark" actually looked like. It was one thing to have Barry describe it but another to really see it and be able to say I had been there and done so. So at six a.m. with a couple of scrambled eggs under my belt, off I go, thinking getting there and back by ten would be a lead pipe cinch. It was my first cross country venture in the wilds of the Montana Rockies and I was a little excited. There is no blazed and graded trail to follow, no nothing. Like Lewis and Clark, I am my own pathfinder through the virgin wilderness. Both my own Sliderock peak and the bench mark point were quickly lost to sight in the timber, but no matter. I have looked at the point hundreds of times and know exactly where I am headed. On account of the thick lodgepole that is all the same girth and height and huckleberry bushes and other brush, the going was a little rough and slower than anticipated. Every now and then, there is a game trail that I can follow going in exactly the right direction. The rising sun is approximately where it should be and all I need to do is just keep going. So faster and faster, I just keep going. When out of nowhere came a sudden blood curdling scream freezing me in my tracks. A mountain lion, there were a few, for sure, in the area. Of all things, I had left my pea shooter back at the peak. I heard another scream guaranteed to scare pee out of a wooden Indian. It was worse than that of an about-to-be-executed cottontail rabbit! This time, however, I zeroed in on that direction—straight up. Looking up, I saw the soaring screamer. What the heck—only an eagle! This mundane discovery had a sobering effect on something I had been feeling and fighting off.

Bathed in perspiration and exhausted from trying to get somewhere—just anywhere—fast, I parked myself on a down log, wiped the sweat from my eyes, and came to the impossible, unbelievable realization that, in my own

backyard—no less—I was simply downright *lost* and
verging on panic. There is no way of describing this lost
sensation. The only way to know it is to experience it.
The mind is completely disoriented. The inclination is to
just get somewhere else. Everything is strange, dis-
located and out of order—so run. It may not be anywhere you may get to, but it cannot be any worse . . .
any place but this place . . . escape . . . run. The urge is
inexplicable, inexorable, insane.

In my experience, the one defense against the lost
feeling is to know it and accept it. You settle down, keep
your wits, and save your energy. There is nothing wrong
or disgraceful about getting lost. I have been temporarily lost in mountain wilderness of numerous occasions
and I would bet the early day mountain men were lost
and lived with being lost most of the time. That first
time of experiencing the lost feeling, as anyone who has
been there will tell you, is simply hell asunder, and
indescribable. I sympathize.

Sitting there on my windfall, my thoughts were a
jumble of doubts, uncertainties, and a few positive facts.
One thing I knew, I had covered a distance from the
lookout but not any great distance. Somewhere in the
vicinity had to be that darned bench mark point, but
just how close and in what direction was the question.
The same applied to the lookout. I was in no real danger
even without food or water. Rock Creek and the road or
Clark's Fork and the railroad were a long, downhill
hike, but well within reach. I could come out at either
place and be Ranger Nichol's lost Sliderock lookout and
the natives would laugh me out of the country—a fate
worse than death and a very last resort. The trouble was
the thick timber. If I could get up where I could see
something, like the eagle . . .

Instantly, I was on my feet sizing up the trees.
Picking a tree that looked to me like being a little, but
not much, taller than all the others, I went shinnying
up. Pole size, I could get good hand holds on the trunk
but the branches were small and brittle and kept

snapping off. One I trusted too much broke. Slipping downward, I put a six inch rip in my Levis and a painful scratch on the inside of my upper leg. Lucky I didn't get hung up. Higher up, I hit better going. And a little higher—there was my tower. It was not at all where I expected it to be, about the right direction but much closer than I thought. The bench mark point was not in sight, but off to the right about where I'd been headed. I just hadn't gone far enough. My panic turned to jubilation. Self confidence in my sense of direction was fully restored, but I had learned an invaluable lesson. I would do no more running, panicking, and brush beating like a madman. What the heck—why had I been carried away? Taking another bearing on the tower, I eased down from my perch and refusing to be balked by uncertainty, once more took off for the bench mark point.

Shortly, I broke out of the timber and there it was. Colter, when he discovered Old Faithful in Yellowstone Park, could not have felt any greater sense of accomplishment than I did on finding that little metal marker planted in the rock on that inconsequential Northern Rockies point. I looked back at the high standing tower on Sliderock, threw back my shoulders and let go with a Tarzan scream calculated to outdo even the scream of the still-soaring and circling eagle.

In plenty of time, I was back for my ten o'clock report to Barry. Very casually, I reported to him that I had taken a little walk over to my orientation point just to find out what a bench mark marker looked like. Surprisingly, mention of this brought on not the expected accolade but pause in the conversation. Then: "Umm. Did you have any trouble finding it?" "Heck no. Why would I have trouble?" "Well, that country between Sliderock and the point is a little confusing. No trails. Heavy timber. Not sure you should just take off like that." "What do you mean?" "Well, I mean in that country you could get yourself lost and I'd have to come lookin for a lost lookout. You decide to take off like that again you report in where you're goin'. Okay?" "Yeah," I said, ending the conversation. "Okay." Maybe my accomplishment had been bigger than I'd thought.

Minus needle and thread, the long ragged limb tear on the inside of my pants leg provided more ventilation than needed the rest of the summer. Next time, I would bring along some thread and needles, and, just in case, a few buttons. Next time, too, going cross country like that, I would pack my gun, pea shooter or not.

Though the loudest and most terrifying, the screaming eagle was not the only feathered inhabitant of the mountain to give me a chilling start. While hiking happily, carefree, and absentmindedly down my water haul trail between the tower and spring house a few days after arrival on the peak, I was brought to a skidding halt by the loud and very close by sound of someone or something beating a pillow with a carpet beater too fast to maintain the pace. As suddenly as it started, the sound stopped. Carefully, rooted to the spot, I looked around me for the source. This high on the mountain, there were no rattlesnakes and the sound was not that of a rattler at any odds. Vaguely once before, but only once, I had heard that peculiarly distinctive muffled drumbeat in the past. Flashing back, I remembered Uncle Bill and Burr's cornfield! Prairie chicken! No prairie chicken in these precipitous parts!

Almost perfectly camouflaged with the dark, down lodge pole, the beater-drummer's identity and location was revealed only when my eye caught a slight movement as he eased along the top log of a pile of closeby windfall—not away from, but directly toward me. Suddenly again as though for my special benefit, the bird with a brilliant red patch above his eyes now visible raised his head, erected and fanned his tail, threw out his chest, puffed out a windsack through a cleft in his lower neck feathers and beat his wings against his sides fast and furiously, producing the drumming sound that had stopped me in my tracks.

This was no prairie chicken, but it was a mountain

cousin chicken I came to know as the "fool hen." Why both sexes were lumped under the term for female chicken was always a good question. This particular bird was a "fool rooster," as only the rooster puts on the wing-beating performance. To get technical, this member of the grouse family is a Franklin, and the "fool" appellation is most appropriate. The bird is stupid beyond belief. Apparently absolutely fearless of man, it can be approached and killed with a stick. Many a one has met his end in this shabby fashion as they are good to eat, unless they have been feeding largely on pine needles in which case they have the acrid flavor of pitch.

To demonstrate just how foolish a fool hen can be, a friend of mine once put a "jake stick" (a broomstick size "stick" for mounting a surveyor's compass) over his shoulders, backed up to a limb on which a fool hen sat, worked the stick under the bird's feet and marched off with the stupid thing riding abaft. It was a cute trick and not the first time he'd pulled it off.

Another quieter—if he ever did the drummer stunt, I never saw or heard him do it—relative of the fool hen on my peak was the blue Richardson grouse. Considerably larger than the fool hen, the only start he furnished was when he might loudly get up practically underfoot. Along toward the first of August when the spring hatch might be three-fourths full-grown and stuffed with berries, grasshoppers, and seeds, the blue grouse— though not as suicide-bent as the fool hen—had a tendency to run head on with rocks, lead, and other solid objects that might be flying through the air. When these sad fatalities occurred, the roving lookout, starved for fresh meat, was obliged to do his duty and not let the deceased bird go to waste. He must pluck, clean, and separate it into skillet or pot-sized parts, subject it to heat, consume it to the last tender and delicious scrap, then appreciatively lick his fingers.

Cat and his voracious adolescent appetite was a special hazard I failed to take into account till too late. Once, having performed my duty and carried a defeathered bird home to the top, I put it to stew along with some rice. I used too much rice as usual, so by the time the rice was done, practically all the fine broth was gone. What remained was largely rice with pieces of chicken. Since I could not possibly consume it all at one sitting, I put the residual in a smaller pan, covered the pan with a too-big lid and made the mistake of leaving breakfast on the table next to the open, unscreened window. Come dark, Cat entered through the window, pushed the lid off, and managed to extract every last shred of chicken apparently without touching a grain of rice. For breakfast, rather than the picked-over rice, I settled on oatmeal and raisins with butter and sugar for my pitiful supply of condensed milk by then was long gone.

Another hazard was an unexpected mealtime visit from the ranger. At that time of few, widely scattered game wardens, he served not only the U.S. Forest Service as ranger but the State of Montana as deputy game warden. The population of grouse in the back country was large and never hunted. It was taken for granted that lookouts added an occasional grouse to their menu even though it was technically illegal.

Once upon a time, according to a fellow lookout, he happened to have a choice young bird in the pot for lunch, when coming up the trail at some distance, he spotted the ranger. Rather than hide or throw the planned lunch in his garbage pit, he ran to the stove and added a can of stewed beef. Come lunch, while the lookout carefully avoided doing so, the ranger equally pointedly picked out all the pieces of grouse from the conglomeration and ate them with great gusto and relish never saying a word till meal's end. When, with obvious appreciation, he wiped his fingers on his Levis and settled comfortably back to roll a cigarette. "You know, Pete," he said reflectively, "That canned beef is good eating. So help me every time I have to eat it, I get to thinking it tastes more and more like chicken. You noticed that?" "No, sir, Mack, I never noticed," the petrified culprit stuttered. "To me it still tastes just like it should taste—canned beef." "Umm. Well, next time don't let me catch you tryin' to change it. Might be embarrassing to both of us—and for you, expensive. Understand?" "Next time I see you coming, we'll have fried ham." He thought he heard the ranger mumble to himself: "God forbid."

One more hazard to anything placed or left uncovered on the two-man table in the cook shack were the ever-present swarming assorted species of flies—everything from huge horse and blow-flies, common house flies and deer flies, bees and yellow-jackets. No knowledgeable lookout was without at least one strategically located homemade trap for these unwelcome and hazardous pests, nor more delighted than watching them meet their end.

The usual trap was simple, effective, and required little maintenance. Take any old pickle jar and till it about half full of one or several kinds of syrup off the canned fruit furnished as part of the diet. Let said juice ferment as it rapidly did and sit back and delight in seeing the darned flies and yellow jackets crawl in, drink, get drunk, fall back, and drown. Then the bait became overfull of insect cadavers, strain off the deceased and start over. Very entertaining.

One lookout of my acquaintance, however, claimed this was a wanton waste of good syrup. Having once worked in a California winery, he collected all the syrup off his canned fruit, let it ferment in insect proof containers, and drank the high potency product himself. Thereby, as he said, "finding relief from the tedium of the work, while at the same time improving efficiency by occasionally seeing double."

As a kind of screen protection against biting insects, it occurred to me to grow a beard. Early day mountain men were generally depicted sportive of beards as were the prophets, like Moses who went to the mountain and came back with the Ten Commandments.

In my experience, long hair in any form was (and is) nothing but a nuisance. The thin-whiskered, bald-pated man has many advantages and just a few important disadvantages. Biblical and frontier beards I always figured were easily excusable to the unavailability of a good sharp cutting tool and lack of soap for lather. All others I had considered explainable only by a careless, shiftless, downright lazy, and filthy personal disposition. Since Uncle Bill was none of these, the reason for his face mask and lengthy mop were forever a puzzle concerning which, I decided, I had best not inquire. At this place and time, as a means of warding off mosquitoes, gnats, deer flies and such, I could see where a good thick beard might possibly be desirable. Maybe, in addition to a dearth of razors and soap, the pests were another good reason for the mountain man and prophet hairy look. So, shortly after Lou had surprisingly come and gone and there was little likelihood of anyone else happening along and catching me in a messy, hairy state, I abandoned the daily morning shave rite and let come what would.

What came was never again: bugs or no bugs, *no more beards!* About the third day, with a fairly respectable stubble developing, I also developed an itch. Where the chin ends and the neck begins began to itch. Then the cheeks and under the nose began to itch, itch, itch, scratch, scratch, scratch. Along with the itch, here and there, a hair perversely grew in rather than out, resulting in irritating pimples. Albeit as the days and weeks wore on, the itching and pimpling wore out and as it lengthened, the stubble softened. What I progressively beheld in the ragged piece of broken mirror fastened on the wall beside my hanging five gallon water bag was, to me, anything but what one might be able to live with. Blond, light-complexioned, and blue eyed, as was my lot, the emerging bug inhibitor was turning out to be a sickly, nondescript pink.

Having proven to myself that the beard was possible, after six weeks the beard did not come off easily, even with the help of a new Gillette razor blade. When I descended the mountain in September, I asked Barry if he had ever tried to grow a beard. "Why, yes," he said. "You don't think I shave every morning, sometimes even with cold water, just for the fun of it, do you?"

There was no rule that I ever heard of barring the cultivation and wearing of a beard of long hair, but among all the mountain-going foresters (including packers) I knew over forty years, I cannot recall a one who wore a beard or long hair. Helpful as a bug screen or as a bib to keep from getting gravy or spaghetti sauce on your shirt, I gladly give you the beard, preferring to resort to alternate protection.

Items like water, fresh milk, fresh vegetables, fresh meat, bakery goods and mail service were scarce on Sliderock, but the occupant was as long on a few things as short on others. Of canned spinach, carrots, and hominy, there was never any insufficiency and of one thing, in particular, there was a huge surplus: time to think. From out of this excess evolved a thought that backfired, like a rifle with a barrel plugged with mud, and was far worse than growing a beard.

Exuberantly sensing the unlimited freedom and isolation of my exotic wilderness estate one bright and shining day, I was unfortunately inspired to soak up a measure of nature's bounty that might be carried away with me as a fond memento of a heavenly home. I would strip down to skivvies, stretch my length on the flat, smooth, and handy topside of one of the several four feet by eight feet shutters off the lookout windows in full unobstructed view of the glorious sun, and take on a Tarzan tan in less time than it takes to tell it. The near fatal flaw in this grand plan was failure to account for how close to heaven my heavenly home happened to be.

Revolving so as to expose one side and the other at what I wrongly judged to be proper intervals, the end result of my miscalculation was multiplied to about the fifth dimension due to the original error in orientation. What started out to be a Tarzan tan turned out to be a rosy cooked-lobster pink. Except for the purely habitual retention of shorts, I shuddered to think. The potent rays of the alpine sun played havoc with my body except for a narrow white band luckily encompassing male pendants and the sitting part of my posterior. Even the soles of my feet were burned.

Happily, I had an adequate supply of water and did not have to go anywhere except up and down the ladder to my shaded aerie and the telephone. With no alleviating ointment, I crippled around in unlaced boots, unbuttoned shirt, shorts, and no skintight Levis for what seemed a week but was only a few days. Days were hot but nights were chilly and rough WWI surplus wool blankets against sunburned bare hide were simply intolerable.

My transient "tan" memento of heavenly home was the everlasting memory of a night spent in shorts only from chilly sunset to chillier sunup with a large supply of firewood and my blessed little stove.

Even though almost complete failure to bake anything in the tiny oven of said stove was virtually guaranteed at the outset, the first part of this night was whiled away in an attempt to bake a batch of baking powder biscuits. In the process of this exciting endeavor, as usual, I managed to spill large amounts of flour over most everything including parts of my sun-baked anatomy. Since this oddly seemed to have a cooling effect, just testing, I sprinkled on a little more until I was fairly well-powdered all over. Once my biscuits were baked, I opened a can of red raspberry jam, extracted a quarter pound of butter from the brine in another can, and sat there and gorged myself while feeding the fire as well almost till midnight. The seemingly endless remainder of the night I spent dozing as best as possible sitting on a hard backless bench, feeding the fire only.

Come morning and the outside temperature being tolerable to a near nudist, I eased downward to the spring and with a two-pound coffee can dipped and poured on the icy water, theorizing that this torture would either kill or cure. At least it mostly cleaned me of flour. Even with swarms of mosquitoes and gnats spurring me on, the return to the top was by far the slowest I recorded all summer. In due course came the itching, flaking, and peeling—comparable in this case to the snake's annual shedding of old skin for new.

I have been a strong proponent of solar heating ever since—extremely wary of exposing any part of my hide even to the extent of wearing short sleeves. The hats I favor come equipped with a brim so wide, I can barely see out from under.

There is certainly no doubt that a surplus of time to think has spawned some of the world's greatest philosophies but it can also be hazardous to your health.

Speaking of surpluses and shortages and philosophers, the reading material I found on Sliderock would have made the works of Plato, Descartes, Marx, or whomever seem like the most exciting fiction. What library was present consisted of a miscellany of two, three, and four year old out-of-sequence issues of *Cosmopolitan, Saturday Evening Post, Red Book,* and a few other similar periodicals I had never heard of. All of them had covers torn off, pages missing, cartoons cut out, and chewed on by mice. There is nothing more aggravating and frustrating than having the end of a complete or continued story or article and no beginning, or worse yet, the beginning and no end. If ever I went back on another lookout, I swore more than once, I would haul along *The Unabridged Complete Works of Shakespeare* or something similar even if the additional weight broke the mule's back. Rather than in hotel rooms, the place where the distributor of a *Bible* or *The Book of Mormon* should leave them, with a better than average chance they would be used, is a wilderness lookout. A miracle might come to pass and the occupant "get religion."

If the wilderness lookout had not already contracted some kind of religion from experiencing the fearsome electrifying storms, there were the breathtaking, spellbinding sunsets, beside which the splendor of the rainbow fades to a minor phenomenon. Sliderock sunsets were celestial pageants of the hosts of heaven parading an infinite assortment of colors. Ever changing as day gave way to dusk and darkness, the wonder of these spectaculars transcended the wonder of life itself.

On occasion, following or in advance of a storm when the western lowering sun rays over the dark ridges and thrusting peaks were painting and scintillating off stupendous billowing thunderheads, a mere human like me was left either completely choked up or wildly screaming appreciation of being alive and witness to the glorious scene. When the air was heavy with driftsmoke from distant upwind conflagrations, which was and still is, sadly all too frequently the case during summers in the Northern Rockies, the hue predominate in the sunset was an awesome blood red—as though reflecting the agony of the torched trees and ravished land. As I watched, occasionally through an unaccountable lachrymose film, all the riches of the earth and the universe were revealed to me; and I did not want for any. No words, music, song, or artist's brush can ever fully capture the mysterious, primitive flooding emotions generated by certain mountain sunsets.

My measly monetary wage appeared as a fabulous bonus. What was mine was treasure beyond reckoning. Written in the mountain sunset was early-on understanding of utter humility. In the Great Spirit's inscutably omniscient scheme, there is the marvelous human being, who with all, all is little more than another ant, seeking a place and way of total fulfillment, until inevitably, he dies. Seldom, but on rare occasion, is he actually fulfilled. After Sliderock, I always felt that, come whenever, my own Crossing-of-the-Divide should warrant little regret and minimum intercession with whoever or whatever might be on the receiving end.

As the long days of summer wound down, so did the short season. It was especially short in 1928 with a protracted cold wet spring and early wet fall. While the lightning strikes were no less numerous, most of the storms were luckily accompanied by heavy rains. The one "smoke" I spotted all summer turned out to be latent fog. In the tower early, on account of a late afternoon storm with unusually vicious lighting, I called in early to alert Barry that I had a smoke on a bearing where I had marked down what looked to me like a particularly hot strike, but I wasn't yet sure it might not be fog as the rain was almost a cloudburst. The difficulty was that it was over a ridge in a draw where I could not see the bottom. By ten o'clock, I had no doubt. With the warming sun, my "smoke," instead of changing location or increasing in volume, had slowly entirely evaporated.

It was when I reported this fact that Barry wanted to know how I had spotted this strike on exactly the bearing I gave him when I was supposed to be in the cook shack where the only window faced the opposite direction. I told him with all the receivers off the hook, or maybe on account of a tree across the line somewhere after the storm, I couldn't hear his question. He hollered in the phone for people to hang up their receivers, that this was important official business, as usual. When I didn't answer anymore, I heard him mumble something about "darn fool lookouts" and finally hung up. He knew I had been in the tower watching the storm and didn't need to ask embarrassing questions in the first place. When I reported in again at six o'clock, he was so happy that the line was still working, he forgot all about it.

After that particular storm, the last week in August, I started slipping into my jacket after washing the evening dishes and into my shirt, socks, and jacket before stepping out of bed on the packed dirt floor of the tent at sunup. For several mornings, when I threw back the tent flap, I found my alpine world shiny and crisp with frost. The pool in the shaded spring box when I arrived as late as eight o'clock still had a fragile rim of ice on it. As I passed down and up the trail, the chattered pine squirrel greetings suddenly seemed much more infrequent and notably less prolonged. Cat caught grasshoppers with much less difficulty and the buzzing and humming around my fly and yellow jacket trap, other than at midday was greatly diminished. Though I could not put a finger on it, I sensed a strange, guarded expectancy of something portentous soon to come—like the world and all was holding its breath just listening and waiting for an unknown happening.

And on September 2, unbelievably, it happened. Heavy black clouds moved in from the northwest pushing a gale force wind ahead of them that had a mean, cold, no nonsense bite, but oddly no lightning. Then came subsiding blasts and soft, not hard or heavy, rain. It started to half rain, half snow, then all snow came. They were big lazy falling flakes so thick I could hardly make out a clear outline of the cook shack below the tower. With no more watching or waiting, I got down the wet cold ladder, picked up an extra armload of firewood, and started a fire in the stove.

If there is anything more satisfying than sitting in a snug warm cabin with plenty of firewood, water, bacon and beans, and watching the first snowfall, I have yet to discover same. On the other hand, in this case, it would have been much more satisfying if the cabin had been big enough to accommodate a bed as well as a stove, firewood, food, and water, and I did not have to sit there worrying about how badly my bedroom was leaking. Would the old canvas hold up under the weight of the accumulating wet snow? After about day three of sitting and watching out the window, the supply of water and firewood can pose somewhat of a shortage problem, and the sitting and watching can become darn monotonous, even if the cabin is big enough to also accommodate a bed. After a full week, the feeling of snug satisfaction can deteriorate to a certainty that unless the snow stops instantly, you will go stark raving nuts, especially if you do not happen to have along snowshoes, skis, deck of cards, or anything to read.

This was no three day or full week snow. After

carpeting the peak and surrounding ridgetops with about three inches of good tracking snow, precipitation gave way to a dense milky fog, as though a cloud, too moisture-pregnant to float, had settled in on the peak blotting out all sight and sound. There in the vacuum created, on the summit at trail's end, I saw in my one rough knocked-together chair, snug in my too-small cabin, sensing with a strange mixture of regret, relief, and excitement other imminent endings like the early end of one more fire season, and the end of my usefulness as a lookout.

When I mounted the clammy cold ladder in the soggy gloom and checked in with Barry, he was far less optimistic. "Aw, heck," he said, "we got no snow or fog down here. Just a good rain. Tomorrow it'll be bright and shiny and the snow all gone. It dries out fast. I wish we were, but we're not out of the fire business yet. Hang tough and go bake yourself a cake." "Yeah," I agreed, "with a little flour and the last of my plum jam in place of sugar."

Next morning when I called in, it was Lou instead of Barry on the phone. "Squirtah, how does it look up theh?" "As far as I can see, just like down there. The fog's lifted but heavy overcast, like more rain. Snow's mostly all gone but still pretty chilly." "Umm. Barry says you may be runnin' short of grub." "Sort of short but not down to carrots or spinach more than once a day." "Umm. Don't want to pack more grub up theh unless we have to. Think you can get by another week or so?" "I won't starve." "Tell you what—it's lookin' mighty good but we don't want to take chances on this weatheh. You set tight up theh till we see what happens. Maybe today you oughtah take off and throw some rocks outah the trail between the top and the head of Harvey Creek. Reckon you can do that?"

The trail between the top and head of Harvey Creek was as clean of rocks as any rock cleaned trail anywhere and Lou well knew it. "You bet," I answered, enthusiastically. "I'm on the way!" It is a proven fact that the

beautiful black and red trout inhabiting beaver ponds at
the head of Harvey Creek are just as foolishly eager to
hit a grey hackle-yellow wet fly following the first snow
of autumn as during a summer drizzle. At least it was a
proven fact in 1928.

Since consequences are so often critical, probably
more decisions are delayed due to waiting to see what
happens or doesn't happen to the weather in the Rockies,
than for any other single reason. Possibilities are almost
infinite. Will it rain? Or will it be all dry lightning? If it
rains, will the rain be general and really wet things
down? Or will it be spotty—here but not there? The way
summer rains are scattered, the old saying is that you
can set a double barrel shotgun upright against a fence
or log and it will rain down one barrel and leave the
other dry. Will it freeze? Hard enough to break the
block in the truck with no antifreeze—or just a light
frost? Should the hay be cut or should we wait a couple
days? Do we try to make it out with horses over that
steep slick trail today—or wait it out till tomorrow?
Snow looks good for skis or snowshoes now, but what'll
it be by noon? If the wind comes up, the fire will crown
out and run—do we put ten men on the line and take
chances of holding it or send twenty?

"Chancy" is the word for it. About as many wrong
decisions are made due to weather estimates as right.
And, if wrong, we have the price to pay. Great going
fires make their own weather. Lives of men and livestock can be and all too often have been lost. Bones have
been broken, lungs singed, frost-bitten extremities am-
putated all on account of bum estimates of the vagaries
of mountain weather.

For whatever else, the weather is never "usual."
Always in the memory of the oldest natives, it is "very
unusual": unusually wet, unusually dry, unusually calm,
unusually windy, unusually hot, unusually cold. Only
fools and foreigners predict the weather in the Rockies.
With those who live there, it is always a game of hurry
up and wait, hurry up and wait. If you do, never be

caught in an unprepared or indefensible position, and never make a precipitous decision. To do so can cost money, misery, and lives of man and beast. So there on my peak, I sat tight and waited on the weather—and it wasn't easy.

Like piano playing, I have always considered the ability "to wait" something enviably inherent. To an extent, it can be and in certain occupations and places must be developed, but there are just naturally easy waiters and others with whom waiting is literally anathema. They are the ones who feel the need to hurry every chance they get, develop ulcers, and pace in circles while a woman powders her nose.

Once in later years when I had reached an exalted position, one of my good friends with whom I had covered many a mile and waited in many a duck blind (and was my boss), called me into his sanctum during a particularly trying time, saying he had something to talk about. When I came hurrying in between times vaguely wondering what was so important, I found him lighting his everlasting pipe with kitchen matches as usual and easily waiting, as usual. "Hessel," he greeted. "Take the weight off your feet and sit down for a minute. Your problem is you're impatient, impulsive, impetuous. You need to slow down." Before I realized that this was what he wanted to talk about, I answered, "Aw heck, Ed, we both know I've always had that trouble. But one way and another, I get things done. What was it you want to talk about?" Ulcers, I had. He never suffered a twinge.

As it turned out on this occasion, Barry's guess was right. The clouds cleared out and the days were gloriously warm, shiny, and bright. Somehow things were different, inviting indolence and lazy contemplation. The nights were crisper early following in the hours of darkness by a hard heavy frost. In my tent, I shivered and burrowed deeper in my six blankets. The cobweb ice in the spring box became a thin crust. The green ground cover under the dark lodgepole donned a color-contrasting coat ranging from dwarf huckleberry scarlet to gold, yellow, and wilted greys and brown. The clatter of a few hardy grasshoppers taking flight was heard only in late morning and early afternoon. Less frequent screams of the ever soaring and circling eagles seemed more garrulous and searching than fearsome.

I swept the rough cook cabin floor and scrubbed it till it was almost white, reorganized what little of my supplies remained on the shelves, and split more firewood to make sure of having plenty to fill the woodbox on departure. A cardinal rule learned early: Never leave an empty woodbox and always leave a box of kitchen matches in a covered coffee can nearby.

When the day of departure would arrive, I would be physically ready to leave the accommodations cleaner and more orderly than on arrival. Regardless of what happened to the weather, my days were numbered due to limited financing for the position. Come 15 September, the Ranger's allotment ran dry and without highly unlikely emergency supplemental fire money, Sliderock lookout was out of business.

Like its beginning on a shoestring, the Forest Service in 1928 was still a struggling barebones outfit with a budget allowing for only custodial protection and maintenance of the vast national forest lands and hardly that. Except for broad basic guidelines such as "the greatest good for the greatest number in the long run" and "timber cutting commensurate with sustained yield," scientific development and management of the lands and resources was being dreamed of by the leaders at the top and the new breed coming out of University Schools of Forestry like Supervisor Jim Brooks. However, planned and applied land and resource management was still to come.

Painfully under-manned and under-financed, it was more than the original largely untrained firstcomers could do to simply protect the rich, vulnerable holdings against holocaust and thievery. What existed was a penny-pinching, make-do operation, and it was advantageous to loggers and range users to keep it that way. The general public could have cared less for this was a land of rocks and savages. Have at it. Let it burn.

To me—bred, born and brought up in the routine, orthodox flatlands—the magnificent rugged wilderness mystically closeting the secrets of eternity and the universe was Heaven on Earth. The vast forested lands accessible only by foot and horseback sparsely populated by humans was still excitingly replete with pristine pockets and drainages known only to deer, elk, bear, and other forms of wildlife, big and little. Fearsome and forbidding to many, nothing other than a wasteland to be ransacked of any inherent treasure and forgotten to most, this wild, far-flung mass of mountains reaching for the firmament and dividing East from West, to me was sheer Utopia.

A stranger to homesickness for the land and life where I was born, I was acutely aware within me that, though physically ready to leave my peak when the weather dictated, and to leave these mountains as dictated by the skinny financing for my tour of duty, I would not be separated from either more than five minutes prior to suffering all the soul-searching agonies of homesickness fourfold. This I would be stuck with on every separation from the mountains ever after.

No matter where one is bred and born, it was never more truly said than that, "Home is where affection calls" or "Home is where the heart is." Mine was a disciplined no-nonsense childhood and upbringing with affection playing little part. Until the mountains, I had never known what consummate affection or love for an entity animate or inanimate could be.

The definitive departure day came sooner than even I had anticipated. Those "bright and shiny" Barry-predicted days were not long lasting. Switching ended almost overnight, and the fickle summer-end weather brought heavy grey-black clouds barreling in out of nowhere the afternoon of September 11. What followed foretold a long hard winter and left many a man with loose purse strings wondering where his summer wages had gone.

As to wages, in my own case, during the three months since arrival at Bonita, I had yet to see cent one, much less spend one. Hardly a hobnail was left in my used-up leaky boots. One pair of Levis was more white than blue with wear and washing, and where ripped (on sliding down a lodgepole one memorable day when badly confused if not actually lost) held together with safety pins out of the first-aid box. One work shirt was not worth packing off the mountain, but with $195 coming, financially I was flying high.

That night on checking in, it was Lou, instead of Barry again. "Squirtah," he greeted, "you got any snowballs hittin' you?" "Yes, sir. By morning, I'll be like that tall Arapaho you tell about—up to my behind in the stuff." "Well, come mornin' get on down to Grizzly an' Barry'll meet you with the truck. He's got some fence fixin' you can help out on. Tie up that pad and bedroll an' hang them from the ridgepole in the cookshack where the rats can't get to it. Plenty moh blankets down heh. Leave the tent standin' to dry out aftah this stohm. Ben an' somebody'll be up to shut the place down latah on. What time you think you'll be down?" "Eight to nine miles downhill—10:30. Maybe sooner." "You been sproutin' wings, or figurin' on buildin' a toboggan? Barry'll figure on you bein' there by noon." "Okay. Might be I'll have trouble gettin' Cat to fit in my packsack or breakin' him to lead but I'll be there." "Forget that darn cat. Why don't you shoot the sonofagun an' leave him theh?" "Uh—uh. You're going to love Cat. Best mouse and rat trap between Rock Creek and Missoula or Rock Creek and Butte." "Huh! If you say so, bring him back. See if he can earn his keep."

Cat, I knew would be no problem. I had made him a collar out of the top of an old boot and taught him to lead some time ago. Several times I had taken him with me on the water haul and was pretty sure he would follow off the peak as well as lead. By getting up before sunup, when I knew I would be up without much sleeping during my last night on Sliderock, Cat and I would make it to Grizzly with time to spare. If they were biting in the beaver pond below the trail as usual, we'd catch a mess of trout for lunch or supper to boot.

All too soon, on the once-again-sunny afternoon of September 15, with an Earl Barry-special hand clipper haircut, and decked out in my worn out boots, last pair of Levis, work shirt and beat up hat, Lou, Miss Maud and I stood on the right of way cinders by the Bonita return milk train stop, awaiting westbound mail and for me to board. When it came to talking, I somehow had a lump in my windpipe and to hide it, said the least possible. As the train came clattering, steaming and grinding up, Miss Maud quickly and surprisingly gave me a motherly peck on the cheek along with her firm handshake. Grasping my hand in his big fist, Lou said, "Squirtah, you want to come back, you write to me. If we got any money, you got a job. Heh?" All I could do was give his hand a last little squeeze, nod my head with a weak grin, and pack on back, swing aboard without looking back. That lump in my throat had suddenly grown to the size of a goose egg.

On the dusty day coach, the hard mohair-upholstered seats were mostly all occupied, but at the far end I spotted what I was looking for—a left side window seat. Because of the brush and heavy growth of cottonwood and pine trees, I knew I could not get a last glimpse of Rock Creek Station. I sat with face close to the window watching for the spot where in my birthday suit, I had entertained the Milwaukee freight crew while taking my first icy dip in the famous Clark Fork River. When shortly I spotted the big flat rock and shallow backwater where I had shivered, I knew, more happily than sadly, that never again in this "land of rocks and savages" would I rank as a flatlands greenhorn.

Not after Sliderock! After the timeless silence and solitude of Sliderock I knew that for once in my time under the sun, if never again, I had found total self-fulfillment. In this "land of rocks and savages," I had found my place.